ISBN 978-1-331-84585-0
PIBN 10241354

1 MONTH OF
FREE
READING

at

www.ForgottenBooks.com

By purchasing this book you are eligible for one month membership to ForgottenBooks.com, giving you unlimited access to our entire collection of over 1,000,000 titles via our web site and mobile apps.

To claim your free month visit:

www.forgottenbooks.com/free241354

NARRATIVE AND EXPOSITION

OF THE LATE PROCEEDINGS OF

NEW-ENGLAND YEARLY MEETING,

WITH SOME OF ITS

SUBORDINATE MEETINGS & THEIR COMMITTEES,

IN RELATION TO

THE DOCTRINAL CONTROVERSY

NOW EXISTING IN THE SOCIETY OF FRIENDS:

PREFACED BY A CONCISE VIEW OF THE CHURCH, SHOWING THE OCCASION OF ITS APOSTACY,

BOTH UNDER THE FORMER AND PRESENT DISPENSATIONS.

WITH AN APPENDIX.

EDITED FROM RECORDS KEPT, FROM TIME TO TIME, OF THOSE PROCEEDINGS, AND INTERSPERSED WITH OCCASIONAL REMARKS AND OBSERVATIONS.

Addressed to the Members of the said Yearly Meeting.

BY JOHN WILBUR.

" For it had been better for them not to have known the way of righteousness, than, after they have known it, to turn from the holy commandment delivered unto them."—2 PETER II. 21.

" Men talk as if we ought to speak lenlently of the faults of a man who delights us by his genius or his talents. This precisely is the man whose faults we should be prompt to mark, because he is the man whose faults are the most seducing to the world."—DYMOND, 186-7.

NEW-YORK;

PIERCY & REED, PRINTERS, IX SPRUCE STREET

1845.

PREFACE.

INASMUCH as our first parents, as individuals, were subject, through the wiles of the enemy, to a departure from the purity of the condition in which they were created, so it will be admitted by all true believers, who have been conversant with sacred and profane history, that throughout every generation of their descendants, men have been liable, through the same beguiling influence, to fall from a better to a worse condition.

Hence it follows, that as all religious associations are made up of individuals, that all such bodies of men are exposed to the same danger of a declension; and for this reason it undoubtedly was, that the Lord God of Israel, through his servants Moses and Joshua, labored abundantly with his chosen people in exhorting them to a continuance of fidelity and obedience, in the keeping of his covenant with them, and commands to them—warning them against a lapsed condition, and assuring them of his judgments and indignation that must surely follow a departure from his commands.

And thus we see that their future safety and preservation, consisted not in his having once chosen them from amongst all the families of the earth with whom to place his name, but in their continuing to keep a single eye to the pattern which he had showed them in the mount.

He had done wonders for them in delivering them from bondage,—he had brought them out with a high hand and an out-stretched arm, and had established his covenant with them as his peculiar church and people, and therefore required faithfulness at their hands, answerable to the favours which he had bestowed upon them.

He had required them to love him, and to do justice, righteousness and judgment in all things, throughout their generations—to abstain from idolatry, and from all the evils against which he had warned them : he had prohibited them from mixing with the surrounding nations in their ways and manners of devotion—to come out from among them, and to be separate from them.

Notwithstanding some of those nations believed in the same God in whom they believed, and held and practised some rites in common with them, and coincided with certain things which he had commanded them, such as their altars, their sacrifices, and their priest's services in offering upon them—rites which had been handed down from the first ages of time; figurative and prophetic of that most acceptable sacrifice of the Saviour of men, for the blotting out of the sins of all men, on condition of true repentance towards God, and faith in our Lord Jesus Christ.

Yet, as the practices of those nations were in many essential points diverse and not according to the covenant which he had made with his Israel, and tended to idolatry and the serving of other gods ; his people were therefore strictly forbidden to mingle with them ; not because there were no sincere people among those nations, but because their ways were not in accordance with the pattern shown to Israel in the mount.

We find by following the history of this once favored and chosen people, and beholding, as we do, their gross departure from God's covenant, abundant evidence to show the necessity there was of warning them in the outset against an apostacy, and no less of his mercy in continuing from age to age to send his prophets and messengers unto them, to testify against the forsaking of his law, lest his statutes should be altogether disregarded and trodden down by them.

But, alas ! how many sufferings, reproaches and persecutions these his messengers had to endure, from the hands of those who had departed from the Lord's testimonies, because of their faithfulness to him. On the other hand, how many of those *called* prophets were induced by bribery, were lured by the love, and driven by the fear of man, to prophecy smooth things —to flatter those in power, and to cry peace, peace! when there was no peace. How many and unsparing were the gifts and honors bestowed upon men by those in power, for the strengthening of their own hands in iniquity, and for working devices against the Lord and his faithful servants !

But blessed be the Lord, a faithful remnant there was, (among the many hundreds that were called prophets,) who feared the Lord, that could neither be bought nor driven to forego the word of the Lord, nor to baulk his testimonies to please men. But an apostacy had so prevailed over the rulers of Israel in that day, that many of the prophets were persecuted and slain for their constancy and faithfulness to their Lord and Master. The rulers of the people had become so lost to all that was good, that they took light for darkness, and darkness for light, and so persecuted the Lord's true messengers.

But a reformation—a better day and a better covenant was seen to be coming, and was foretold by those persecuted messengers. And however long the darkness of that apostacy prevailed—however long the coming of a better day was protracted, it was not deferred until human nature had ceased to be human nature in the fall—a condition from which the Gospel power is only able ever to redeem ; but this redemption is effected only upon the condition of *faith and obedience,* so essential under the former dispensation, and without which fallen nature has been the same in every age, is abundantly evinced by the grievous lapse which has befallen the church under both covenants.

Thus we see, however better the day, that without the obedience of faith, fallen nature, or the natural man, is the same, and no better under this than under the former dispensation. And those who are favored with the New Testament, and do not live in conformity with its precepts, and come to experience the power of that religion which it inculcates, are even more reprehensible than those under the former covenant ; of whom many, with less outward advantage, came to witness in an eminent degree, that which was then, as now, the power of God unto salvation.

By the events which have transpired, it would seem that the same liability of departing from the law of the Lord which existed in the Jewish Church, exists in the

Christian Church, and that individuals, as well as bodies of Christians, are as liable to degenerate through disobedience and unfaithfulness to the commands of Christ, as were those under the former covenant; inasmuch as the temptations of the old enemy are as artfully directed against the Chrstian as against the Jewish Church, and only detected by abiding in Him who is the Light of the world, and the Lamb slain from the foundation of the world.

The lapse of the Lord's people, under the former covenant, is strikingly observable in the lamentation over them : "Yet I had planted thee a noble vine, wholly a right seed : how then art thou turned into the degenerate plant of a strange vine unto me ? "— Jer. ii. 21.

But to mark the consummation of the declension and final apostacy of the Jewish Church, we must refer to the time when Jesus Christ came into the world, and call to mind the great enmity and bitterness which the whole sanhedrim and rulers of that body betrayed ; their madness against Him and His doctrines, His ministry and mighty works.

They denied Him and his mission, although Moses, in whom they trusted, had spoken so plainly of him,— they made and spread abroad among the people, all manner of false reports and wicked accusations against him; and made a decree that any one who confessed him to be the Christ should be put out of the synagogue; and their influence and the fear of them,— the bribery, the friendship and other means to which they resorted, succeeded to an astonishing degree in bringing the Saviour of men into great disrepute among the people; and even made the Jewish nation generally believe him to be a deceiver, a dangerous person, and a disturber of the peace, and that therefore he ought to be put to death.

Finally, they bribed Judas Iscariot to betray him into their hands; and in that great concourse which was assembled at his trial before Pilate, (where only two of his disciples dared to come,) there was not so much as one who raised his voice against his being put to death.

By these high professors he *was* put to death—under great pretensions, and professions of religion, and a zeal for the support of the law and covenant which God had ordained to them as a people; making great boasts of their ancestors, and of being the children of Abraham, whilst they were doing the works of their father, the devil, and were his children.

We are assured that eleven out of the twelve of his Apostles, and many others who stood faithful to His Gospel, suffered the like from their cruel hands.

With these wicked rulers, the chief Priests, the Scribes, the Pharisees, and the learned Rabbis, terminated the Jewish dispensation.

When the spirit of this world rules in the hearts of the children of disobedience, whatever they profess as to religion, or whether they make no profession at all; whether priests or levites, scribes or pharisees, or mere men of the world, it matters not, if destitute of the spirit and love of God, they persecute the Saviour of men, and his disciples the children of light: for there is an enmity existing between the spirit of the world and the spirit of God—the flesh warreth against the spirit, and the spirit against the flesh—consequently the children of this world war against the children of God.

It was, by that spirit of this world and of darkness which rebels against the light, that Christ and his followers were persecuted and put to death, by the Jews first, and also by the Gentiles : for his religion truly was, to the high professing Jews, a stumbling block, and to the wisdom of the Greeks foolishness ; because the darkness which was in them, could not comprehend it.

But after the Jewish nation was dispersed, the Christian church continued to grow and increase greatly, although her sons were persecuted and slain in large numbers by the heathen nations : and death —to them welcome death—was almost continually inflicted by the hand of man, and became to them the happy passport to an entrance into the fruition of light, and the realms of eternal glory with Him, for whose cause they had dared to die.

Thus the tribulations of those who were loyal to their Lord, whose mission to this lower world was made perfect through sufferings, were sanctified and productive of a crown of life ; whilst those who were not faithful unto death, through the fear of man or love of the world, were cast off forever and denied the tree of life.

What a glorious pattern, therefore, were the early Christians in suffering for the name of Him who had given the example before them ; and to which example has been added these precepts—that it is enough for the servant to be *as* his Master, and the disciple *as* his Lord. Fear not them that kill the body, and have no more that they can do ; but I will forewarn you whom ye ought to fear, &c.; for to those who know God, and the Will of God, his fear surpasses the fear of man.

What shame and blushing, therefore, ought modern professors to take to themselves, flinching as they do, when their sufferings, whether by the hand of false brethren, or from the world, are so entirely incomparable with the sufferings of Christ and his early followers.

But in process of time the Head of the Church was pleased to say it is enough, and saw meet to prove his people by the reverse of personal suffering; then persecution ceased, and ease and luxury succeeded; a soil in which the life and power of religion was less prolific: and a *trust and reliance* on the Divine support was gradually less apparent, the *love* and *friendship* of the world began to take root in too many of the influential members of the Church; a plant which could not so well flourish under persecution.

Subsequently, for want of sufficient self-denial and true humility, the love of power increased in some of the honorable, and in time a junction with the earthly power ensued, and a disposition for greatness, and to give and receive honor one from another, began to prevail, and that honor which cometh from God and belongeth unto God, was less regarded and less inculcated, and at length profanely transferred to men.

And the title of Reverend, Right Reverend, Holy Father, and Most Holy Father, was ascribed to men —was called for and most sacrilegiously given and received by men! by vain and sinful men! to the pampering of the pride and haughtiness of man: thus shamefully robbing God of that reverence and honor only due to His Great and Holy Name. This constitutes idolatry in its legitimate form.

The sin of avarice, and love of rule, and of absolute power, took deep root in the hearts of those seekers after divine honors.   And as their authority increased and became established, great and most oppressive requisitions were made upon men's consciences and estates : and the Christian discipline by which the church in its purer days had been conscientiously and faithfully governed, was now disregarded and made to give place to the will and pleasure of Popes, Bishops, and Synods.

These men, or this body of men, thus assuming divine honors, did, in their collective capacity, claim to be the Church, or body of Christ—the Holy Mother Church, and with great boldness asserted their own infallibility, and that the Church could not err—that her decrees and determinations were imperious and paramount to all former doctrines or discipline, or even to the Holy Scriptures themselves ; and punished all gainsayers of their doctrines and practices, with excommunication, or imprisonment, or with death.

It is abundantly evident, that the deeper the church became involved in error, the more boldly she proclaimed her authority and infallibility.   It is no less evident that an apostacy of the church has always led to persecution ; and that sufferings under persecution, faithfully and patiently endured, have tended to a reformation.

The Christian exercise of the true church's labor and care towards those who have lost their way, is *Discipline*.   But the annoyance of honest men and women for well doing, is *Persecution*.   The former was ordained of him who is supremely good—the latter is an abomination in the sight of God.   Again, the former is exercised in the love of God, but the latter in the hatred of the wicked One.

The advancement of any people, in moral or religious righteousness, is truly more cheering and hopeful to an honest mind,.and vastly more well pleasing in the sight of God, than a retrograde course, and that without any reference to the point already arrived at.

But that body which descended from the primitive Christian church, and became degenerated, has never been wholly reformed, although divers notable attempts were made for that purpose, at different times between the third and sixteenth centuries, notwithstanding a solitary remnant of sincere believers came out and stood in a situation of detachment from it, during that period. But the regal power of the Romish church was exceedingly great—combining with, and encompassing the authorities of many earthly kingdoms and empires; and before whom, with a Pope at their head, a Huss and a Jerome, with a great number of others, fell victims to their ferocity.

Will any protestant say, that these martyrs were not raised up of God as witnesses against the ecclesiastical corruptions, because of their failure of success? Will any such presume to make that failure chargeable upon a want, on their part, of integrity or purity of intentions, or yet upon the want of a Divine commission, to testify against the atrocities of the church? For is it not a true saying, that the blood of the Martyrs is the seed of the church? And can there be a doubt, that the death of those unflinching and undaunted men, gave energy and resolve to those who followed after? So that their lives and sufferings are not lost, but cherished in the sympathies of all honest protestants: and does not their patient indurance of the most cruel persecutions, tend to encourage every tender heart to greater faithfulness in suffering?

But the enquiry arises, what could induce these rulers to inflict the punishment of death upon the Martyrs? Not the spirit of the meek and lowly Jesus, whose kingdom was not to be supported by carnal weapons, but whose religion is love; and who came not to destroy men's lives but to save them.

Was it not their insatiable avarice and voracious love of power, grounded in malice, which led to many crafty inventions for their own aggrandizement, and the grasping of wealth, and carnal indulgences, that led them on to those atrocious deeds? For their craft they saw was in great danger, if men of such principles, and such Christian eminence as the martyrs were, should be suffered to go at large, and to promulgate their doctrines.

In time, through the good providence of Almighty power, more men were raised up and made instrumental in bringing about a partial, though notable reformation; to the breaking down in some degree, the power of the Roman Hierarchy. And although this beam of gospel light, did not at once fully dispel the whole cloud of papal darkness, yet it did discover to the reformers, some of the greater evils.

Whether the minds of men in that day were not prepared to endure the full radiance of the gospel light, as it shone upon the primitive believers; or whether the papal yoke was too strong to be entirely broken off by the hands of these witnesses, I will not pretend to determine: suffice it to say, that God saw mete that such advancement should then be made. And be it remembered, that even this was at the expense of many lives of his faithful martyrs ; though not to the full accomplishment of a perfect reformation.

And, however, they broke the ground by faithfully renouncing some of the grosser errors of the popish church, yet they retained and unhappily brought out with them the spirit of war, retaliation and persecution, which never existed in the primitive Christian Church, together with a deal of formality and useless ceremonials, which had been imbibed and accumulated during the dark ages of the church's apostate condition.

And in some instances, in the escaping of one great error, the reformers invariably fell into another in an opposite direction. They were right in denying the merits and works of Romish observances, of likenesses, and imagery, of holy relics, the mass, indulgences, &c., &c. But at the same time entirely overlooked the spiritual work of God to be wrought *in man*, and through the gift of the Holy Ghost *by man*, in the obedience of faith, to the regenerating of the heart : they erred in placing their trust in faith alone without regard to that work wrought by the power and spirit of Christ ;in the heart, to the regeneration of the soul, whereby He subdues and crucifies the old man with his deeds ;—in a dependence upon a faith which stands alone, and which is not the gift of God ; and, therefore, not a living faith that worketh by love ; but a faith that is well pleasing to the unregenerate man. If barely believing in Christ, and that his death and sufferings *alone*, would save men, who would refuse so much as to believe, and to ascribe much honor to Christ for justifying and saving them through his own sufferings without them, and without the painful endurance of the baptism of fire and Holy Ghost in themselves.

Under these and other like circumstances it was, that the protestant believers, although they had faithfully witnessed against many of the Romish superstitions, fell into a state of ease, relaxation, and the indulgences of a carnal mind ; still trusting in man, and in the advancement which they had made, and so rested far short of fully attaining to the life and power of true Christianity which had been lost in the apostacy. Then the Lord was graciously pleased to stir up and to visit many minds, with the day spring from on high, for the blessed purpose, not only for salvation to those individuals, but for a further reformation, and final consummation, and establishment of true vital Christianity among men.

And by means of this visitation, many became uneasy and dissatisfied, with the lifeless formalities which yet remained in the Church, and longed in their minds to find the living and sustaining substance, of which the customary rituals and outward performances then practiced, were but a figure ; and of which they took place, not to the satisfying or removal of the sins of the flesh.

Among these seeking and awakening souls, was George Fox. He, through deep meditation ; waiting upon and dwelling with God in spirit, was made a chosen instrument in unfolding the religion of Jesus Christ, more perfectly agreeable to the New Testament ; and was endued with a remarkable gift of discernment of the condition of men, and in the mystery of true godliness ; that it stood not in form but in power. And with great meekness and Christian courage, was enabled to combat the sins of the age in which he lived : and more clearly to instruct and to direct those seeking souls to the teaching of Christ in the inner man, by his light and good spirit : and to bring them off from trusting in man, and from those, who like the Papists, were still making a *trade* of the Gospel, a thing unknown in the primitive days of the Church.

To this faith and ministry, and to the covenant of the pure Gospel of peace, many were gathered. These separated themselves from the spirit and friendship of the world, (so prevalent among the professors of that day,) for the purpose of restoring primitive Christianity in the life and power of it, to the purging of the consciences of men, through the inward operations and purgations of the Holy Ghost, to the doing away, (at least among themselves,) of war, retaliation, and oppression, as well as a hireling ministry : all of which had been introduced into the Church under its degenerated condition.

This doctrine, which inculcates the belief in Christ's teaching his people himself ; and the faith that every true believer has access to God through him ; as also the testimony against war and a hireling ministry, spread alarm among the clergy of that day.

Hence, as the number of the Quakers increased, the clergy began to have fearful apprehensions as to the safety of their callings, or the continued enjoyment of their salaries ; and consequently, resorted to the exercise of their influence, (which was then great in England,) for the purpose of disaffecting the minds of the people against this, to them, new doctrine, of free grace, and a free ministry ; and soon succeeded in raising a storm of persecution against these unresist-

ing Christians. And they, the priests, successfully invoked the civil powers to their assistance ; so that the
spoiling of goods, imprisonment, and even death itself
was often inflicted upon this unoffending people ; when
nothing could be laid to their charge, but obedience to
the law of their God, in honestly promulgating the
doctrines of Christ and his Apostles as exemplified in
the New Testament, and thereby to carry out the
reformation which the first reformers had begun

Here then was seen, protestants inflicting persecution upon their fellow protestants; (similar to that
which those of the Roman Church inflicted upon one
another ;) and only for the reason that the latter were
consummating the good work that the former, or their
predecessors, had begun. And the evidence to prove
that the first reformation was not complete, will be
found in the consideration that the former had not
arrived fully to the ground of primitive Christianity, in
that they yet retained the spirit of domination, war,
and a hireling ministry, creating jealousy and hatred
against the *greater* excellency—against the free teaching of the Gospel. And no greater evidence need be
called for, to establish this point, than to show that they
persecuted their fellow professors for well doing.

And God's permission of the deep sufferings of the
many messengers whom he had sent to bear witness
for him, is no evidence against the validity of their
mission or calling. Their sufferings were as seed
sown, and the fruit to be gathered in God's providence
in after generations—by those who are accounted
worthy also to suffer for the name of Him who died
for them ; whilst those who have lifted up their cruel
hands against the Lord's humble messengers, are
equally reprehensible, whether those messengers were

prophets or apostles, or early Christians, or modern reformers, however unsuccessful any of them may appear to have been, in obviously reforming the church from a lapsed condition, or of having effected a reformation. Here allusion is made to such instances as those of Huss and Jerome.

It appears by the testimony of Jesus Christ our Lord, that the persecutors of that day were chargeable with the blood of the prophets that were slain, from righteous Abel to the days of Zacharias, who perished between the altar and the temple; and whether more or less reprehensible, modern persecutors are, under the light of the gospel day, and themselves professing to be Christians, the reader will judge.

Suffering for righteousness' sake, is diffusive of the spirit of righteousness, not only for the time being, but to after generations. And this diffusion of the Spirit tends to *gather* to the cause espoused by the sufferers.— " A sword shall pass through thine own soul, that the hearts of many may be revealed"—"If I be lifted up I will draw all men unto me." His gathering spirit should extend to all men, through the power of his death.

But among the sufferers for righteousness' sake, Jesus Christ stands above all and over all—*His* sufferings were propitiatory, and a sacrifice for the sins of others, as well as procurative in the ordering of God's power and wisdom, of an immediate and universal pouring forth of his good spirit; whilst the sufferings of prophets and apostles, and all the faithful martyrs, though not propitiatory, nor immediately influential, are mediately influential, through our outward knowledge of their great and unflinching faithfulness to Christ the Head over all.

Human nature itself would never be a Christian martyr; and human reason alone could never comprehend why God should yield his faithful servants to the power of wicked men, because it sees not as He sees —he cannot see how success can grow out of a defeat. And even the disciples of our Lord themselves, whilst his body lay in the grave, felt as though his mission was defeated. But after his resurrection, and after he had taught them of the necessity and purpose of his sufferings, and had breathed the Holy Ghost upon them, then their understandings were opened, and they were made not only to see the power of his sufferings for the establishment of his cause, but were made willing to suffer themselves, for his sake and for their own sake, as well as for the honour of that cause and those testimonies which he had published and ordained, and to follow his example of non-resistance.

But the successors of Huss and Jerome, for want of more of the understanding here alluded to, seemed to apprehend a defeat in *their* death; and to retrieve their cause unhappily resorted to unchristian means, as did also the Waldenses, *eventually*, in support of themselves and their good cause, and the result plainly shows, that the cause of God cannot be promoted, nor his work made to prosper, by resorting to an arm of flesh, instead of trusting in *His* power.

One thing is very observable, that the peaceable, unresisting, and patient endurance of persecution, by our early friends, as dictated by the precepts and spirit of Christ, has hitherto been apparently instrumental in terminating to a great extent, persecution among protestants; an influence, which we have reason to believe, has also reached the Roman Catholics.

And persecution is a thing so heinous, and so irre-

concileable with the law of Christ, that we may well
say it was never inflicted by one true Christian upon
another, or upon any other person. Discipline, the
church of Christ has always had—not for wounding
but for curing—not for the annoyance nor restraining
of him who *reprobates* the evil, but for reproof to him
who *doeth* evil.

But seeing the liability of men and Christians to a
declension and departure from the immediate government of truth, as individuals and as a body, induced
George Fox and his fellow helpers to institute and establish a written disclipine, both for the Church and
for the members, as a guide to the ordering of Church
government, and for the deciding of all questions that
might after arise in the society.

They were aware that the same liability existed in
the primitive church; and that a sad departure from
the meekness and true Christian spirit of right government, did by degrees actually take place with their
successors, and saw the great benefit that a just and
wholesome system of discipline set up and established
during the purer condition of the church, under the
authority of truth, *would have been* to those who followed after, if adhered to by all.

Under these considerations, it undoubtedly was, that
the discerning minds of our first Friends saw the importance of a written system of Christian discipline,
set up and established under the dictates of truth, and
by the consent and authority of the whole church collectively, for the future government of the yearly
meeting, and its subordinate branches, and for the reproof and reclaiming of disorderly walkers, as well as
for the praise of them that do well.

Coincident with a written discipline, a written con-

fession of faith was also adopted in the society, as exemplified in the writings of the first friends, and agreed
to by the whole society. And these doctrines were
fully recognized by the discipline, and summarily incorporated in it. And whosoever therefore deviated
either in faith or practice, became subjects of dealing
by the true intent of that discipline, be their outward
standing or condition in the church what it may.

Hopeful, and in a good degree successful had the
administration of this discipline been, when in the
hands of faithful men and women, acting under the
authority and benign influence of the spirit by which
it was dictated, in guarding against innovation, and honestly laboring for the safety of the society. And the
only ground of fear which may be entertained, of a
final lapse or departure from that discipline, is a defection of principle—in the ruling members of the body.

But notwithstanding the many advantages with
which the society is favored, the reasoning is undeniable, that if unhappily the "leaders of the people"
should become apostate in principle and practice, as
did the successors of the Primitive church, that excellent system of doctrine and discipline handed down
by George Fox and his cotemporaries, would not
govern their proceedings; but would be disregarded
or shaped into a mere automaton, and turned in an
unhallowed manner to almost any direction, or made
to serve almost any purpose that such men might
choose, and finally be changed into an instrument of
persecution!

Notwithstanding the great and helping hand of such
a system of discipline; is not the deepest concern-
ment to the church under our name, involved in the
rectitude of the rulers? And in the inquiry whether

this people are more secure and less liable to an apostacy than was the primitive church. Is it not obvious that when the heads of the tribes begin to cry *peace, peace,* and to preach up the safety and infallibility of the church and of themselves, that the greater danger awaits it, as in the middle ages Yes; and then it is that the wakeful and faithful sentinel sees the greater cause of alarm and the most imminent danger.

And how many deeply exercised and afflicted laborers could be named, from the days of George Fox down to the present time, who have watched over this people as they have watched over their own souls: and how often have they trembled with fear for the church's safety, when they were made to see, in the visions of light, that an enemy had entered the camp: and how faithful to give the watchword of alarm, and to cry aloud for the awakening of the armor bearers, lest, while men slept in security, the city should be broken up.

And whether there is danger of a departure from doctrine or discipline, or of the leaders of the people, lording of it over the heritage, and causing the people to err, at the present time, the watchful and sincere reader of the following history of measures and proceedings, will be prepared to judge.

The following narrative has been taken from records made at the time when the events took place, and is offered to the members of the Society of Friends in New England, and, if practicable, to the awakening of all to a sense of our condition, and to the necessity of a soundness of faith, and a scrupulous regard to our discipline.

INTRODUCTION.

By way of introduction, it appears proper to add the following, taken from the author's documents, or records of things which transpired in England, or came to his observation during his visit to that country, in the early part whereof his mind was brought into deep exercise by the unexpected discovery of a spirit at work, in the minds of some of the influential members of our society; which appeared to him to be at variance with the established and well known doctrines and testimonies of friends : and as he advanced in his religious engagements, more and more of this spirit was brought to view, in a manner which led him to suspect that the society was, at least in some danger, either of a retrograde lapse, as a body into a similar state of things from whence it came out; or otherwise of a rent or division; if its members generally could not be awakened to the perils which he thought awaited them, or induced more decidedly to rally to the standard which George Fox and his fellow helpers set up against the spirit and friendship of the world: as well as against the ceremonials and false doctrines which then remained among the protestant professors of christianity.

Finding this departure so formidable, on account of the talent and station of many of those concerned in it, his mind was brought into great distress, and mourning over the flock of God, once so loyal to the precepts of Christ, the Mediator of the New Covenant. But now alas ! in this very land where this standard was first set up, (after the apostacy,) a departure from first principles was seen among some of the leading members ; the consideration of which was very afflicting at times during his sojourn in that land.

He saw, or thought he saw, the great subtilty of the enemy, (in taking advantage of the Hicksite heresy, which led off on the one side from the true doctrine,) working on the minds of those who were the most prepared to forsake the original ground of vitality : so that whilst they were guarding against a fatal lapse on the one hand, he might the more easily and unsuspectedly plunge them into another as destructive on the other hand,—both insiduous and defective in relation to the true faith in the offices and attributes of the Saviour of men.

It was under these circumstances and apprehensions, that the author wrote a series of letters whilst in that country, to his friend G. C., which were by him published, for the purpose of apprising, at least, some of his friends, of this exercise and concern, and with a desire that both of these extremes and departures might be avoided.

These letters drew upon their author, as well as their publisher, the great displeasure of those in England, who were disposed to confound Hicksism with primitive Quakerism. They came out on the eve of the publication of their avowed sentiments to that effect; which they soon after published in a work called the " Beacon," and which also contained *many other sentiments*, which stand directly at variance with the fundamental doctrines of friends. Many of the abettors of these opinions soon after separated them- selves from the society, and set up meetings of their own; and much better would it have been for the society, if *all* at that time, who held opinions discord- ant with those of R. Barclay, had withdrawn from friends, and openly avowed their real sentiments on the Christian religion; if indeed they were beyond the reach of being reclaimed.

Subsequently, when the author returned to America, a number were not wanting in New England, who instead of strengthening his hands in that important concern, as they ought to have done, hesitated not to condemn his letters and the publication of them, and thereby much too nearly committed themselves to the views which those letters were intended to counteract, affirming, " that the state of things in England was not such as called for the writing of those letters." They professed to know more of the state of things in that country, than one who had mingled largely with the society there, and had held conversation with most or all of their principal characters.

But the coming out of the " Beacon" soon after, and the author of it being strongly supported, as he was, by divers leading and influential characters, put the question out of all dispute with sound friends, that those letters were needful on the occasion and publish- ed at the right time,—that it was highly important that something of the kind should have been laid before the society at that time.

The author of these letters does not pretend to say, by any means, that they were the *best* thing that could have been done on the occasion; but he does say, that seeing the sentiment was getting abroad in England that primitive Quakerism was nearly allied to, if not the same thing as Hicksism, that something of the kind was very needful to set forth and define the vast difference between them, as well as to controvert another idea put forth there, viz. "that the leading characters now in England, were equal, if not superior to G. Fox, W. Penn, R. Barclay, and their cotemporaries; and that if the early Friends had not come out until the present day, Quakerism would have been a very different thing!"

Whosoever attentively reads that publication called the "Beacon" will find its grand object was to confound primitive Quakerism with Hicksism; and then by reading the letters above mentioned, it will be plainly seen that one of the leading objects of them was, to show the distinction, and to set forth the utter disparity between the sound Christian doctrines of our first friends, and the doctrines of Elias Hicks.*

When that pernicious book called the "Beacon," so subversive of Quakerism, as well as of vital Christianity, reached this country, the writer of this, under

---

* In attempting to prove that Hicksism is in accordance with primitive Quakerism, the Beaconites and Hicksites are in this one thing well agreed, and equally dislike and condemn those letters. By a reference to Joseph J. Gurney's Brief Remarks upon Scripture Passages, it will be found that his views evidently approximate to theirs upon the same subject.

In that book, in his attempt to refute our early Friend's doctrine, he boldly charges their views of Scripture passages with "error and heresy"—with aiding that tremendous process of heresy in America

the same concern, used his best endeavours to prevail on the meeting for sufferings for New England to testify against its sentiments, but his labours in this respect were unsuccessful.

It is believed to be due to the editor of the following narrative, to state that he did unwaveringly, on all suitable occasions, express his dissatisfaction with the sentiments of Elisha Bates, when he last attended New England Yearly Meeting as a minister, and afterwards until his apostacy was fully developed, whilst some of the prominent members of our **Yearly Meeting** spoke highly in commendation of him.

But the denial of the writings of our early Friends, by Joseph John Gurney,* is no less palpable than either E. Bates or Isaac Crewdson's ; which is easily proved by a reference to the writings of the former, hereinafter brought to view. And it is as easily proved that the prominent members aforesaid did, and have continued to support and defend the said J. J. G.,

---

* Our frequent and almost only recurrence, by way of objection, to the doctrines of J. J. Gurney in this exposition, is not on account of any thing of a personal nature, nor yet because there have been no other objectionable sentiments written by any who are now members of the Society ; but because *his* are of the greatest notoriety, and very extensively spread in America, as well as in Great Britain and Ireland.

The writings of Edward Ash, of Bristol, (England,) are probably as defective as those of J. J. G., but not of so much celebrity, nor yet spread much, if at all, in America ; and therefore unknown to the American reader ; as also are others of less note.

Waln says, " But every man who makes a public declaration of his opinions, with the avowed design of converting others, subjects them to public discussion, and has no right to complain, if those who believe them to be unsound, endeavour to counteract their effects."

although he rejects and openly controverts some of the essential doctrines of Robert Barclay, and others of the early approved writers!

The doctrines of J. J. G. contained in his "brief remarks on impartiality in the interpretation of Scripture, are of the same cast with the "Beacon," and so nearly agreeing in substance, that a wise man could scarcely distinguish the purport of the one from the other. This book has been fully endorsed before the public, by the Beaconites. And we are most credibly informed, that they declare their sentiments, such as are at variance with those of Friends, were suggested to them by the writings of J. J. Gurney.

Each of these writers have published doctrines essentially at variance with those of the religious society of Friends, which being carried out and adopted, must unavoidably undermine Quakerism, and it is self evident, that whosoever *openly defends or advocates either of these men*, commits himself to, and identifies himself with the doctrines of the man whom he thus defends against the Society; and the more especially so, if that defence be made upon the occasion of others opposing such doctrines. This course has been unhappily pursued, and to a fearful extent, by those prominent members of New England Yearly Meeting, to whom allusion has been already, and will be more frequently hereafter made.

The intelligent reader will readily recognize in such committal, the groundwork of the present controversy, as will fully appear in the subsequent part of this work.

It is apprehended that a loss, in a greater or less degree, of the Virtue, Life, and Power, of pure Christianity, has prepared the minds of too many in the

Society of Friends, to imbibe sentiments which are at variance with true self-denial, and a full conformity to the Cross of our Lord Jesus Christ, and, consequently, with his doctrines, as held and laid down by the early writers in our Society. That a great tendency outward, and to outward views and outward things, has, of late, been apparent in this once greatly favored Society, is very obvious.

Consequently the sentiments of some writers, who have not known the living savour of the Divine life to predominate in their own hearts, (or otherwise have lost its unction,) have sorrowfully spread and taken root in many minds.

And the authors of such sentiments appear to have obtained great place with many of our members, and to have much influence over them.

Moreover the great schism and fearful departure from the Christian covenant on the one hand, in the Society farther west, has furnished the enemy with vast and powerful machinery, to delude, deceive, and draw off, from the same covenant on the other hand, insomuch that many of those who were not caught in the snare of that apostacy, called Hicksism, have been of late in great jeopardy, by the influence and insidious sentiments of persons of genius, high standing, and great learning in the schools of men, tending to draw away from the same gospel covenant in an opposite direction.

These having lost, or never found that hidden treasure of this covenant, as revealed by the Divine Power in the inner man of the heart, have taken offence at the law and the restraints of a meek and lowly Saviour, and so far imbibed the spirit of this world and of the age, as to despise the foolishness of the Cross, which

is the power of God and the wisdom of God, and not
of man, nor of the flesh, but of God.

Instead of submitting, therefore, to die with Christ,
and to abide the painful struggle of yielding up the
will and wisdom of the flesh, these have moulded and
fashioned to themselves a substitute, by professionally
extolling and claiming the faith of Christ's incarnate
sufferings and propitiatory sacrifice upon the Cross
without the gates of Jerusalem, as the *whole* covenant
of salvation, and by Him thus accomplished without
them ; and, consequently, it is feared are carnally believing and trusting in this alone for justification, without its essential concomitant, the true obedience of
faith, and the work of sanctification wrought in the
heart.

These views, and many other of the like tendency,
having been avowed and published by Joseph John
Gurney, a member and professed minister of the Society of Friends in Norwich, Old England, and spread
far and wide among Friends, have been the cause of
great uneasiness and much dissatisfaction in the minds
of faithful Friends ; and the more, because many are
found among us who are disposed to advocate and defend the author of them, without, and in the refusal of
an examination of his published sentiments, or a comparison of them with our acknowledged and well -
known doctrines.

The fact that the author of these views is a man of
great influence, and having many supporters of a
similar description, does indeed give cause for much
alarm among the living members of this Society, well
knowing, as they do, by the history of things that are
past, as well as by those which have transpired in their
own time, that the existence of these troubles, in the

church of Christ, as occasioned by an apostacy from sound doctrines, have always had their beginning in a little obvious diverging, or departure from some essential points of doctrine.

As two direct lines which begin to diverge from each other, (though barely apparent at first,) if they continue, will, in time, come to be at a great distance asunder.

So these have seen, that when men of a strong and independent temperament begin to depart from the fundamental testimonies and doctrines of a religious society, they go wider and wider therefrom, until a great departure from the true meridian is effected, or, to speak more plainly, until they adopt sentiments entirely foreign to those from which they at first, (but perceivably,) departed.

Some of these concerned Friends, who have remained at their posts, have watched over the "landmarks" of Israel's inheritance, as they have watched over their own souls, and can but tremble for the safety of the Ark of his testimonies, when, with their eyes, they behold the demolishing of those stakes, of which the good Shepherd of the fold ordained that "not one of them should be removed."

And, notwithstanding what they have fearfully beheld, of that which they apprehended was an attempt to obliterate and to cancel those distinguishing signals of our profession and its defence, they have marvelled to hear so many of the watchmen cry peace! peace! when the citadel itself is beset by a troop of strong men. They believe that so great a loss cannot otherwise be sustained, either by us or by the world at large, as would be sustained by the breaking down of our distinguishing doctrines and testimonies. And, consequently, they see the great necessity of keeping a single eye to their safety, and a scrupulous watchfulness against " every appearance of evil," that may in the least forebode an apostacy of principle, inasmuch as such did happen, to a sorrowful extent, to the primitive church—the best of bodies—and that too by small beginnings.

Furthermore, these concerned friends have felt not a little responsibility resting upon themselves, and upon the church at large, by reason of the committal to its charge and keeping of the most exalted, efficient, and dignified principles vouchsafed to the hand of man in these modern times, or in any age of the world, because they are the same as committed to the primitive church, in all that relates to Christian redemption and salvation. And they have also felt something of the weight of that appeal which was made of God to his Servant, the Prophet Ezekiel, chap. iii. 28; also xxxiii. 8, 9. " If thou do not warn my people from their ways, they shall die in their iniquity, but their blood will I require at thy hands," &c.

Moreover, the late attempts at innovation, by those above alluded to, speak loudly as a warning to us of the jeopardy which awaits us as a people; for our unfaithfulness and disloyalty to the blessed Truth is such, that Satan appears to have availed himself of the advantage of our relaxation, and seems resolved to divide and scatter us from the true faith; still we hear the cry of peace! still we hear the language of safety reiterated among us! still we see a prevalent disposition to trust in man, and to make flesh our arm!

NARRATIVE AND EXPOSITION.

THE above-named J. J. Gurney, on a visit to America, came to New England, in the 6th month, 1838, and found the ground already prepared in many minds to receive and defend him, notwithstanding the defection of his doctrines.

These persons whose minds had been thus prepared, had evidently been for some years seeking for the control and dominion over New England Yearly Meeting, and over all its concerns, in which they had been successful.

And being men of influence, and disposed to avail themselves of all means within their reach, (which were not in any wise very limited,) whereby, to clothe themselves with rule and with power—have drawn many *to* them, or *after* them, by their proffered friendship—by promotion in appointments—by the honor of man, and by temporal favors, bestowed in many ways. By these means they have encompassed (however unsuspected their object by many) a great proportion of those who were active members, as well as others, and have promoted and made active, many who were not so before.

And those who have not fallen into these new views, have not been desirous of office or control in

2*

the church, and consequently have not put themselves or one another forward much for appointments. And, more especially of late, perceiving a disposition in those of the new ground to exclude them, have mostly refrained from action. And at the last annual assembly, these were entirely excluded from taking a part in its concerns, by the supporters of unsound men and their doctrines, deciding to reject from any service the names of all such as had expressed themselves opposed to the previous proceedings of the Yearly Meeting—thus declaring such out of unity—a measure which had already been adopted and acted upon by Rhode Island Quarterly Meeting.

Those who had thus assumed the control in the Yearly Meeting, formed from their own number, standing committees therein, as also committees of Rhode Island Quarterly Meeting, and clothed themselves with authority to visit and control subordinate meetings, and consequently to control the religious rights of all their members: and these committees have not been backward in exercising this authority. And further, the Yearly Meeting, through their influence, has of late made its committee's advice and decisions conclusive and final; so that appeals from their advice, either by individuals or subordinate meetings, to the Yearly Meeting, is unavailing, however contrary to discipline their advice or decisions may have been.

In the 11th month of 1839, John Wilbur felt himself bound under a religious concern, to visit most of the Quarterly Meetings in the Yearly Meeting, and was cordially liberated by his own Monthly Meeting for that service: and after having visited one Quarter and some of its subordinate meetings, was cited by one of these committees, to appear before a deputation from their body. But their letter not arriving seasonably for him to meet them at the time and place assigned, he called on the

writer of that letter as he passed on in pursuance
of his journey—his having made a stand against the
new doctrines by writing to some ministers and
elders, as well as by conversation, was alleged by
the writer of the letter as a disqualification for
travelling in the ministry; but J. W. was enabled
to convince him that he ought to be left at liberty to
pursue his journey—and he did so.

When the said J. J. Gurney first arrived in New
England, there was a report in circulation that he
had made satisfaction to his friends at home on account of his exceptionable writings; but J. W.
being aware, through direct communications from
England, that the report was unfounded, (a matter
of great importance for the Society to know) took
an opportunity with J. J. Gurney, and informed
him of the apprehensions of many friends in regard
to his sentiments, as set forth in his books, and so
extensively abroad in the Society: and suggested
to him the desirableness of his satisfying friends in
relation to such of his doctrines as were not in
conformity with our acknowledged principles, and
thereby open his own way among us.

But instead of giving any encouragement of doing so, he entered into a prompt defence and justification of all his writings, without exception.

In consequence, therefore, of the result of J. W.'s
visit to the author, he believed it to be his religious
duty to caution friends, on suitable occasions,
against receiving or imbibing the unsound doctrines
alluded to; and at the same time making direct
reference to some of the most exceptionable among
them.

On John Wilbur's return from his eastern visit,
he produced certificates from all the Quarterly and
Monthly Meetings which he attended, expressive
of their satisfaction with his services among them.
And soon after his return from this journey, he ob-

tained the concurrence of his Monthly Meeting, and attended the Yearly Meeting in Philadelphia.

But his travelling as a minister, on account of his objection to those doctrines, was displeasing to those who were supporting and defending the author of them.

It being apparently too much of a circumstance frequently to call together the Committee of the Yearly Meeting of Ministers and Elders: and further, as the Committee of the Yearly Meeting at large was not authorized to recognize ministerial service, a way was devised to get a committee appointed in the Select *Quarterly* Meeting; and if practicable, to be vested with authority to take hold of him, and to stop his speaking against the doctrines of J. J. Gurney; or travelling as a minister.

To effect this, deficient accounts were brought up in relation to unity, from two subordinate meetings, where themselves predominated, professedly for the purpose, and under the pretention of bestowing labor in the cases referred to in those accounts, a committee was appointed, ostensibly for the restoration of unity and harmony.* Howbeit, if their own confession is sufficient evidence, we are warranted in saying, that they never attempted any labor of the kind, whatever, within the limits of those two meetings from which the defective accounts came up; although more than four years have since elapsed, and the committee have been dismissed from their appointment.

John Wilbur was called upon to meet this committee the next morning after its appointment; and they artfully attempted to make him a subject of dealing, and to decoy him to place himself within the purview of their appointment, by asking him

---

* The accounts which went up at this time from South Kingston Monthly Meeting, to which J. W. belonged, were unexceptionable as to unity.

the question, " whether he believed any of the members of our Select Meeting were unsound?" expecting, as was supposed, an affirmative answer; and if so, then here, as they might think, would be a case of disunity fairly within their reach. But their object was seen, and the question not answered, although all the committee, save one, joined in pressing him to answer it. Being defeated in this, they severely reprimanded him for having been to Philadelphia, accusing him of having *known* that they were unwilling he should travel in the ministry. But this charge, of knowing it, he was able to meet, by adducing what some of them had said to him and others, during his eastern journey. One of the committee had said, in a letter to his daughter, that "*they had no desire to stop his travelling in the ministry,*" and another, who met with him on the journey, said "he was glad to meet with him *there.*"

But they brought many other complaints and accusations against him, of which the principal was, that "he had written and spoken against J. J. Gurney, and had spread long lists of extracts from his doctrines." [For an account of these charges and his defence see his letter to this committee, and the vindication of it, further on.]

He now informed them that he had not spoken to the disadvantage of J. J. G., otherwise than by a recital and disavowal of some parts of his doctrines: and in order to show them that those parts of his writings to which he had made exceptions were unsound, and consequently that the course which he had taken was correct and agreeable to discipline, he proposed reading to them the extracts which he had taken ; and which they had charged him with spreading.

But they were unwilling to hear him read these extracts, and conceded there might possibly be some things in the manner of his expressions that would be deemed exceptionable. But J. W. insisted on reading these extracts, in order that the committee might know *how unsound his doctrines were*, (believing that his defence rested upon their demerits,) but the committee appeared exceedingly unwilling to allow the reading of them, and the dilemma in which they were now placed, apparently drew from D. B., one of their number, the expression, "I acknowledge that some of J. J. Gurney's writings are very unsound." But for this imprudence, D. B. was immediately jogged by J. M., one of his colleagues who sat near him, and who dissented from his concession, by saying, "*I* should not have said so."

Finally they utterly refused to hear his defence or the reading of the extracts from Gurney's doctrines, and gave him very little opportunity of any oral vindication of himself in relation to the charges brought against him, by reason of their own claims upon the time; freely and in close succession bestowing upon him their censures, and demanding from him immediate concessions, accompanied with the advice "to stay at home and to be quiet." And so this interview ended.

Thus being denied a full, and fair personal hearing which truth and justice always allows, even to the greatest offenders, John Wilbur resorted to pen, ink and paper; and through this medium addressed T. A., the first named of the committee, with whom he had heretofore stood in the relation of great intimacy; which address is further on.

To this letter, both himself and his colleages declined altogether to make any reply, or to attempt a refutation in writing; yet they did not fail to resort to personal declamation and high sounding words in an interview which they called for in the early part of the Yearly Meeting at Newport, 1840, with an evident design to alarm him; and to induce him to condemn, not only the course which he had taken, but also the letter which he had written to them. And because he hesitated, conscientiously doing so, cast upon him many reproaches, and the epithet of stubbornness, and a disposition to resist his friends and the good order of society. They also now denied the intimation in the letter, that one of their number had said that *some of J. J. Gurney's doctrines were very unsound.* And D. B. himself denied ever saying any such thing. And they further declared that no one would know by reading the letter, any thing about what transpired at their meeting at Greenwich.

At a second interview, during the same Yearly Meeting, they read to him a paper, which, as they said, was from a friend who felt much concern for him; but at the same time withheld from him the name of the writer, as well as the document itself; proceedings which he thought reflected no great honor upon the writer or the presenters thereof. But its contents were not such as to give any uneasiness to him whom it was evidently designed to annoy.

During these interviews, in which the committee evinced much excitement, J. W. was favored to endure their reproaches and revilings without reviling again; and to make no concession or compromise of principle.

In justice to one of the committee, Andrew Nichols, (since deceased) a fellow member with J. W., of the same Monthly Meeting, it ought to be said, that he was a minister of sound principles; and that he was named incidentally on the committee. He was, whilst living, of singular service to J. W., and to the good cause which he was concerned to support. He saw the letter in question, read and approved its contents; and of its being forwarded to the committee, previously thereto.

The fourth meeting of the committee, with some additions to their number, was held at Portsmouth,

R. I., and J. W. was cited again to meet with them, to which he acceded.

The committee now attempted reading extracts from his letter to them, against which they were intending to join issue ; but he objected to their reading *extracts* from his letter without first reading the *whole letter*, and the more, because a number of the committee now present had never became acquainted with its contents, except by hearsay ; and because also, T. A., one of their number, had told him that he had placed upon it, with pen and ink, the inscription of *falsehood*.   J. Wilbur's arguments for either reading the whole letter, or else for not reading the extracts from it, though strongly opposed by some, finally prevailed.

After the letter was read, some attempts were made, (though feeble) to read extracts from it, in order for refutation, but in this course they proceeded not far ; inasmuch as J. W. now called for their objections in writing, both to the course which he had taken in the first place, and to the letter itself, distinctly and severally giving their reasons for such objections.

This seemed to throw the committee into considerable disorder ; after which their proceedings were irregular and desultory.   At one time they would declaim against his making a defence against his friends ; and at another time they would accuse him of having taken false premises in his letter : and again D. B. came forward in a denial of saying at Greenwich, "that some of J. J. G.'s writings were very unsound," (Why need he, for the saying was very true,) and attempted to change the ground, by now adopting this version of it, to wit, "For argument sake I will admit that some of J. J. G.'s writings are very unsound." And J. M., the one who jogged him at Greenwich, and remarked, "*I* should not have said so," now responded to the truth of D. B.'s present version of it, and said, I remember these were D.'s expressions. Why then, asked J. W., did thou jog D. at Greenwich and say, "*I* should not have said so.?" But before this query, to which J. M. made no reply, several of the committee had endorsed his present statement of it.

Finally, as Andrew Nichols had said nothing to this disputed point, they called on him to testify in regard to it: and though a diffident man, he did say to David, the words which thou hast now prefixed, were not prefixed at Greenwich, thy words then were, "I acknowledge that some of the doctrines of J. J. Gurney are very unsound." And so ended this part of the discussion.

After having been together near four hours, they began to talk of what course should be taken, inasmuch as the object of their meeting had not been attained. Two of the committee proposed to burn the papers and drop the subject altogether; but others hesitated. J. Wilbur had complained of the injustice and severity of their charges thrown out against him—of the aspersion of falsehood endorsed upon his letter, saying, that he had never, in speaking of them, or of J. J. Gurney, made use of such language. In answer to which T. A. said, "I don't think that John Wilbur *meant* to say any thing in that letter which was untrue." J. W., after resuming his request to be furnished with their complaint in writing, withdrew in order to remove all embarrassment from their deliberations.

From this time J. W. heard nothing of the intentions of the committee until the holding of the select Quarterly Meeting at Sommerset, in the 11th month following, wherein his sufferings were by no means inconsiderable in consequence of their bringing the case to view before that meeting; but silence was believed to be his lot and ground of safety. After meeting, he was called upon to meet them that afternoon at 3 o'clock; but not feeling ready in his own mind therefor; and having other good reasons therefor, he declined an interview on that day, but informed them that he would wait on them the next day, or at any future time, as they would best like. Accordingly he was notified the next day, after Quarterly Meeting, to meet them on the following morning at the Boarding School at Providence, to which he agreed, and met them there accordingly on 6th day, morning, the 6th of 11th month, to wit, six men and two women. And after a short pause R. G. rose and said, that passing over J. W.'s speaking of a friend travelling in the ministry to his disadvantage, they would proceed to read such passages from his letter as were not satisfactory to the committee, and so proceeded to read them. To which objections J. W. now felt at liberty to make some remarks and to reply somewhat in course; but withal again claiming the right of being put in possession of their objections on paper.

With a view of sustaining their charge of falsehood against his letter they had taken the ground at a former interview, that their censure of him was not for objecting to Jos. J. Gurney's *doctrines*, but for speaking against J. J. Gurney himself. But, nevertheless, their first and prominent charge against him at the first interview, was that he had " spread long lists of extracts from Jos. J. Gurney's doctrines." It is true, that when at that interview, J. W. attempted to justify his having done so, by showing the unsoundness of those doctrines, they feigned to make shift, in order to avoid the exposure of them even among themselves, to let go the complaint, which they had thus emphatically preferred against him,— and attempting to discriminate between the man and his doctrines, to make their charge against him for objections to the man only. Which latter charge they never could, nor can they ever substantiate, and consequently by this wily contrivance to shift their hold, their whole fabric falls to the ground.

Now, at this meeting at Providence, in order to bring them back to their first charge, and the only one as is believed which they can make lie against him; he enquired of R. G., who in opening the case at this time, spoke "of passing over what J. W. had said against a friend travelling in the ministry," as above; J. W. enquired of them whether they were now disposed to relinquish their first charge against him of "spreading long lists of extracts from that friend's doctrines," to which several of them responded, No, oh no. And although J. W., at Newport, did not feel himself at liberty, even to clear himself from many of their accusations; yet now such restraint was removed, and his mind was free, and opened in clearness, and strength was given to speak in defence of the good cause, and to exculpate himself from blame in so far as he had been endeavoring to guard it against innovation.

And it was not long the committee pursued reading extracts, because of their objections being so fully answered, choosing rather to object to the letter in a more summary way; and alleged that J. W. had, by that letter, "implied that the committee were unsound as to their religious sentiments." To this he replied, " that no body of people, or individuals, had any occasion to fear that a charge of unsoundness could be made to lie against them, if they had not accused or identified *themselves* therein by things which they had said or done— that if this committee would come forward and now disavow and condemn the *unsound doctrines* of J. J. Gurney, as himself had done, there was no one who would attempt to implicate them therewith: and " he earnestly and affectionately entreated them to do so for the clearing of themselves from all imputation."

This proposition and entreaty brought much solemnity over the company, and silence prevailed until he found it right to speak further, and to tell them, that they had found much fault with him in relation to expressions in the letter, and that himself had susceptible feelings as well as they, and if they would give him leave, he would remind them of a few expressions and . movements of their own which had been afflictive to him, and then paused for liberty to proceed. After standing for some time, he subjoined, if friends are unwilling to be thus reminded, I will take my seat; but soon rose again, and revived the saying that *silence gives consent*, and then proceeded to tell them that because he conscientiously hesitated to condemn his letter at Newport, that they " charged him with *stubbornness;* and also, divers times, said " that no one could tell by his letter any thing about what transpired at the first interview," [making the whole document a fabrication.] And further, at Portsmouth, had " pronounced the premises therein taken to be false, and the conclusions therefore to be false and unsound," and had inscribed this upon the letter. And in the select Quarterly Meeting but a day or two previous, had opened the subject in a manner altogether uncalled for and unnecessary, unless it was needful to reproach him in that open manner. Silence again reigned, until he again proceeded, the committee also required of him to hear them read to him an anonymous letter, reflecting unfairly upon his proceedings, and which letter or paper was withheld from his possession. An act which he thought the most extraordinary that he had ever known to be practiced by those called friends.

Not the least reply was made to this exposure of their injustice.

It was now very observable that the committee (for the present) were somewhat softened and moderated ; and consented that J. W. should be furnished with their objections to his letter on paper, or with a copy of his letter with their objec-

tions designated in the margin.   And agreed that
T. A., who was not present, should, if he was willing, furnish him with them in the one form or the
other.   But still before we parted, they so far re-
covered their former feelings, that they, or individuals of them, were disposed to annoy him with
questions, if not to entrap him, in an unprovoked
manner, a process, in such a case, as dishonorable
as it is unchristian.   But the result was, that the
answer to every question they asked, as well as to
every accusation they made, tended to their own
disappointment.

On the 28th of 12th month following, came R.
G. and T. A. of the Select Quarterly Meeting Committee to South Kingston Monthly Meetings, and at
the close thereof, called together the ministers and
elders ; and when convened, R. G. stated to them,
that a misunderstanding existed between the Quarterly Meeting's Committee and John Wilbur, a member of this meeting, on account of a letter which he
wrote to them, and which letter was very dissatis-
factory, and apprehended that the members of this
select meeting had been misinformed, and therefore
had not a correct knowledge of the case.   That
they of the committee had now called the members
together in order to give them a right understanding of it.   To this T. A. subjoined, that the letter
alluded to, *contained things that were untrue*, and
again repeated it, *contained things that were not
true*.   And then proposed reading extracts from
the said letter, for the information of the meeting.
But J. W. proposed the reading of the whole letter,
because divers of the members had never seen it,
and because there was a chain of connection
throughout, showing a relation of one part with
another.   And, however, the reading of the whole
letter was strongly opposed by these two committee men, yet the proposition for reading the whole
prevailed, and the letter was deliberately read.

And now the committee, instead of offering their extracts, and instead of going about to prove their assertions of falsehood, which they had said it contained, proposed, and as they said, in order to put an end to the controversy, to destroy the letter, with the copy retained by the writer. And at the same time stoutly affirmed, and repeated it again and again, that the letter was altogether inapplicable to what they said to him at Greenwich, that he, the writer, had made his own premises and drawn his own conclusions, &c. Wherefore J. W. desired them to put a finger on one of his seven references to their charges at Greenwich, and to refute it. This he pressed them earnestly several times to do. But instead of doing it they boldly affirmed that they never made any charge against him there, that they only made some friendly enquiries of him, and thus evaded an examination of the premises so distinctly grounded upon their own charge. They had, in this meeting, made both a formal and formidable complaint of something which he had said or done, and he now earnestly called upon them to show what it was, that thereby it might be seen what it was not, alleging that in the civil department, a man was never so much as brought to trial for defaming others, without propounding the words charged upon him, and much less subjected, without proving them.

But they now declined altogether an examination of those items in the letter which refers to their charges against him, which charges were the whole occasion and ground work of the letter.

And again, inasmuch as they had inscribed upon the letter this condemnatory sentence, viz: that " the premises therein taken were *false*, and consequently that the conclusions were *false* and *unsound*," which inscription had been read in this meeting ; and they had also declared at the same time, without reserve, that " the letter contained things which were not true;" he now called upon them to make good those high charges.

So that, finally, after being thus closely pressed to do the thing which they at first professed to have come for, they referred to the passage relating to their "endeavors to put down those who honestly withstand J. J. Gurney's sentiments," and said, "those expressions which they understood to have been applied to the committee, were untrue."

J. W. now reminded them of what one of them, (R. G.) said to him whilst at Greenwich, viz:—"Thou knew that the Yearly Meeting's Committee were not willing that thou should travel in the ministry, and therefore thou ought not to have gone to Philadelphia," and subjoined, "and my advice to thee is to stay at home and be quiet." To which advice every one of the committee then present, except A. N., responded. Knowing that these were their own words, they appeared to feel the weight of their defeat.

It was observed by one of the members of South Kingston Select Meeting, and seen by every one present, that the truth of the passage referred to was sustained. To this observation they of the committee made no reply. And then again J. W. asked them for other objections, if any they had, tending to prove their charge, but without effect—they wholly declined challenging any other item in the whole letter, though once and again called on to do so.

Hence the writer of it is fully justified in assuming the ground that the letter contains no tangible evidence which goes to sustain their high charges.

And inasmuch as the committee had pressingly proposed the burning of the letter, and had given the assurance that such measure would put an end to the whole controversy, one or two members of the meeting, seeing the utter failure of the committee, and, as it may be, feeling a little for them, and great-

ly desiring the restoration of peace among us, proposed to John Wilbur that he consent to the con-
suming of the papers that related to this unhappy
controversy; being also unduly credulous as to the
assurance given, that this measure would accomplish its termination,—not seeing the consequences
that would most likely follow it; for should this
letter become extinct, and therefore could no longer
bear witness for itself, false charges *might* be
brought against it, in which case the writer would
be left in a very unpleasant predicament, on account of the difficulty of proving a negative without
a record. Moreover, another good reason why
the letter ought not to be burnt is, because the
charge of *falsehood* was written and remained upon
it, and because the writer of it was now charged in
a meeting of ministers and elders, with writing
things therein that are *untrue.* Consequently, for
him to consent to the destruction of the papers, until those slanderous charges are removed and retracted, it might, and not very unfairly, be construed as an acknowledgment on the part of the writer
that those accusations of falsehood were correct.
Hence he saw it much safer to preserve a correct
copy of the letter, and resolved to do so.

The great efforts and unhallowed means resorted
to heretofore by the committee, to calumniate J.
W., and to prevent his having an opportunity to
vindicate his cause, induced him to suspect their
integrity in a professed desire and assurance of a
settlement through the destruction of this letter.

And this suspicion has been since abundantly
confirmed by the acknowledgment of other members of the Select Yearly Meeting's Committee.—
The one who first cited J. W. before them, having
said in a letter to a friend, "The burning of that
letter would, I conceive, have done little if any
thing at all, towards settling the difficulty."

On parting, he called on T. A. to take from that

letter his charge of falsehood, which he had placed upon it, inasmuch as the writer had now been able to substantiate the truth of every line of it: to which **T. A.** answered, as being disposed to alter it, if that would produce a settlement. [If that would procure its destruction?]

But the writer was soon after informed by a message from A. N. that the said T. A. said to him, that himself placed that endorsement on J. W.'s letter, therefore he had a right to take it off; and *he would take it off;* to which message J. W. made this reply, that time would determine, whether that promise were fulfilled or not.

At the close of this interview, J. W. asked **T. A.** for the extracts which they at first proposed to read in that meeting, but he declined giving them, but handed him a copy of the letter with some pencil marks in the margin.

At our Select Quarterly Meeting at Providence, 2nd month, 3d, 1841, the committee presented a report setting forth, as near as can be remembered, (for J. W. has been denied a copy) that " a member of this meeting having spread reports to the injury of the order of society, was labored with on that account by your committee, whereupon the said member wrote a letter to them containing things that were *unjust,*" &c.

This report produced considerable expression, mingled with censure and exhortation, pointedly to the individual, with professions of sympathy for and travail with the committee. And it was concluded that the subject should remain with the same committee. It was perceived by J. W., that the committee at large, was resolved to disregard and overlook the proceedings of those two of their number at South Kingston, he rose, on behalf of the person alluded to in that report: requested that the meeting would either take up the subject itself and allow that individual a fair opportunity of

making his innocency appear, or otherwise instruct
their committee to do so; stating that some of their
number had convened the select meeting, of which
he was a member, and there openly in the meeting
brought complaints against him of a more aggravated nature than those stated in this report, but
which complaints they were not able to sustain,
and which failure he believed was obvious to every
member of that meeting, that he had been suing
for six months past for distinct objections to the
course which he had taken; and as he thought obtained a promise three months before to furnish him
with those objections. But that promise had not yet
been redeemed; and referred to the trial of W.
Penn and W. Mead, in London, to whom a full and
fair hearing was promised, but which promise was
not fulfilled. And the court seemed disposed to
condemn them upon the reports abroad and the prejudice against them. By which reference J. W.
suggested whether the reports abroad tending to
produce unfavorable feelings towards the person alluded to in the report, had not influenced the minds
of some of his friends against him.

The committee now seemed to be brought to a
stand what to say to this statement, but one or two
of them did say that much opportunity had been allowed him; and referred to the time of one sitting,
which they said continued for five hours in discussion of the case. But he reminded them, and informed the meeting, that his solicitation, through
that meeting were the same as now, to give him a
plain statement, on paper, of their ground of uneasiness, and thus the subject was left. But before
leaving Providence, J. W. asked T. A. (the one who
furnished him with the copy of the letter,) whether
those pencil marks on the margin were intended to
designate their objections? and to which he replied
that " he did not know."

John Wilbur received from one of the same committee a previous notice to meet them at Greenwich on the 4th of 5th month, 1841, the day before the Select Quarterly Meeting there. He went accordingly, and met with nine friends of the before-mentioned committee, and six of the standing committee of the Yearly Meeting. And after a time of silence one of the former said, that inasmuch as J. W. had expressed a desire for an opportunity to make his defence, the committee had now met to give him that opportunity.

He now waited some time for their complaint to be brought forward; but not being presented, he mentioned that he had been waiting in expectation, that a complaint, if any they had against him, would be presented: and that nothing to that effect had been given him—that although there were pencil marks on the copy of his letter handed him by T. A., yet T. A. said he did not know whether those pencil marks covered the committee's objections or not; and that therefore he was not prepared to respond to their complaint, having received no other designation in writing of their uneasiness. But J. M. said that " John Wilbur, having received that marked copy from the hands of the committee, *he might have known* that it contained their objections." But as one of their own number had spoken doubtfully in relation to it, J. W. was not now prepared to meet those objections specifically. But the committee decided on going into the consideration of the case at this time. Whereupon he requested that they would allow him the rightful privilege of one of two things, viz: that they would either give him their objections in writing, and time to canvass them; or that they would constitute an individual of their number as their organ to speak on their behalf, intimating that for one individual to be laid under the necessity of replying to the objections and allegations of so many, might tend to an unreasonable embarrassment—these requests were both denied. The Quarterly Meeting's committee plead that he had been furnished as above, and that their objections were marked upon that copy, and that he might have known that it defined their objections, &c.

It was now proposed, as he thinks, by the Yearly Meeting committee, that the letter should be read, and that the Quarterly Meeting's committee should discuss the objectionable passages as the reading went on. To this proposal J. W. objected, for the reason that the Yearly Meeting's committee, (who were presumed not to have seen it,) could not in that way so well comprehend it as a whole. And so the whole letter was read without any interruption. And quite a solemnity prevailed throughout, and for some time after: inasmuch that it did almost seem doubtful whether the Quarterly Meeting's committee would make any objections, nor did they do so until the Yearly Meeting's committee encouraged them to bring them forward, saying that it contained the insinuation that the Quarterly Meeting's committee were unsound, &c. Finally they attempted, but in so feeble a manner, and so indefinite, that the Yearly Meeting's committee proffered their help, (though brought here professedly to judge in a case of uneasiness between the Quarterly Meeting's committee and J. W.,) in pointing out a paragraph or two which they said by a reasonable construction, appeared to them to bear upon the doctrinal views of the Quarterly Meeting's committee.

But to this J. W. said, as he had heretofore said, that it was not his intention to *charge* the committee with unsoundness; and if it would give the committee any satisfaction he was still prepared so to say, [by way of explanation] and as they had asked the question, he would say, that he was as willing to say it in writing as verbally, as it could not then be misconstrued.

These committees held three meetings at this time at Greenwich. And it was at the first that they gave occasion to J. W. to mention the substance of the interview of two of the Quarterly Meeting committee with the ministers and elders at South Kingston, and he was astonished to hear them disclaim having any remembrance of what he related ; and in the sequel they denied it ! although proveable by every member of that meeting.

During this sitting W. J. accused J. W. of setting himself up against the Yearly Meetings of London and New England ; and said that J. J. Gurney's certificate from London pronounced him *to be sound in doctrine*, and that his returning certificate from New England Yearly Meeting also said that he was *sound in doctrine;* but on being disputed as to the latter, said it was to that amount. And as to the former, viz : whether his certificate of liberation pronounced him *sound in doctrine*, the clerk of the Yearly Meeting, now present, was asked to inform the committee of the correctness of that assertion, who said he did not remember ! But there was one present, who did know that assertion to be without foundation ; and W. J. was informed of his error in both cases.

D. B. now said, (though uncalled for) " that he had never read *any thing* in J. J. Gurney's writings, which he considered unsound," (probably to redeem what he had at first said against them.) And at the close of the sitting, whilst many members were yet present, A. S., jr., said that he believed that J. J. Gurney's doctrines, when compared one with another, would very nearly, if not entirely, comport with the doctrines of our early friends. To which W. J. and one or two more responded, and no objection to either of these affirmations was expressed by any one of the committees then present.*

---

* Here then, we find those committees voluntarily identifying themselves in the doctrines of J. J. Gurney. And J. W. thinks,

After the close of this sitting, A. S., jr., put into
the hands of J. W. a sheet of paper, folded in form
of a letter, but not sealed, and offered it for his consideration.   J. W. enquired who the author was, but
did not obtain the name.   He then enquired if the
document was to be his property ?   The answer
was, No, I expect to have it returned to me in the
morning ; and by this time A. S. was retiring, and
so J. W. just put the paper into his outer pocket, and
returned it to the same person next day without unfolding it, or of seeing one word of its contents, and
with it this information, that he had made up his
mind to read no more anonymous letters, and especially if not to be his property, and therefore had
not unfolded it ; and desired to be excused.   And
then referred to such an one read to him at Newport
by the committee, and further said, if any one has
not enough of religious concern to venture his name,
he may as well withhold his writing ; and moreover
said to A. S., that he was willing to receive a letter
from *his hands* at any time, and would pay due attention to it.

On 4th day, morning, J. W. met again with
the committee, and in a recurrence to the great
question of doctrines, as treated of the preceding
evening, he told them that his fears had not diminished by reason of what passed yesterday ; that one of
the Quarterly Meeting Committee had said that he
had never read any thing in J. J. Gurney's writings
which he thought unsound.   And that one of the
Yearly Meeting's Committees had also said, that he
believed, if we were to compare one thing with
another, that we should find J. J. Gurney's doctrines
to be nearly, if not entirely conformable to the doctrines of our early friends ; and that one or two more

no possible construction can be placed, and made to hold upon any
part of the letter in question, implicating them, or as implying that
they had implicated themselves in any sentiments more unsound
than those of J. J. G.

responded to that sentiment. But no reply to these remarks is recollected to have been made. Subsequently, and after some conversation not recollected, R. G. spoke at considerable length, in commendation of J. J. Gurney, bestowing high encomiums and much praise upon him and his services in this country. Soon after, they asked J. W. if he were willing to commit to writing his expressions, that he had no intention of charging the committee with unsoundness? to which he answered in the affirmative, inasmuch as he had quite a choice that such explanation, if made at all, should be in writing; and proposed, if A. S. had a pencil, that he should sketch it out, [meaning then while we were sitting.] But, contrary to his expectation, the committee proposed to rise, and did so. After the sitting of the select Quarterly Meeting, he was requested to meet the committee again next morning at 9 o'clock.

On 5th day, morning, when assembled, A. S. read a paper, not only embracing the explanation agreed to, but a condemnation of expressions contained in his letter, and so shaped as J. W. thought that they could apply it to any part of the letter they might choose, and thereby, if they pleased, make him to retract the whole letter, and the whole ground which he had taken against the doctrines of J. J. Gurney, as well as his objection to the proceedings of the Quarterly Meeting's Committee; hence, of course, he refused to sign it, but asked them to what expressions in the letter they alluded? A. S., the writer of the paper, first referred to J. W.'s saying that D. B. " acknowledged that some of J. J. Gurney's writings were very unsound," when D. B. arose and denied making such expressions. But J. W. now related the conversation that led to it, and mentioned J. M.'s expressions of dissatisfaction with it at the time, when he, J. M. repeated, to wit, " *I* should not have said so," and then called on Andrew Nichols (who had not arrived until this morning) to state his understanding of what D. B. said at the time

alluded to.   And he, although backward about testifying, gave it verbatim as the letter stated; and
immediately that subject was dropped.

A. S. then referred to the passage in the letter
which says, "When you say that I have spoken
against the doctrines of J. J. G., &c.," and said, "that
the committee alleged that J. W. had attributed expressions to them which they had not made use of,"
a matter in which it seems that the Quarterly Meeting Committee and J. W. are at issue.

He now plainly stated to them, that at the first
interview, (and previously to his proposing to read
extracts,) they *did*, and with some *severity,* "censure him for spreading extracts from the doctrines
of J. J. Gurney," but that on his producing those
extracts, and proposing to read them, for their information, as to the extent of their unsoundness, thereby to evince the propriety of his showing those
extracts; then it was that they came round and
said that the unsoundness of the doctrines of J. J.
G. had nothing to do with (J. W.'s) defence.

But even now, (continued he) suppose we were
to waive this impassable ground, and mark the restraints which the select Quarterly Meeting Committee essayed to lay upon him at that time, and
enquire for what cause?   Let the answer be in
their own language for his having spoken against
J. J. Gurney.

This was effectually, and to every intent and purpose, making him, so far as such could make him,
an offender, for speaking against the *doctrines* of J.
J. Gurney, and not otherwise, because it was his
doctrinal characteristics *only* that were implied in
these animadversions.

And if the committee can separate the *doctrines*
from the man, so he, as well, can separate the man
from his doctrines.

In the next place, A. S. spoke at some length in
denunciation of the course which J. W. had taken,
and much in the same strain as did the Quarterly

Meeting's Committee, in the first place at Greenwich, affirming it to have been a breach of order,
&c. The speaker appeared to understand how to
foreclose a reply, by immediately proposing an adjournment on taking his seat, viz: to meet again
on first day evening, at the time of the Yearly
Meeting at Newport, which was agreed to.

At Newport, 1st day evening, the 13th of 6th
month, 1841, the committee again met; J. W.
being present, let them know that he had responded
to, or rather vindicated the passages marked on
their copy of his letter to the Quarterly Meeting's
Committee—and now desired to be furnished with
their objections in writing in relation to the stand
which he had made against the writings of J. J. G.

They now denied having said at their last meeting, that the marked passages included the committee's objections, and J. M., the very man who then
said that " J. W. might have known that the marked passages, coming from the committee, did in-
clude their objections to the letter," now said, that
it was himself, unauthorized by the committee, who
marked those passages, and that they did not in-
clude all the committee's objections to that letter,
and to the last assertion, to wit, that *they did not in-
clude all their objections*, several others responded.

Then, after reminding them of the promise in the
11th month, to furnish him with their objections,
and of their assumption in the 5th month, that they
had done so, as related to the letter, he called upon
the committee, most seriously to furnish him with a
plain account of their dissatisfaction with him on
paper, in a manner which could no more be changed, averring that the allegations and complaints
against him had been several times changed! But
they said he knew enough already of their dissatisfaction, and utterly refused to give him a written
recital of their uneasiness.

Howbeit, he told them, that such was not only his

right, but altogether reasonable, [they had once
promised to give him their objections on paper, and
essayed to do it; and afterwards did not know as
they had, and subsequently assured him that they
had, and now again they assure him that they have
not!!]

Wherefore he now told them that if they persisted in a refusal, there would be no use in his meeting them any more.

Much, however, was said by this committee,* (which now amounted to about thirty persons together, at this time,) and endeavors were
not wanting to place him in a fearful and alarming position. And they ultimately resorted in
turn to persuasion, exhortation and denunciation,
in order to obtain concessions from him. And
at one time, repeatedly said, that it was but a
little they would require of him to say. And at
another time, proclaimed him to be in a dangerous
position; and again they told him, that he was in a
dark, hard state of mind! And after laboring in
this way for some time, they concluded that a smaller number would be better, to labor in a more private way, and so appointed about half a dozen out
of the number for the purpose, and adjourned till 3rd
day, evening. This sub-committee requested him
to meet them next morning at 7 o'clock, which he
did. But during the recess, and on much deliberation, he became more and more confirmed in the
belief, that he could not safely, in any manner whatever, retract the course which he had taken. In
which conclusion he had the unity as well as the
sympathy of his friends.

When this sub-committee met, he told them that
he had but very little to say, that his mind had been

---

* The Select Quarterly Meeting's Committee had now, as they
said, resigned their authority to the Yearly Meeting's Committee,
of which they were all members save two, and by this manœuvre
Andrew Nichols was excluded.

deliberately made up, that he could make no concessions, and therefore was disposed to withdraw;
that the committee could take such course as they
thought proper. But they seemed very unwilling
he should go out, and proposed that he read his defence to such objections as he had already received
from the committee, but he said there would be no
use in answering to a part of an indictment, before
it was finished, or the whole brought into court,
which they could not gainsay, but seemed inclined
to administer more exhortation, and to show him
the danger of his condition; and so he staid until
he supposed all had done. They were quite impor-
tunate, however, that he would meet the full committee the next evening, but he gave them no encouragement of doing so, and did not meet them.

At the close of the Yearly Meeting he was invited into the committee room, where he met with
three or four of the committee, and where the question, whether he would take the advice of his
friends, was urged by one of them, which was only
answered by asking him, whether he was prepared
to give advice? Intimating that it would be time
enough for them to ascertain that fact when their
advice was given.

Some allusion, he thinks, was made by them
at this time, to the passage in his letter which
stated that one of them had demurred to the doctrines of J. J. Gurney, affirming, that although he
had proved it by one witness, that they, the committee, could disprove it by half a dozen witnesses.
And to which J. W. replied, that a negative cannot
be proved, not even by any number of witnesses,
when by one credible individual the thing had been
proved by an affirmative. But one of them, S.
T., jr., said that he was a greater *lawyer* than J.
W., and that a negative can be proved, but did not
tell how. [Howbeit, in this case, the negative
could only be proved by an affirmative witness,

testifying that D. B., instead of being with the committee at the time, was at some other place.]

These few now importuned most earnestly that J. W. would make at least some little concession, and asked him if he would not say this, viz: "If I have done wrong, I am sorry for it." To which he replied, this is by no means a proper way [for a transgressor] to make satisfaction. They finally asked him if he would not meet the whole committee next-morning, and pressed him to do so, but he did not promise, telling them he should take the advice of his friends.

Sixth day morning, agreeable to the counsel of his friends, he again met the Yearly Meeting's Committee, and was there again pressed to make them satisfaction by acknowledgment, and R. G. undertook to give a history of the case, but stated it in the most aggravated point of view, omitting the circumstances militating against the committee, and in favor of J. W. However, as the latter had before concluded to make no defence before the committee, until they had allowed him the just right of having a plain account, in writing, of all their charges against him; he told them, that however unjust and aggravated that statement was, he should make no formal defence. Subsequently, his letter to the committee was read, and when accomplished, reference was made by them to the denial therein contained, of the right or authority of that committee to reprehend him in the form and manner they had done. He now called for a copy of the minute of the appointment of the Select Quarterly Meeting's Committee, but it was not produced; and then stated that he had applied to the clerk of the meeting which appointed them, for a copy of that minute, but he refused to give it. And so they were pleading for assumed powers while they refused to produce evidence of having such powers. He then related the purport of the minute of their appointment, substantially as it was, which they had no right to gainsay, as the only evidence was in their hands, and *that* a matter of record, which only could be admitted to prove their authority.

He stated to them a supposed case where defective accounts should be sent from one of the Quarters to the Yearly Meeting, and a committee appointed on that account, and asked whether such committee would have a right, under that appointment, to go all over the Yearly Meeting in the exercise of the authority thus conferred upon it. To this they made no reply, and it was deemed by J. W. as conclusive against them.

They now professed, and that, as he thought, most dishonorably, to *have in their possession, other complaints against him, of which they had not yet told him.* He then desired, that if they had other charges against him, they would be so good as to bring them forward, as well as those of which they professed that he had sufficient knowledge, so that he might have a plain list of the whole. To which one of them replied, that they had *many others!* [He supposed that they made this pretension to having more charges in store, for the purpose of alarming him, and to induce him to yield to their demands.] But no encouragement was given of letting him know what they were, nor yet of making tangible on paper any thing of the kind whatever. In answer to their frequent demands for concessions, he replied, now near the close, that there were many friends, and probably in all parts of the society, who were nearly united in making a stand against the unsound doctrines spread abroad among us, and that with them, and in the same cause, he had taken a pretty prominent part; therefore, if he should now condemn his having withstood those doctrines, he would inflict a wound upon the good cause, and upon the feelings of his friends, as well as upon his own conscience. To

this one replied, that those alluded to in other parts
of the society, were as likely to be mistaken as was
John Wilbur. To which he saw fit to make no reply. This remark, however, was an assent that the
question should rest upon the ground of doctrines.

This committee, as it appears, were desirous that
he should say something that they could call *a condemnation of errors which he had committed*, and then
to liberate him by *their pardon*, and in that way to
cast a stigma upon him, and on the cause which he
had supported; and which would go to strengthen
the doctrines which he had reprobated. This he
could no more agree to, than G. Fox and others
could agree to be released from prison, under the
sentence of a premunire, by a *pardon* from the king,
the acceptance of which would have implied a confession of guilt. George Fox therefore declared,
that he would rather have lain in jail all his days,
than to act in any way dishonorable to the truth,
or as implying transgression on his part.

Considerable more passed in the course of these
discussions, that was not essential to the merits of
the controversy, and is therefore omitted.

At our Select Quarterly Meeting in the 11th
month following, and in the forepart thereof, divers
pointed declarations were thrown out, evidently
aimed at J. W., which passed without remark ; but
near the close of the business part of that meeting,
one of its committee fell to censuring South Kingston select meeting, for sending up to that meeting,
as representative, one who was under the care of
a committee of that meeting. And now, although
J. W. had let pass, without remark, those pointed
declarations which were aimed at *him*, (he having
a right to do so) yet when the proceedings of that
meeting from which he was there as a representative, were condemned, he felt it his duty to come
forward in vindication of its rights; and he informed the meeting that the friends of South Kingston

meeting believed that this Meeting's Committee, not being appointed for that purpose, had interfered with, and had invaded the *rights* which the Yearly Meeting had confided to it, and to all others within its limits, of that description, and that in a manner unauthorized by Discipline, and that this interference was therefore gratuitous. And further said, that superior meetings and their committees were bound to move through the regular and defined channels of the same discipline which was to govern those of an inferior order as well as individuals. To which no one responded, for the meeting immediately rose.

One of the pointed communications above alluded to, was delivered by T. A., in which he referred to the passage, "When thou bring thy gift to the altar, and there find that thy brother hath ought against thee, leave there thy gift and go and first be reconciled to thy brother, and then come and offer thy gift." This was evidently said with a design to make it appear that J. W. had no right to be exercised in the ministry until he had become reconciled to the committee. A suggestion which came, as it was thought, with no very good grace, from one of a committee, who had strenuously defended J. J. Gurney and his ministry, a man whose mission and ministerial service, in a proposed and extensive visit abroad, was objected to by a number nearly equal to those who united with it, in his own select Yearly Meeting, and *he* desired to forbear going on the proposed service, until he were reconciled to his friends by a suspension of his lecturing, and a correction of his writings : an objection founded upon the palpable *unsoundness* of his views, and consequently it was of immense importance that those views should be retracted previous to his liberation for such a mission, and upon which the passage before us has a most direct and strong bearing.

And evidence is not wanting to prove, that the want of reconciliation between J. W. and the committee originated in the fact, that he, (like those who objected in J. J. Gurney's own Yearly Meeting,) was not satisfied with his travelling as a minister, until he retracted his offensive doctrines.

Under existing circumstances, if sound ministers were bound to conform to the wishes of the defenders of J. J. Gurney, by suspending their gospel services, it results in a concession of truth to error. Has therefore a conformity to their desires and injunctions, in the nature of things, any greater claim upon the true messengers than had the command to Amos the Prophet by Zedekiah, or to Peter and John by the Chief Priests and Pharisees; or to our early Friends by their opposers; however clothed all of these were with constituted authority?

When order, law or discipline, however good in their primitive institution, whilst in the hands of good men, are perverted and turned into instruments of oppression, and made to suppress the gift of God, in bearing testimony to the truth; the consideration becomes of serious and deep import.

Was it wrong for Amos to disregard the authority of the king's court? Was it wrong for Peter and John to forego the constituted authority of the Jewish church, when by that authority they were forbidden to preach Christ? Was it wrong for our early friends to disobey the injunction of the ecclesiastical and civil authorities of their day, in preaching the true gospel of Christ? No,—because the authorities under which they acted, were perverted and made the engine of an unhallowed purpose—were exercised for the purpose of restraining religious duty.

In the cases alluded to, the very intention of restraining the right, was to make way for the establishment and perpetuation of the wrong!

But the intentions of God, in moving his servants to preach the truth, was the reverse of theirs,—was for the purpose of exposing and eradicating the wrong, and establishing the right. It was so, as we have seen, both under the Jewish and Christian dispensations,—that the reformers under the latter, whether earlier or later, though marked as offenders, could not hold their peace—though forbidden by those in authority, could not flinch from their religious duty, from testifying against the evil, or for the advancement of that which was good.

Under the best of church government that has ever been instituted, when it is abused, and a party of unsound leaders have grasped the reins of that government, and in violation of its discipline, attempt to silence the honest supporters of it, as well as its doctrines, shall these, or ought these to hold their peace when their faithful labors, under the guidance of best Wisdom, are the means appointed for sustaining her doctrines, discipline and testimonies? But it is no marvel that a party, designing an innovation upon the doctrines of a religious society, should be disposed to silence and to put down all who make a stand against them.

Another of the committee, (J. M.,) made an effort in that meeting to put J. W. in the place of the old prophet who deceived and misled the prophet of the Lord—he that was sent to declare against Jeroboam's idolatry and his altar at Bethel.

But J. M. found some difficulty in making his parable to bear on any one point of that scripture account. Whereas, if J. J. G. and his apostacy from the doctrines and testimonies of our Israel, were compared to Jeroboam and his departure, and those who feel themselves bound to testify against him and his views with the prophet of the Lord, the parable would bear on most, if not on every point.

And again, if those who have resorted to so many unhallowed efforts to turn the conscientious aside from truth's direction, were compared to the old man, who professed to be a prophet, and who probably had been a true prophet, the comparison would apply in a most striking manner in almost every point. Jeroboam had in many respects departed from the doctrines and testimonies of the Lord's people, and so has J. J. G. A servant of the Lord testified against Jeroboam and his altar, and so J. W. and many others have testified against J. J. G. and his altar.

The Lord commanded *his servant* formally not to turn aside from his direction to eat or drink in that place,—that is, not with Jeroboam, nor with his priests nor prophets. And so the Lord has instructed these in the same sense not to turn aside from his purpose by a compromise, likened to eating or drinking with the prophets of J. J. Gurney. And it is very likely, that if J. W. had been prevailed upon to turn aside from the course prescribed, that the devourer would have had power over him. And there is much reason to fear, that many are in danger of losing the precious life, by being prevailed upon to abandon the word of the Lord, and to believe that J. J. G., and those who advocate him, are the prophets of the Lord, and to listen to their testimony.

On the 13th of 1st month, 1842, two of the committee, as noticed in the complaint, did come to the house of J. W., under the profession, as repeatedly avowed by one of them, that they came upon their own individual concern, but it afterwards appeared by information from another of the committee, that they came by direction and as a deputation from the committee. Their object and labor apparently was, to obtain from him a condemnation of the course he had taken as before pressed by the committee.

But it is due to them to say, that they did allow him pretty fully to vindicate his cause; which was done in a manner that they were not prepared to gainsay; but one of them, though unable to point out error in his proceedings, said, " that as the committee called for something from him, his confidence was such in the committee, it was his opinion that something was due from J. W. to them."

During the interview, J. W. asked them if they believed J. J. Gurney to be a sound Friend? and was answered, by one of them, unhesitatingly, in the affirmative.

In the 4th month, 1842, fifteen in number of the Yearly Meeting's Committee attended South Kingston Monthly Meeting, and brought a voluminous complaint against him, without any previous notice, and literally made good their assertions eight or ten months before, viz: that they had many things against him, of which they had not yet told him. So they did indeed, couch divers charges in this complaint which they had never before brought against him as such.

This attempt by force of numbers, as it appeared, to compel the Monthly Meeting to take immediate measures, contrary to the usual course of business, by overseers, and through a preparative meeting, produced a want of confidence, both in the Monthly Meeting and in the preparative meeting and overseers: and raised the question in many minds, What can be the merits of a complaint which they dare not venture with the overseers and preparative meeting, nor even with the Monthly Meeting, without so great a number to enforce it? Not that the Monthly Meeting was unwilling to recognize it, through the usual channel prescribed by discipline and the order of society. Nor was J. W. unwilling that this case should be submitted to South Kingston Monthly Meeting for decision in a regular manner according to discipline.

The following account of proceedings relative to
the case is compiled from minutes thereof kept by
members of South Kingston Monthly Meeting.

*In the 4th month, 1842, a large number of the Yearly
Meeting's Committee, attended South Kingston
Monthly Meeting, and brought a complaint in
writing against John Wilbur, a member of that
meeting ; which is as follows :*

" *To South Kingston Monthly Meeting of Friends :*

We, the Committee appointed by the Yearly Meeting to extend a general care on its behalf, for the
maintenance of our Christian principles and testimonies, and the preservation of love and unity among our
members ; and in the ability that may be afforded us
to assist and advise such meetings and members,
as circumstances may require, and way open for,
under the direction of best Wisdom ; having had our
minds introduced into deep concern and exercise on
account of the course pursued for some time past, by
John Wilbur, a member of South Kingston Monthly
Meeting, in the station of a minister ; believe the time
has now come, for us to state some of the particulars,
wherein he has departed from the good order of our
religious society, in the disregard of our Christian discipline.

He has circulated an anonymous pamphlet, which
impeaches the character of our Society, and in which,
some of its important doctrines, as exemplified in the
religious engagements of some of its faithful ministers,
are reproachfully held up to view ; and purports to
contain the proceedings of London Yearly Meeting of
Ministers and Elders, with the sentiments of divers
Friends therein named, when the subject of liberating
a minister to visit this country was before that meeting.
The object of which together with sundry letters which
he has circulated, appears to be to induce the belief
that the concern did not receive the unity of the meeting, and that the clerk did not act in conformity with

the true sense and judgment of the meeting in signing the certificate, thus endeavoring to invalidate both the proceedings and conclusion of a meeting, in unity with this Yearly Meeting, and whose certificate on behalf of the same friend was received and united with, as entered on our records. And while the friend was in this country, and engaged in the discharge of his apprehended - religious duty, with full certificates of unity from the Monthly and Quarterly Meetings of which he is a member, and the Yearly Meeting of Ministers and Elders of London, and which were duly presented, received, and accredited, in all the Yearly Meetings in this country except one, which he did not attend. And thus was he at liberty for religious service within their limits in the full and acknowledged character of an approved and authenticated minister of the society of Friends ;—John Wilbur, for the want, as we believe, of an humble abiding in the truth, has circulated divers letters, one or more of which appear to have been written in England, and others originating with himself, addressed to different Friends in this country, which were intended to show that the minister thus liberated to religious service was not in unity with his friends at home, contrary to the long established order of our religious society, and designed to close his way in the minds of Friends. And we also believe, that for the want of maintaining his integrity in that dependence upon the Holy Spirit, which would have preserved him in unity with Friends, he has indulged in a spirit of detraction, in speaking and writing, by which the religious character of divers Friends in our own and other Yearly Meetings has been much misrepresented.

Many friends were introduced into deep concern on his account, and several of them treated with him in tenderness and love in relation to it, but without producing any apparent change in his mind, and there having been a committee appointed by Rhode Island Quarterly Meeting of Ministers and Elders, in the fifth month, 1840, of which body he was a member, on ac-

count of existing deficiencies as manifest from the
answers to the queries, and under a concern for the
cause of truth ; and they having been made acquainted
with John Wilbur's course as last above stated, and he
having made divers assertions tending to induce dissatisfaction among Friends, and with the proceedings of
our Yearly Meeting in various particulars, and calculated to produce division therein, and also to disturb
the unity of different Yearly Meetings, and to alienate
the feelings of their members from each other, sought
an opportunity with him, in which they endeavored to
show him the effects of his proceedings both upon himself and others ; but he so far from receiving these
labors of love in the spirit in which they were administered, soon after wrote a letter to one of the committee, in which he made unjust insinuations, and preferred charges against them which they deny in point
of fact.

They, nevertheless, continued their care and labor,
but his mind appearing closed against their advice in
the 5th month, 1841 ; we, at their request, believed
it to be our duty to extend care in his case ; and it is
with deep regret and sorrow we have observed the
effect his course of conduct has produced, in lessening
that regard for the wholesome restraints of the discipline, and for the labor of faithful Friends, for the
preservation of that good order, love, and unity,
which are essential to the peace and welfare of the
body.

We have had repeated opportunities with him in
which we have labored to convince him of his errors,
but this desirable object not having been accomplished, and after waiting several months to afford him opportunity to make satisfaction for his deviation, and
two of the committee having unavailingly visited him
on this account at his own house, and there not appearing that change in his mind, which is necessary to his
being restored to the unity of Friends, we now believe
it incumbent upon us in discharge of the service confided to us by the Yearly Meeting, to recommend his

case to the immediate notice and care of South Kingston Monthly Meeting.

Providence, 4th Mo. 23, 1842.

(Signed,)

ROWLAND GREENE,	ALLEN WING,
JOHN OSBORNE,	PEREZ PECK,
CALEB NICHOLS,	DAVID BUFFUM,
DANIEL TABER,	JOHN MEADER,
EDWARD WING,	WILLIAM JENKINS,
THOMAS ANTHONY,	MARY WING,
ELIZABETH MEADER,	OLIVE WING,
	MARY B. ALLEN.

After the reading of the complaint, the Yearly
Meeting's Committee proposed that the meeting
should take action upon it, by appointing a committee on the case at that time.

The Friend complained of, and others, took the
ground that the complaint should come to the
Monthly Meeting through the overseers and Preparative Meeting—agreeably to our uniform practice,—but the committee said, their authority from
the Yearly Meeting was such as to obviate the necessity of such preliminary proceedings—and when
it was proposed that the case should be referred for
a month on the ground that the Monthly Meeting
was hardly in a situation to act in so important a
matter on account of the small number present,*
the Yearly Meeting's Committee insisted upon immediate proceedings—saying an addition could be
made at a future time to the committee now appointed, if the meeting desired it ; and threatened,
if the Monthly Meeting did not comply with their
advice, to carry a complaint against it to the Quarterly Meeting.

---

* The meeting was at this time held at the most remote place
from the greater number of Friends—and the day was wet, and
consequently a smaller number than usual were present.

After an expression by the meeting, in which the greater number objected to the proposed immediate action ; the clerk proposed to refer the decision of the question to the Yearly Meeting's Committee, who had been urging it upon the meeting.

They recommended the clerk to decide; which he then did in favor of their views.

The members of South Kingston Monthly Meeting generally knew very little of the merits of this case before it was brought to them by the Yearly Meeting's Committee; but the unusual solicitude and determination manifested by that committee in regard to it, and their apparent control over the clerk, induced many to believe that if a fair and impartial investigation of the case was had, it was important to have an independent and impartial clerk appointed, and accordingly, at the Monthly Meeting in the 5th month, the time for which the clerk was appointed having expired, a new clerk was chosen, having the unity of more than three-fourths of those who expressed themselves ; and those who opposed the appointment did it on the ground of postponing the action of the meeting, and not from any expressed objection to the person appointed. The former clerk having left the table, the one newly appointed was requested to take his seat, but before doing so, he proposed for the former clerk to make a minute of the appointment, but the former clerk said it was not customary. The new clerk then went to the table, and the business of the meeting proceeded ; the former clerk and those who had advocated the postponement of the appointment of the clerk, participated therein. At this time one of the committee in the case of J. Wilbur proposed that an addition be made to that committee, the case being, as he said, a very important one, and the meeting, when they were appointed, small. An addition of five Friends was then made to the committee.

At the Monthly Meeting in the 6th month, several of the Yearly Meeting's Committee attended, and proposed that the new clerk should resign, and that the meeting should re-appoint the former one ; giving it as their opinion that this course would tend to restore *unity* and *harmony* in the meeting, which they professed to be the object of their visit. The committee said, their reason for this advice was, that they had heard that the appointment of the clerk was made in a disorderly manner, and that it was planned out of meeting ; b ut they were unable to sustain these charges when called upon to do so. A large part of the meeting expressed their satisfaction with the appointment of the new clerk—making it evident that the change proposed would not tend to unite the meeting ; and the subject was passed from without making the change.

A committee being appointed at this time to transfer the books and papers of the Monthly Meeting from the former to the present clerk, the Yearly Meeting's Committee stated, that they had advised the former clerk to retain them ; and gave as a reason, that they had cause to apprehend that a *separation* was contemplated by South Kingston Monthly Meeting. This was disclaimed by the Monthly Meeting, and no evidence of it was adduced by the committee.

In the 7th month the committee in the case of John Wilbur met for the investigation of that case, and six of the Yearly Meeting's Committee attended. Before the examination of the case was commenced, J. W. desired to have one or two of his friends to sit with him and assist him ; and after some discussion, in which the Yearly Meeting's Committee made objection to his having this privilege—the respective parties withdrew, submitting the matter to the Monthly Meeting's Committee, who unanimously decided to allow J. W. the assistance of two of his friends. Upon their return, the Yearly Meeting's

4

Committee still objected, and again retired a short
time for consultation among themselves. On again
coming in, they took decided ground that the decls-
ion of the Monthly Meeting's Committee must be
reversed or they should not proceed with the opening of the case, but should leave. The Monthly
Meeting's Committee, on being again appealed to,
declined to take from J. W. the privilege they had
granted, without he should consent thereto. J. W.
subsequently did consent to proceed without the
help of his friends, as from the determination of the
Yearly Meeting's Committee, no other way appeared to go forward with the case, with said committee present, which was to him desirable. During
the discussion of this question of allowing him assistance, which occupied the whole of the first day,
the Yearly Meeting's Committee claimed that it
was their province, after representing the case on
their part, to join the Monthly Meeting's Committee
in judging the same ; a position which the Monthly
Meeting's Committee were not ready to allow. The
Yearly Meeting's Committee also during the same
discussion, denied that they were complainants in
this case—and when, the next morning, they were
asked by J. W. whether they still persisted in this
denial, notwithstanding their names were attached
to the complaint ; they made no reply. In the early
part of the trial, the Yearly Meeting's Committee
introduced the pamphlet alluded to in the complaint,
and which, J. W. was therein charged with circulating. He requested the pamphlet might be read, but
this the Yearly Meeting's Committee opposed, proposing to read only certain extracts which they had
selected from it ; and said if it was read at length,
they should leave ; they opposed it strongly, saying
it would make them accessory to the *further* circulation of an improper book, and responsible for it,
if read before the Monthly Meeting's Committee, but
subsequently said they were willing the committee

should have the pamphlet for examination ! The Monthly Meeting's Committee, however, decided to have it read, and it was read accordingly. The evidence of the Yearly Meeting's Committee in support of charges in the complaint being gone through with, J. W. proposed in his defence to go into the examination of certain fundamental doctrines of the Society as held by the early Friends, and also of certain other doctrines promulgated by Joseph John Gurney, as those of the Society, because it was on account of his objection to the latter, that he was complained of. This was objected to by the Yearly Meeting's Committee.

In support of his right to do so, J. W. refered to the Discipline, p. 74, which is as follows:

" The importance of steadfastly maintaining our ancient principles, respecting the doctrines of the Gospel, coming renewedly under our consideration, we earnestly recommend and enjoin upon Quarterly and Monthly Meetings, and upon all faithful Friends, to be watchful over our members, as it regards the profession of their faith in our Lord Jesus Christ, both as to his outward coming in the flesh, wherein he tasted death for every man, and was the propitiatory sacrifice for our sins, and not for ours only, but also for the sins of the whole world, suffering the just for the unjust, that we might be brought unto God through Him ;— and to his spiritual appearance in the heart, for, " unto them that look for him, shall he appear the second time, without sin, unto salvation." And if in any instance there should be manifested any deviation from our Christian principles in these respects, that they proceed to labor with such in the spirit of meekness and wisdom, endeavoring to bring them to a sense of their departure from our acknowledged principles, that if possible they may be restored to soundness of faith. And if there should be any who should persist in their errors, notwithstanding such labor in brotherly love, that our testimony be maintained by testifying against such."

The Yearly Meeting's Committee took the ground that the Monthly Meeting's Committee had no right to set themselves up as judges of doctrine, and that only two bodies are in any case authorized to judge of doctrines, to wit, the Yearly Meeting and the Meeting for Sufferings; that if they entered into doctrines they would assume authority to decide that the great body of the Yearly Meeting are unsound, taking into view the great unanimity of it, in granting Joseph John Gurney a returning certificate.

The Yearly Meeting's Committee asked a decision of this question, and after taking time for deliberation the committee of the Monthly Meeting gave the following written decision:

" Inasmuch as the complaint against John Wilbur, charges him with circulating an anonymous pamphlet, in which some of the important *doctrines* of our religious society are reproachfully held up to view; and inasmuch as the merits of that matter have been fully gone into, on the part of the Yearly Meeting's Committee: and further, as it appears to us, that the merits of this essentially depends upon the doctrines which have been called in question by John Wilbur; we have concluded to allow him to proceed with his defence, introducing such evidence and documents on these subjects, as shall appear essentially to relate to the same."

And, subsequently, the committee gave the following reasons for their decisions, namely:

" That they came to this conclusion on the ground that John Wilbur had been charged with circulating information, both in writing and print, calculated and intended to close the way of a Friend, from England, travelling among us as an approved and accredited minister,—as well as certain other offences against the discipline and order of society;—and he pleads in defence, that what he has done has been in the faithful discharge of his apprehended religious duty, in guard ing the Society against the introduction of unsound and pernicious doctrines, subversive of Quakerism, which doctrines he maintained were held and promulgated by the individual alluded to. Now, since our Christian discipline *enjoins* upon all faithful friends to be watchful against such doctrines, and to testify against them; it appears to us, that no less could be done, than to allow the person so charged, to show, if he can, that he has been acting in conformity with the Discipline in such cases.

In answer to the assumption of the Yearly Meeting's Committee, that we have no right to judge of doctrines; and that the only bodies authorized to do so, are the Yearly Meeting, and the Meeting for Sufferings; we would observe, that Monthly Meetings and Committees appointed by them, are required to judge of doctrines in many cases; as on receiving members, whether they embrace our principles, and sometimes in disowning members for an abandonment of them. And it will be seen that the discipline above alluded to, would involve an absurdity if this was not the case, for therein *all* faithful friends are *enjoined* to be watchful against the manifestation of unsound doctrines among our members.

We acknowledge, that the Yearly Meeting has very properly constituted its Meeting for Sufferings, the body to judge of the soundness of doctrines proposed to be published as those of the Society; and whose especial duty it is to guard against every inroad of error among us;—but this does not, and cannot debar subordinate meetings and their members, from the *right* and *duty* of judging for themselves in so vital a matter as the doctrines they embrace; and bearing their testimony against manifest unsoundness, in whomsoever it may appear. And, so far as our meetings and members are guided by the Spirit of Truth, which leads into all truth, so far there will be an unity of sentiment among them, and all, as we believe, in full accordance with those doctrines and principles so clearly and fully

testified of, in the early days of the Society by George
Fox, and the primitive Friends."

The Yearly Meeting's Committee being informed
of the decision of the committee of the Monthly
Meeting on this question, immediately withdrew,
taking with them all the papers and documents
which they had introduced to sustain their charges.
The Monthly Meeting's Committee continued their
sittings to the conclusion of the investigation.

At the monthly meeting in the seventh month a
number of the Yearly Meeting's Committee attended. The committee appointed to transfer the books
and papers, reported that they were unabled to obtain them; the former clerk refusing to give them
up; alleging as a reason, that the Yearly Meeting's
Committee advised him to retain them. It was proposed to take him under dealing for the offence, and
the meeting took the case into consideration, denying the right of the committee to interfere with the
records. The Yearly Meeting's Committee objected to his being taken under dealing, but expressed
their satisfaction with the continuance of the same
committee for the same purpose as before, and were
willing, if Friends thought best, that one or two
names be added !

(A member of Greenwich Monthly Meeting having a few words to say, not referring to the merits
of the case, one of the Yearly Meeting's Committee
denied his right to speak, because he was not a
member of South Kingston Monthly Meeting,
thus interfering with that religious freedom of expression which has always characterized Friends;
and this, notwithstanding a member of another
Monthly Meeting who accompanied them, spoke
freely and without any interruption, in condemnation of South Kingston Monthly Meeting.)

The committee again said, that from what they
had seen and heard, they were induced to believe

that a separation was contemplated on the part of South Kingston Monthly Meeting, in which event they said it was very important that the *Society* should have its records, and gave this as a reason for advising the former clerk to retain them. Regret was expressed by the meeting that the committee should again allude to that subject, and they were reminded of the great inconsistency and impropriety of such a course; professing to be laboring to restore unity and at the same time talking about a separation.

The committee in the case of John Wilbur, stated that they were not prepared to report at present. One of the Yearly Meeting's Committee made inquiry whether no part of the committee were ready; upon which one of the committee stated, that two or them had a report in readiness.

The Yearly Meeting's Committee advocated the reading of this report of *two* out of a committee of nine, but the meeting decided against it.

The seven members of the committee who did not sign this report had never had an opportunity to see it, this introduction of it to the meeting being their first knowledge of it.

Near the close of this meeting, that member of the Committee who said two of them had a report in readiness, proposed that those in unity with the Yearly Meeting, and the Yearly Meeting's Committee and their doings, be requested to stop in the house a short time, at the close of the meeting. With this, the former clerk united, and wished the same request made to the women. The Yearly Meeting's Committee, encouraged and approbated this proposal, but the *meeting generally* objected to it, on the ground that it appeared to be a scheme for a separation, which it was hoped would not receive any encouragement, and objected to this *test* of unity with them, as an improper one, fully expressing unity with the doctrines of the Society, as held

by the early Friends, choosing rather to commit
themselves to principles than to men. The Yearly
Meeting's Committee made no charge of unsoundness against any ; but one of them said that a man
might be entirely *sound in doctrine*, and yet be very
far from being in unity with the Yearly Meeting.
The judgment of the meeting was fully acquiesced
in, by him who made the proposition, upon a suggestion of a member of the Yearly Meeting's Committee, and the subject was passed from.

This was the condition of things relative to South
Kingston Monthly Meeting at the time of the Quarterly Meeting in the eighth month, when the Yearly
Meetings's Committee reported it in a state of disunity, disorder and insubordination ; and a Quarterly
Meeting's Committee was appointed to unite with
them in visiting that Monthly Meeting, while the
case of John Wilbur, about which the Yearly Meeting's Committee had manifested such extreme anxi-
ty, was still in the hands of the committee of the
Monthly Meeting, who had not yet reported.

At the Monthly Meeting in the eighth month,
several of the Yearly Meeting's Committee, and all
the committee of the men's Quarterly Meeting attended, and claimed that the Quarterly Meeting's
Committee were incorporated with the meeting,
having a right to act as members, and to advise and
assist the Monthly Meeting, and that the meeting
was bound to act according to their advice, even to
the abrogation of its recorded acts for months past.

The Monthly Meeting did not allow this claim ; it
expressed its willingness to hear and consider whatever advice the committee might offer, and give it
all proper weight, but claimed the right to exercise
its own final judgment as to adopting it; acknowledging itself responsible to the Quarterly and Yearly Meetings in the manner and form prescribod by
the Discipline, for any breach of the discipline and
order of Society.

Seven of the committee in the case of J. W. made the following report.

" *To South Kingston Monthly Meeting of Friends, to be held at Hopkinton, the* 22d *of* 8th *Mo.*, 1842.

The committee appointed by South Kingston Monthly Meeting, to treat with John Wilbur, on account of the complaint brought against him by the Yearly Meeting's Committee, have attended to that service; having given notice to the parties of the time and place of our meeting John Wilbur, and several of the Yearly Meeting's Committee attended, and were heard upon the several matters contained in said complaint.

Upon a full and deliberate investigation of the case, our judgment is that the charges against John Wilbur, have not been sustained; but that his defence is sufficient to exonerate him from the same :—it appearing from the evidence brought before us, that the complaint originated on account of John Wilbur's labors under an apprehension of his religious duty, and in conformity with our Christian discipline, against the introduction into our Society of defective principles and doctrines, and for the preservation of those ancient testimonies of Truth, committed to us as a people. We, therefore recommend that the complaint against him be dismissed.

Hopkinton, 8th Mo., 1842.

OTHNIEL FOSTER,
WILLIAM NICHOLS,
JOHN FOSTER,
ISAAC COLLINS,
JOSHUA GARDNER, JR.
SAMUEL SHEFFIELD,
CHARLES PERRY."

Two of the committee made a counter report. The consideration of the first was then entered upon by the meeting, and the Quarterly Meeting's Committee advised against its adoption.

One of the Yearly Meeting's Committee called for

an explanation of the causes which led that committee to leave, before the investigation of the case of J.
W. was concluded.   The clerk of the Monthly
Meeting's Committee then read an extract from the
committee's minutes, giving their reasons for allowing him to go into an investigation of doctrines in his
defence.   *These reasons were not attempted to be
controverted or answered.*   The meeting gave a very
full expression in favor of receiving the report of the
committee, four-fifths of the number of those who
spoke in relation to it, supporting it, and at its final
adoption only one member of the Monthly Meeting
spoke decidedly against it.   The meeting deliberat-
ed long upon the subject, hearing all the committees
had to say, and when all discussions had ceased,
and the meeting had remained some time in silence,
the clerk made a minute accepting the report, and it
was sent to the women's meeting for their consideration.   The Quarterly Meeting's Committee united
with the Yearly Meeting's Committee in advising
the former clerk to retain the records of the Monthly
Meeting.

Before the report was returned by the women,
an attempt was made by two of the Yearly Meeting's Committee, sitting at the head of the meeting,
to break it up, but it was not successful, and the report *was* united with by the women's meeting.

At the Monthly Meeting in the ninth month a
committee was appointed to labor with T. C. C.,
the former clerk, on account of his withholding from
the Monthly Meeting its records, and the committee
had an opportunity with him on that account; after
the opportunity was ended, he informed one of the
committee that he had delivered our records over to
the Quarterly Meeting's Committee, who had given
him a receipt for them, and taken them away out of
the limits of our Monthly Meeting!   Thus, by this
bold depredation upon our property, effectually de-

priving our members of the right secured to them by the Discipline, of having access to our records.

At the Monthly Meeting in the 10th month, four of the Quarterly Meeting's Committee attended and presented the following written advice to the Monthly Meeting.

" The committee appointed by the Quarterly Meeting to visit South Kingston Monthly Meeting, and for other services, as will appear by the minute of the Quarterly Meeting herewith presented, now believe it right to state to South Kingston Monthly Meeting, that having taken into our deliberate consideration, the proceedings of that meeting in the 8th month last; and other previous proceedings connected with it; which have had the effect to produce the present unhappy differences existing in that meeting, and the state of insubordination in which it now is,—have come to the conclusion that the placing of Samuel Sheffield, at the table, to act as Clerk in the 5th month last, in the irregular and disorderly manner in which it was effected, and by which procedure the feelings and views of many of the members were wholly disregarded; and being satisfied that he took his seat at the table, and made the minute appointing himself out of the usual and long established order of said meeting in appointing their Clerk. We did therefore unite with the advice previously given to Timothy C. Collins, by the Yearly Meeting's Committee, that he should continue for the present to retain the Records of that Meeting.

And as this committee were also fully united in the advice given in the 8th month last to South Kingston Monthly Meeting, not to accept the report presented by that portion of the committee, five of whom were added (contrary to the general usage of our Society,) to the committee appointed in the 4th month, to have charge of the case; after Samuel Sheffield took his seat at the table in the 5th month; and as we have cause to apprehend from the manner in which they were selected. and from their relationship to the individual under care, it was with a view to prevent an impartial exercise of our Christian discipline.

We, therefore, now on behalf of the Quarterly Meeting, advise South Kingston Monthly Meeting at this time, to remove Samuel Sheffield from acting as Clerk, and to re-appoint Timothy C. Collins to the service, to dismiss the case of Timothy C. Collins from their records, and discharge the committee appointed last month to visit him as an offender, for retaining the records of said meeting, as advised to do by this committee, and likewise that the decision in the 8th month last, as entered on their minutes in relation to John Wilbur, against the judgment of concerned friends of that meeting and against the united advice of this committee, be now set aside and be made void and of no effect.

Signed by the committee appointed by Rhode Island Quarterly Meeting to visit South Kingston Monthly Meeting and advise it on its behalf.

> ASA SHERMAN,
> BERIAH COLLINS,
> JOSEPH METCALF,
> ARNOLD CONGDON.

Members of the Committee present.

Hopkinton, 10th Mo., 24th, 1842.

The advice having been twice read, and embracing matters of great moment, and wholly unprecedented, involving not only the rights of individuals, but of meetings, it was proposed to refer it another month for consideration. This document being dated at Hopkinton, the same day, those present were asked if the whole of the committee were consulted in those advices; they answered in the negative. On enquiry of the committee, whether they intended to ask the meeting to act upon it without time for deliberation, one of them replied he thought it reasonable that the meeting should have time to consider of it. But afterwards the committee, and a few members of the Monthly Meeting, advocated the immediate compliance of the meeting. The subject was, however, referred for further consideration to the nexth month.

At the Quarterly Meeting held at Somerset, 3rd of 11th month, 1842, the committee appointed at last Quarterly Meeting, to visit South Kingston and Swanzey Monthly Meetings, reported that they had visited Swanzey Monthly Meeting, and extended such advice as appeared necessary; that they had also visited South Kingston Monthly Meeting in the eighth month, and given their advice in relation to the business of that meeting, which was disregarded, they continuing to manifest a spirit of insubordination, &c., having appointed a committee to deal with their former clerk, for complying with the advice of the Quarterly and Yearly Meeting's Committees in retaining the records of that meeting; that they had also again visited them in the tenth month and given them advice in writing, (here reciting their advice to the Monthly Meeting) which advice was not accepted by the meeting, but they referred the consideration of it another month.

In conclusion, they gave it as their united judgment, (as near as recollected) that South Kingston Monthly Meeting was not in a suitable state to transact business as a Monthly Meeting in conformity with our Christian Discipline, and to the furtherance of the best interests of Society, and therefore recommended that that Monthly Meeting be dissolved, and the members of it joined to Greenwich Monthly Meeting.

The reading of the Discipline under the head of Quarterly Meetings was called for by a member of South Kingston Monthly Meeting, and urged by many Friends, and for a considerable time refused, during which time several united with the report.

At length, after much importunity the Discipline *was* read, and it having been shown that the adop-

tion of the report would be a direct violation of it,
some of the Yearly Meeting's Committee said a
wrong construction was put upon the Discipline, but
did not attempt to point out in what particulars.

Many Friends spoke against the adoption of the
report, insomuch that the meeting appeared nearly
equally divided; but a disposition being plainly
manifested to adopt the report, some of the members
of South Kingston Monthly Meeting strongly remonstrated against the summary dissolution of that
meeting and joining it to another, as a violation of
the plain provisions of the Discipline, and asked for
an opportunity *to be heard* before a committee, or in
some other mode, before the Quarterly Meeting
should proceed to this extremity. This was denied.
It was then stated on the part of South Kingston Monthly Meeting, that if no other opportunity
was to be afforded they should *now* be obliged to
make a statement of the proceedings of the Yearly
and Quarterly Meeting's Committees in that Monthly Meeting, for the information of the Quarterly
Meeting before it should act in so important a case.
Such opportunity being denied, one of the representatives from South Kingston Monthly Meeting, rose
to read such statements ; when he was peremptorily
directed by the clerk to " take his seat and put up
his paper," but he continued to stand, and amidst
great interruption, to plead for the privilege and the
right to be heard. The clerk, however, who was
himself an active member of the Yearly Meeting's
Committee, read the minute dissolving the Monthly
Meeting.*

By the provisions of the minute, South Kingston

* It may be here remarked, that in this meeting the principal and
almost entire actors and managers in this case against the Monthly
Meeting, were members of the Yearly and Quarterly Meeting's
Committee, who have been so often alluded to, in the preceding
pages.

Monthly Meeting is dissolved, and the members thereof annexed to Greenwich Monthly Meeting. It provides that the books be delivered to some person to be appointed by Greenwich Monthly Meeting to receive them, and that all unfinished business be closed by that Monthly Meeting. It declares null and void the appointment of the addition to the committee, in the fifth month, in the case of John Wilbur, and the adoption of the report in his case; also all that has been done in the case of Timothy C. Collins. It continues the same committee, with instructions to visit South Kingston Monthly Meeting, next to be held at Hopkinton, and there to *read* to that meeting this minute of the Quarterly Meeting, and advise those assembled quietly to separate, and hereafter to consider themselves members of Greenwich Monthly Meeting, and under its care; and the committee is authorized and directed to extend its care over all the Monthly Meetings in the Quarter.

When the clerk had concluded reading the minute, the said representative, who had remained standing, stated that he felt it to be due, both to South Kingston Monthly Meeting, and to the Quarterly Meeting, to read the statement, although the dissolution had been consummated, and he proceeded to read.

At first his voice was nearly drowned by the noise and confusion in the house, much of which proceeded from members of the Yearly and Quarterly Meeting's Committees. The clerk attempted to proceed with the business, sending the minute into the woman's meeting, &c. The noise, however, soon nearly subsided, and most of the reading was pretty well heard. When the paper was about half read, the person reading was requested to stop in order to have a passage read from the Discipline, but this he declined, and continued the reading until it was finished.

After he had concluded, the clerk read from the

Discipline, page 154, which advises against the reading of any papers, except such as are from immediate correspondents, without their first being examined by a committee. The Friend who had read the paper said he had no intention to violate the Discipline, but he considered the reading of the statement justifiable under the extraordinary circumstances of the case.*

About ten days after the Quarterly Meeting the representative who read the statement in that meeting, was informed by a young man, a member of South Kingston Monthly Meeting, that he met at Friend's School, Providence, one of the Yearly Meeting's Committee alluded to in the following passage from the statement, viz :

" Before the report was returned by the women, an attempt was made by two of the Yearly Meeting's Committee, sitting at the head of the meeting, to break it up, but it was not successful, and the report was returned united with by the women's meeting."

---

* The reading of this paper was thought to be justifiable for several reasons. First, it was the only opportunity left for a hearing; secondly, a Monthly Meeting is required by the Discipline, page 43, when the Quarterly meeting is dissatisfied with any of its proceedings, to render a satisfactory account to the Quarterly Meeting. Now, the Monthly Meeting being debarred from rendering such an account, it must be done by individuals, if done at all, and was done by one of the representatives. The whole proceedings of the Quarterly Meeting were most irregular and disorderly, depriving the Monthly Meeting at once of all its rights, and even of its existence. A member of the Yearly Meeting's Committee had been allowed to comment on the proceeding of the Monthly Meeting with great severity, misrepresenting and condemning the Monthly Meeting as a whole, and personally reproaching and reviling a member of it in particular. It was felt to be right, under these circumstances, to make a plain statement of facts before the meeting separated. The written statement was read only because it was more strictly accurate, and more concise, than could have been made verbally ; and the character of it was distinctly stated before it was read. The statement read was substantially the same now published, beginning with the 4th month and ending with the 10th month, 1843.

This member of the Yearly Meeting's Committee took him, the young man, aside, and told him that this part of the statement was false, that they had no thought of such a thing, and requested him to correct this mis-statement. On receiving this information the representative aforesaid wrote this member of the Yearly Meeting's Committee, asking him for some explanation, as the attempt alluded to passed under his own eye, and was, besides, susceptible of full proof by others. The propriety of calling upon the person who had made the statement, to correct it if it was claimed to be erroneous, was brought to view in this letter, the writer holding himself fully responsible for it. No reply was made to the letter.

At the conclusion of the Monthly Meeting at Greenwich, 2d of 1st month, 1843, the representative aforesaid, taking two or three Friends with him, sought an interview with both members of the Yearly Meeting's Committee, implicated in the charge. The matter being opened they both denied having done any such thing, or having had any idea of it. A certificate was then read of their denial, from the young man who first gave information of it, which was acknowledged to be essentially correct. This was followed by certificates from five individuals, (two have since been added) who testified that they saw the two friends in question sitting at the head of the meeting, at Hopkinton, in the eighth month, *shake hands* in the common form of breaking up a meeting among Friends, while the report of the committee in the case of John Wilbur was under consideration in the women's meeting; but just as this was done, and before there was time for any others to follow, the women returned the report, and the meeting remained some time longer together. In addition to this was the testimony of several Friends, that both before and after the act of shaking hands, they saw movements

on the part of the two Friends in question which
left no doubts on their minds, that they intended
prematurely to break up the meeting. After this
testimony was read they continued to deny the
act, although one of them seemed to wish to soften
things somewhat; said he could recollect nothing
about it, but *if they did shake hands*, it must be they
thought meeting was through; but the one who first
made the denial said it could not be so, they could
not have forgotten if they had done it. Being asked, after all the testimony which had been adduced,
to retract his charge of falsehood, he said "he had
nothing to retract," and thus the matter was left.

The certificates alluded to are as follows:

CERTIFICATE OF ABEL C. MONROE.

" This may certify that I was at Friend's Boarding
School, in Providence, on the 4th of 11th month last,
on my return from the Quarterly Meeting, held at
Somerset, the previous day; and there met with Thos.
Anthony, who asked me if I lived at my grandmother's
now;—I replied in the affirmative, and he then asked
to speak with me, and we stepped to the door, (in the
porch.) Thomas then said, that the statement made in
the paper read in Quarterly Meeting, in relation to the
attempt to break up the Monthly Meeting, at Hopkinton, was false;—that he and Rowland Greene had no
thought of such a thing. He said he wished me to
correct this mis-statement; that he thought it no more
than right that it should be corrected.

(Signed,)   A. C. MONROE.

1st Mo., 1, 1843.

HOPKINTON, 12TH Mo. 25th, 1842.

" We hereby certify, that at the Monthly Meeting
of Friends, held at Hopkinton, on the 22d of 8th month
last, while the report of the committee in the case of
John Wilbur, was in the hands of the women's meeting, we saw Rowland Greene and Thomas Anthony,
then sitting at the head of the meeting, shake hands

after the manner of Friends when breaking up a meeting; but just at that moment, before there was time for others to follow, the women returned the report, and the meeting remained some time longer together. (Signed,)

> Isaiah Ray,
> Ethan Foster,
> Charles Perry,
> William Foster,
> John Peckham,
> John W. Collins."

"I hereby certify, that at South Kingston Monthly Meeting, held at Hopkinton, on the 22d of 8th month, 1842; that whilst the report of the committee was in the women's meeting, I saw Rowland Greene and Thomas Anthony shake hands, in the common form of breaking up a meeting among Friends.

(Signed,)   Peleg Kenyon."
12th Mo. 28th, 1842.

Westerly, 12th Month 30, 1842.

"I hereby certify that in addition to the act of shaking hands as described in the foregoing certificates, I saw movements on the part of Rowland Greene and Thomas Anthony, in the meeting alluded to, both before and after that act, and before the business was concluded, or the minutes read, such as left no doubt on my mind of their design to break up the meeting."

(signed,)   Ethan Foster.

Westerly, 12th Month 30, 1842.

"I hereby certify that I saw a movement on the part of Rowland Greene and Thomas Anthony in the Monthly Meeting at Hopkinton, in the 8th month last, after the report in the case of John Wilbur was returned by the women, such as satisfied me they intended to break up the meeting. And fearing from these repeated attempts, that the meeting might be prematurely dismissed, I spoke of our practice to read the minutes before the meeting separated, and hoped that

we should conform to that usage; which was after--
wards done."

(Signed,) CHARLES PERRY.

WESTERLY, 12TH MONTH 30TH, 1842.
"We hereby certify that at the Monthly Meeting of
Friends, held at Hopkinton on 22d of 8th month last,
we saw movements made by Rowland Greene and
Thomas Anthony, about the time the report in the case
of John Wilbur was returned from the women's meeting, and before the business of the meeting was concluded, or the minutes of it read, which left no doubt
on our minds that they attempted and intended them
to break up the meeting."

(Signed,) JOHN FOSTER,
THOMAS PERRY,
ISAAC COLLINS.

"I hereby certify that at the Monthly Meeting at
Hopkinton, in the eighth month last, I sat on the seat
directly before Rowland Greene and Thomas Anthony,
and that I heard Thomas ask the clerk if the business
was not through; to which the clerk replied there
would be business from the women; and I then distinctly heard Rowland say, 'We shall have nothing
more from the women,' and turning my head, I saw
motions on their part which appeared like shaking
hands;—at this juncture the door opened, and the
women returned the report united with by their meeting." (Signed,) THOMAS FOSTER.
1st Month 2nd, 1843.

At the Monthly Meeting held at Hopkinton on
the 21st of 11th month, 1842, several of the Quarterly Meeting's Committee attended, and read the
minute of the Quarterly Meeting, dissolving South
Kingston Monthly Meeting, both in the men's and
women's meetings, and advised the members in the
language of that minute, "quietly to separate, and
consider themselves members of Greenwich Month-

ly Meeting, and under its care;" whereupon they withdrew, and eleven members of each meeting with them. Before they left, application was made to them on behalf of South Kingston Monthly Meeting, for a copy of the minute of the Quarterly Meeting, but they declined giving one.

The Monthly Meeting continued together, and concluded to appeal to the next Yearly Meeting, against the decision of the Quarterly Meeting ; and then, notwithstanding the injustice and irregularity of the requirement, it was concluded to suspend the Monthly Meeting, until the Yearly Meeting shall have acted on the appeal. The following is a copy of the minute of appeal :

"The document presented to our last Monthly Meeting, by the Quarterly Meeting's Committee, and then referred, coming now under consideration, and notice being now received through that committee and our representatives, that our Quarterly Meeting has sanctioned the advice therein contained, and has also proceeded at once to dissolve this meeting, and join the members of it to Greenwich Monthly Meeting, as well as to annul a portion of the business heretofore done, and reorded by this meeting ; we have come to the conclusion to appeal to our next Yearly Meeting against the advice of the Quarterly Meeting's Committee, and the judgment of the Quarterly Meeting in confirming it, as not being in accordance with the proper maintenance of the discipline and our ancient Christian testimonies. We also appeal against the decision of our said Quarterly Meeting, dissolving this meeting and the Select Meeting, and their junction with those of Greenwich, as uncalled for by any proceeding of ours, and in its manner premature, and in plain violation of our discipline.

"And we also appeal against such other decrees of the Quarterly Meeting as go to annul or affect the rights, or property, or duties of this meeting, as granted to it, or conferred upon it, and required of it, by the

Yearly Meeting, as set forth in our rules of discipline; and Othniel Foster, John Wilbur, John Foster of Charlestown, Charles Perry, Isaac Collins, John Foster of Hopkinton, Ethan Foster, Samuel Sheffield and Elisha Kenyon, are appointed to represent this meeting and to act on its behalf, in prosecuting this appeal before the Yearly Meeting, or such committee as it shall appoint to hear the same, and our clerk is directed to furnish Rhode Island Quarterly Meeting, Greenwich Monthly Meeting, and the committee of this meeting, named above, with copies of this minute; having the unity of the women's meeting herein."

Extracted from the minutes of South Kingston Monthly Meeting, held at Hopkinton, 21st of 11th month, 1842.

(Signed,)　　SAMUEL SHEFFIELD, *Clerk*.

" And we the undersigned do also for ourselves, and on behalf and in the name of South Kingston Monthly Meeting, or otherwise called the late Monthly Meeting of South Kingston, and on behalf of the members thereof, appeal to our next Yearly Meeting, against the judgment of Rhode Island Quarterly Meeting, held at Somerset, 3d of 11th month, 1842, in relation to the dissolution of said South Kingston Monthly Meeting, and reference is hereby made to the foregoing document, signed by Samuel Sheffield, clerk of said Monthly Meeting, for the manner and form of this our appeal, to be presented to our next Quarterly Meeting, and to our next Yearly Meeting; and the same Friends as named above, are appointed by the signers of this paper, to represent them in the prosecution of this appeal."

(This appeal was signed by eighty-two members of the Monthly Meeting.)

Two of the Committee of South Kingston Monthly Meeting on the appeal, attended Greenwich Monthly Meeting, held at Cranston, in the 11th month, and laid a copy of the appeal on the clerk's table. The meeting did not seem disposed to receive it; the clerk attempted to return it to the person who had placed it upon the table, but he declining to take it back, the clerk finally kept it. The minute of the Quarterly Meeting, by which South Kingston Monthly Meeting is dissolved and joined to Greenwich, was read and acceded to on the part of Greenwich Monthly Meeting.

At Greenwich Monthly Meeting, held at East Greenwich, 2d of 1st month, 1843, two members of the Yearly Meeting's Committee, and one of the Quarterly Meeting's Committee, besides those belonging to Greenwich Monthly Meeting, attended.

A committee being about to be appointed to bring in names for new overseers, &c., including those for the preparative meetings heretofore constituting South Kingston Monthly Meeting; it was proposed and concluded that the clerk should not take the name of any person on the committee, that he should *conscientiously believe* not to be in unity with the Yearly and Quarterly Meetings and their committees.

One of the Yearly Meeting's Committee requested that the minute of the Quarterly Meeting be again read, which was done. He then said it would be seen by this minute that the appointment of a part of the committee, and the report of the committee in the case of John Wilbur, were *annulled*, and that it now became the duty of the committee originally appointed, to report to this meeting.

One of the two of that committee who made the counter report in the eighth month, enquired if it would not be proper for them to have another interview with John Wilbur, and this was concluded on. Objection was made to this proceeding, on the ground that South Kingston Monthly Meeting had appealed from the decision of the Quarterly Meeting; that the action against that meeting was *solely* in consequence of its decision in the case of John Wilbur;—that case was specified and fully brought to view, in the Quarterly Meeting's Committee's advice and the Quarterly Meeting's minute, and the appeal ought to stay all proceedings in the case, until the Yearly Meeting should decide it. This just and reasonable ground was not allowed, but a member of the Yearly Meeting's Committee, who had from the first been very active in the case, said that the appeal and this case were distinct matters. Another member of the same committee urged, that if that Monthly Meeting intended to be subordinate to superior meetings, it must, as the Quarterly Meeting had directed, close the unfinished business of South Kingston Monthly Meeting, and this case was particularly mentioned and brought before them by the Quarterly Meeting's minute. It had annulled the proceedings of South Kingston Monthly Meeting in the case.

It was replied, that South Kingston Monthly Meeting had *appealed against all this*, and that it would only be proper for the Monthly Meeting to carry out the direction of the Quarterly Meeting, after the Yearly Meeting had decided that the Quarterly Meeting had done right,—when a member of the Quarterly Meeting's Committee said, as to this matter of appeal, *there were some doubt whether there was any such meeting as South Kingston Monthly Meeting, when the appeal was made!* thus striking at the right of appeal. This ground, however, was not maintained, and afterwards a member of the Yearly Meeting's Committee said he did not suppose this Friend meant to call in question the right of appeal. He said no!

A minute was made directing the committee in the case of J. W., to report at a future meeting.

At Greenwich Monthly Meeting, held at Coventry, 30th of 1st month, 1843, three members of the Yearly Meeting's Committee attended, besides those belonging to that meeting. The case of John Wilbur was taken up, and one of the committee appointed in the fourth month by South Kingston Monthly Meeting, stated that two of them had met, having given notice of the meeting to the others, and also to John Wilbur, that the latter might be present,* if he saw fit, and make an acknowledgment—but he refused to attend. These two members of the committee made the following report, to wit:

" We, of the committee appointed in the 4th month last, in the case of John Wilbur report: that we have attended to the duties assigned us, by meeting John Wilbur and the Yearly Meeting's Committee, and hearing the evidence in the case, and which was in our judgment sufficient to substantiate all the charges preferred against him, and which charges, having relation altogether to his departure from discipline and good order, it was evident to us his defence ought to be predicated on that ground alone. And whereas the other part of the Monthly Meeting's Committee, were willing to allow him to make his defence, by leaving this only legitimate ground, and go into a justification of his conduct by allusions to doctrines, and which in our view was entirely foreign to the subject matter under consideration. We, therefore, felt ourselves bound to dissent from such a course. And it is our united sense and judgment that he is not in a situation and state of mind, to be continued a member of our religious society, which we submit to the Monthly Meeting.

WILLIAM S. PERRY,
HEZEKIAH BABCOCK.

South Kingston, 7th Mo. 23d, 1842."

This report was in the same words as that presented by the same persons, to South Kingston Monthly Meeting in the eighth month, except that

---

* This was incorrect; he was not asked to be present, but merely notified, by letter, of the time of their meeting, and informed that he might send in an acknowledgment, if so disposed.

in the latter the word " all" occurred before the
words "the charges."

The meeting being now about to act upon the report; some of the Yearly Meeting's Committee
uniting therewith, it was stated that the *complaint*
against J. W. had never been read in that Monthly
Meeting—and upon enquiry it was found that the
complaint was not now present in the meeting.

The clerk sent a messenger for it, and the meeting suspended further proceedings in the case, until
his return.

When the complaint was brought in, it was read,
and the report of the committee was then united with
by most or all the members of the Yearly and Quarterly Meeting's Committees present, and two others.

Objection was made to the report by several
Friends, but the clerk, an active member of the
Yearly Meeting's Committee, made a minute adopt-
ing it, and John Wilbur was *thus* disowned.

At Rhode Island Quarterly Meeting held at Providence, in the 2d month, 1843, one of the Committee of South Kingston Monthly Meeting on their
appeal, laid a copy of the appeal on the clerk's table, in the early part of the meeting, and after a
time the clerk stated that there was a paper on the
table purporting to be an appeal from South Kingston Monthly Meeting, and asked for the direction of
the meeting, as to what disposition should be made
of it. It was proposed to appoint some Friends to
take it and examine it, and report whether it should
be read. The reading of the discipline relating to
such appeals was called for, but the committee was
first appointed, and after they had taken the appeal
out for examination, considerable profession was
made of willingness to have the discipline read, and
it was *then* done. Shortly after, the committee returned the appeal, and recommended that it be
read; which being done, the clerk said Friends
would observe, that there was the name of a Friend

on the Committee of the Monthly Meeting on the
appeal, who had been placed under dealing by the
action of the Quarterly Meeting. He said the
meeting would decide whether they would allow
that name to stand there, in case the appeal should
go on their minutes.

After considerable discussion, in which the injustice and incompatibility with the discipline, of the
act of the Quarterly Meeting was shown,—the
clerk made a minute stating in substance, that although the appeal contained the name of a Friend,
placed under dealing by the action of the Quarterly
Meeting, we have concluded to enter it upon our
minutes, and send it up to our next Yearly Meeting.

One of the Yearly Meeting's Committee corrected
the clerk as to the latter clause, saying that the
conclusion of the meeting was, to refer the consideration of it until next quarter, whereupon he made
that alteration. The same member of that committee proposed that the word "individual" should
be substituted for "Friend," and the clerk at once
made the change.

While the appeal was in the hands of the committee, a member of South Kingston Monthly
Meeting, (one of the committee on the appeal,) stated that at the time that Monthly Meeting was dissolved, a request was made of the Quarterly Meeting's Committee, then present, for a copy of the
minute authorizing the dissolution, but it was refused; that since then application has been made
to the clerk of the Quarterly Meeting for a copy,
who also refused it, on the ground that he was not
authorized to give it, without the authority of that
meeting. He now requested of the meeting, on
behalf of the committee on the appeal, a copy of
that minute.

A member of the Yearly Meeting's Committee
said that the meeting had not come to any conclusion, as to the disposition of the appeal; he thought

it proper to wait until that was decided on, and then the subject might be taken up. The Friend who made the request, expressed his satisfaction with that course. Afterwards, when the appeal had been referred to the next quarter, the clerk being about to proceed to other business, application was renewed on behalf of South Kingston Monthly Meeting, for a copy of the Quarterly Meeting's minute, but it was refused, a member of the Yearly Meeting's Committee saying, that he thought it improper to give a copy! that it would be sufficient for them to furnish the Yearly Meeting with a copy! and this being sustained by other members of the same committee, the meeting proceeded with other business; thus denying South Kingston Monthly Meeting a copy of the document by which it had been dissolved, containing matters of the greatest importance relative to their case.

[It is worthy of remark that *all* who took ground in this meeting, against furnishing South Kingston Monthly Meeting with a copy of this document, were members of the Yearly or Quarterly Meeting's Committees, most of them the same men who had been so active in the case of John Wilbur from the beginning.]

At the Quarterly Meeting held at Greenwich in the 5th month, 1843, the account from Greenwich Monthly Meeting informed, that John Wilbur having given them notice of his intention to appeal from their judgment disowning him, they had appointed a committee to represent the case before a Committee of the Quarterly Meeting. It was stated on behalf of John Wilbur, that he did not intend to prosecute his appeal at that time.

Representatives were appointed to attend the Yearly Meeting, one of whom asked to be excused, which being done, another was named in his place, but being obnoxious to those in authority, his name was rejected, upon the pretence that there were already enough appointed.

The minute of the last meeting, relating to the appeal of South Kingston Monthly Meeting was read. A member of the Yearly Meeting's Committee spoke of the great strait he was in, on account of the name of an individual, standing as one of the committee on the appeal, who had been placed under dealing by the action of the Quarterly Meeting; and said he did not see how the appeal could be carried forward in its present shape. Another member of the Yearly Meeting's Committee expressed himself in a similar manner.

A Friend remarked if this was the case, Greenwich Monthly Meeting might have disowned all the members of the appeal committee, and thus have defeated it altogether. Another Friend said he thought the minute of the Quarterly Meeting carried its own condemnation on the face of it, stating as it did that an individual was placed under dealing by the Quarterly Meeting; he knew no discipline to warrant such a thing.

The clerk said he was *ready to propose that this appeal should be again referred!* A Friend from South Kingston said the appeal was made to the *next* Yearly Meeting, and to refer it again would defeat the appeal.

It was now concluded to appoint a committee to represent the case at the Yearly Meeting,—premising that none should be appointed, who did not unite with the proceedings in laying the Monthly Meeting down.

The following persons were appointed, viz:

Perez Peck, Allen Wing, Beriah Collins, Joseph Metcalf, Nicholas Congdon, Arnold Congdon, William S. Perry and William A. Robinson. By the minute of their appointment, the clerk is directed to furnish them, with all needful extracts from the minutes.

The committee on the appeal of South Kingston Monthly Meeting, made application in writing for access to the records of the Quarterly Meeting, with a view to the timely preparation of the case ; referring to the discipline, " that our records shall be open to any of our meetings, particular members, and to such others as the respective Monthly Meetings may think necessary, for the ascertaining of marriages, births, *or other rights.*" page 43.

This request, after considerable discussion, was refused ; and much severity of expression was indulged in towards the applicants ; after which a member of South Kingston Monthly Meeting rose, and very calmly commenced speaking,—when a large number of persons in the body of the meeting rose and hurried out of the house, those at the head of the meeting shook hands, and it broke up in the greatest confusion and disorder.

The voice of the person speaking was entirely drowned by the noise, and perceiving the meeting really breaking up, he desisted.

At New England Yearly Meeting, held on Rhode Island, 6th month, 1843.

It appeared from the account of Rhode Island Quarterly Meeting, that a portion of Greenwich Monthly Meeting, late members of South Kingston Monthly Meeting had appealed from their judgment dissolving said Monthly Meeting and annexing the same to Greenwich, and that they had appointed Perez Peck and others to represent the Quarterly Meeting before a Committee of the Yearly Meeting to be appointed to hear the appeal.

When this case came up, the clerk read the discipline relating to such appeal, and remarked that it had been customary in cases of appeal to appoint a committee of two Friends from each Quarterly Meeting, but proposed in this case the appointment of three from each Quarter, which was united with.

On behalf of South Kingston Monthly Meeting a desire was expressed to have the case tried in open Yearly Meeting, for the full information of the members generally before acting thereon, and referring to the practice of London Yearly Meeting, in important cases—where *doctrines* are involved. This was objected to on the ground that we must be governed by our own discipline ; and that the usual mode of trying appeal cases should be adhered to.

The clerk said that in cases of defamation, the discipline gave the person complained of the right to object to those named for a committee, provided such objection does not extend to the major part thereof,—but there was no *discipline* which would apply to cases of this kind. He said, however, that the usage of Society had been to allow appellants this privilege in other cases, so far as he knew. He proposed to read from the discipline of another Yearly Meeting ; but objection being made on the ground that the Yearly Meeting had already decided that we must be governed by our own discipline, he did not read it.

A Friend said if he was correctly informed, there was a large Committee of the Yearly Meeting which had been active in this case, having repeatedly attended South Kingston Monthly Meeting, and advised in relation to the proceedings which had taken place in regard to that meeting—and if so, he thought it improper to appoint members of that committee, on this appeal. The clerk replied it might not be proper to appoint those of that committee who had *attended* South Kingston Monthly Meeting and been *active* in the case. Objection was made on behalf of South Kingston Monthly Meeting to the appointment of any portion of the Yearly Meeting's Committee, and allowing them to nominate for this committee.

The clerk proceeded to take names, and having obtained the requisite number, enquiry was made whether any of the Yearly Meeting's Committee was included among them. The clerk replied there was one; that one asked to be excused, which being done, another friend was appointed in his place. It was also stated that several members of the committee had been named by members of the Yearly Meeting's Committee, and objection was made to these.

A member of the Yearly Meeting's Committee said, if these friends were objected to, it would not probably stop there; that objection would be made on the other side, &c. The committee was allowed to stand without further alteration.

A friend from Sandwich Quarterly Meeting said, it appeared evident to him from the Discipline, as read by the clerk, that the Quarterly Meeting had departed from it, in annexing South Kingston Monthly Meeting to another, while at the same time the Monthly Meeting has appealed against the dissolution. If he understood it right, the Discipline only allows such annexation in case the Monthly Meeting *refuses to appeal.*

He requested the clerk again to read that paragraph giving this right of annexation. The assistant clerk then read the succeeding paragraph. The friend said this was not the one, but the preceding one he wished read.

The whole passage was then read; when done, the friend said it was very clear that the Discipline had not been kept to, for the Monthly Meeting not only had not refused to appeal, but the Quarterly Meeting had given us information that it had actually appealed.

The clerk was requested to read the "appeal," a copy of which was in his hands, and several friends expressed a wish to have it read, when one of the Yearly Meeting's Committee said, that by our Discipline, no paper could be read in our meetings not coming from an immediate correspondent, unless first examined by a committee. To this it was replied, that the Discipline made these appellants immediate correspondents by giving the *right of appeal;* and that the Yearly Meeting ought to know the grounds on which the appeal is made.

After considerable discussion it was decided not to read the Appeal, but the copy was by the clerk handed to the committee just appointed.

From the minutes of the meeting for Sufferings, it appeared that a committee was appointed in the 11th month, 1842, to prepare a statement of the condition of things among us, particularly in Rhode Island Quarterly Meeting, which was not generally well understood. This committee reported from time to time their progress, and a few weeks before the Yearly Meeting they reported that they had prepared such a statement, but thought it best to defer the presentation of it for the present, but that they had in the prosecution of this labor, been introduced into a concern to prepare an essay upon the doctrines and testimonies of the Society, which they produced, and it being read, it was referred to a committee then specially appointed, to take it into their consideration, and make such amendments as they may deem proper, and report. The document was subsequently adopted by the meeting for Sufferings, read in Yearly Meeting and directed to be printed.*

Returning minutes were presented and adopted by the meeting for two ministers and their companions, who were in attendance from New York Yearly Meeting. None were prepared for three

---

* The statement respecting Rhode Island Quarterly Meeting, &c.. said to have been prepared as above, has never appeared. The committee was appointed on the subject about the time South Kingston Monthly Meeting was dissolved.

ministers and their companions from Philadelphia Yearly Meeting, nor for a minister and his companion from Ohio Yearly meeting, all of whom, except one of the companions, were present with the usual credentials which had been recognized in the usual manner by the Yearly Meeting.

At the last sitting of the Yearly Meeting the committee on the appeal presented two reports; the first, that the judgment of Rhode Island Quarterly Meeting ought to be confirmed, which was signed as follows:

JOHN PAGE,	WILLIAM FARR,
ISAAC R. GIFFORD,	NATHAN G. CHASE,
STEPHEN JONES,	NATHAN POPE,
MOSES FARNUM,	JAMES N. FRY,
STEPHEN JONES, Jr.,	PAUL TABER,
ELIJAH POPE,	TOBIAS MEADER,
DAVID DOUGLASS.	

The other, that the judgment of the Quarterly Meeting ought to be reversed, because some of its proceedings were in violation of the Discipline. This latter report was signed as follows:

JONATHAN NICHOLS,	JOHN MILTON EARLE,
PRINCE GARDENER,	JONATHAN S. MILLETT,
JAMES TUCKER,	WILLIAM HILL.

Two members of the committee, viz: Joseph Bracket and Samuel Foster did not sign either report.

J. M. Earle, of the committee, said he wished to explain his views, and he thought that when individuals or meetings are subjected to disciplinary proceedings, they were entitled to have the Discipline strictly adhered to; and in this case, while he united in the *conclusion* to which the Quarterly Meeting came, he thought some of its proceedings were not in accordance with the Discipline. Moses

Farnum said he thought, himself, that the Discipline had not been so strictly adhered to by the Quarterly Meeting as would have been desirable, but considering that they acted under the advice of a large committee, with authority from the Yearly Meeting, he thought it would do to confirm their judgment.

The report of the majority was adopted, and after the clerk had commenced making the minute, one of the committee of South Kingston Monthly Meeting on the appeal rose and began to speak by saying, that as this subject was now disposed of and anything he should say could not go to affect the result,—here he was interrupted by the assistant clerk, who said the subject was still open for further expression; and the friend sat down.

Subsequent to this, both before and after the minute was read, many spoke in close succession, exhorting to submission and acquiesence in the conclusions of the body, and one remarked that he thought he could discover the working of a restless and opposing spirit, and expressed his desire that such might be stayed and bound down, &c. J. M. of the Yearly Meeting's Committee said he felt desirous that the meeting should be brought to a close as soon as might be, and not unnecessarily detain Friends. About this time the same member of the appeal committee who had before essayed to speak, rose and said that the longer he sat in this meeting the more he became confirmed in the belief that he should not leave it with peace of mind without adverting to the extraodinary powers claimed by the Yearly Meeting's Committee, who had repeatedly visited South Kingston Monthly Meeting—this duty seemed the more imperative, as that committee had been again re-appointed; they had claimed when with us, that they were clothed with all the authority and power of the Yearly Meeting, that their advice was *discipline;* equally binding with any other;

and this claim has again been set up by the Quarterly Meeting's Committee, during the investigation of this case ; and besides, one of the committee on the investigation has just admitted that he thought the Discipline had not been kept to, but considering the *powers* of this committee (who were advisatory to all these proceedings) he thought the judgment of the Quarterly Meeting might safely be confirmed. He apprehended that the members of this meeting were not generally aware that so much was claimed by this committee. It appeared to him extraordinary and alarming. He wished friends to consider the consequences to which, if admitted by the Yearly Meeting, it will inevitably lead. It appeared to him to strike at that fundamental doctrine of Friends, a belief in the influence of Truth upon the mind, and its paramount authority in transacting the business of Society, and the importance of being governed herein by its monitions ; for, how can we yield to its pointings should they conflict with advice by which we are bound, and which we cannot do otherwise than accept ; or in other words, when under the influence of a counter and irresistible decree of a Yearly Meeting's Committee. It also destroys the benefit of an appeal, for if a member be disowned by a Monthly Meeting acting under such advice, and appeals, he stands no chance for obtaining redress, for he appeals to the very body by whose authority he was disowned in the first instance. These considerations he said had rested with increased weight upon his mind during the present sitting.

Moses Farnum said he had hoped the committee would not now be censured, having acted according to the best of their judgment.

The friend who had last spoken, replied he had not questioned the motives of the friend, and had not intended to, but that he had been led to fear from what he had seen, as well as what that friend had said, that there was danger of a regard for the Discipline becoming lessened if not lost. Several others now spoke in succession, expressing sympathy with those who felt themselves aggrieved, exhorting them to quietness and acquiesence, saying they felt much for them, &c. &c. When these had ceased, the meeting concluded.

At Rhode Island Quarterly Meeting in the 8th month, 1843, a committee of nine was appointed in the case of John Wilbur's appeal, and an attempt was made to appoint members of the Yearly Meeting's Committee. This was opposed, on the ground that they had already prejudged the case, and some of them, several times over; it was relinquished. But a proposition that none should be appointed who were not in unity with "the body," was adopted and acted upon. The name of a friend who had taken no active part in the case, was refused, merely because he was known to disapprove of some of the proceedings of the Quarterly Meeting.

On asking for J. W. the privilege of objecting to a part of the committee, if he should desire it, agreeable to discipline, in cases of detraction, and a usage in all cases; one of the Yearly Meeting's Committee took the ground, that the complaint against J. W. was not for detraction; that if the word *detraction* was in the complaint, it was incidental, and as to usage, it was of no consequence—the meeting could do as it pleased!! It was decided that J. W. could not be allowed to object to any of the committee, unless the committee of Greenwich Monthly Meeting were allowed to object to an equal number, for which no provision is made in the New England Discipline. In the discussion of this question, as many opposed this decision as favored it; and of the latter the Yearly and Quarterly Meeting's Committees were the principal actors.

John Wilbur being called in, and plead for his right of objection, both on ground of Discipline and usage, but without effect, and finally said, if this was the conclusion of the meeting, he should not attempt to exercise the right of objection, as it would be of no value.

The committee appointed at this time, proposed to meet at Sommerset in the 11th month, at which time J. W. attended, when the committee informed him they had ascertained that one of their number was named by a member of Greenwich Monthly Meeting, which was not proper, and they could not consent to proceed on that account. J. Wilbur told them he came there [near fifty miles] prepared to proceed, and was anxious to do so, and that he would waive all objections on account of the irregularity named, but they pressed the objection and adjourned to meet at Providence in the 2nd month, 1844.

At the Quarterly Meeting in the 11th month, 1843, it was stated that a member of the committee on the appeal of J. W. had been improperly named by a member of Greenwich Monthly Meeting, and the clerk suggested that the same friend should be named by one of his own Monthly Meeting, which was done, and the committee stood as it did before. This committee met at Providence previous to the Quarterly Meeting held there in the second month and gave J. W. a hearing.*

At that Quarterly Meeting six of the committee reported in favor of confirming the judgment of Greenwich Monthly Meeting, two signed a contrary report, and one was not present. Both reports were read. One of the Yearly Meeting's Committee was the first to unite with the report of the majority; he was followed by two others, who were not only of the same committee, but also of Green-

---

* John Wilbur's defence before this committee, being substantially the same as before that appointed by the Yearly Meeting; it is omitted here and will be found in its proper place.

wich Monthly Meeting! Both very active in that meeting in favor of J. W.'s disownment! Being also of the number of those who visited South Kingston Monthly Meeting so constantly, and who were before the committee of that meeting as prosecutors in the same case.

On being reminded of the impropriety of this proceeding, another of the Yearly Meeting's Committee, immediately united, and these four were all signers of the complaint against J. Wilbur. Others of the Yearly and Quarterly Meeting's Committee followed, and not more than three or four are believed to have united with the majority report who were not of these committees. Some united with the other report, but the first was decided by the clerk to be adopted, and he made a minute to that effect.

It was enquired whether John Wilbur would be allowed to come in and hear the conclusion; this enquiry being answered in the affirmative, he was called in and the clerk read the report and the minute adopting it.

J. W. informed the meeting that he considered their decision not a rightful one, and that he wished to appeal to the Yearly Meeting against the judgment of this meeting. He then left the house. The appointment of a committee to represent the Quarter was referred to the next meeting.

This case being thus disposed of, the case of T. P. N. was taken up, and a committee of three from each Monthly Meeting, except his own, (Rhode Island) was appointed to hear the parties.*

---

* The case of T. P. N., by appeal from Rhode Island Monthly Meeting, clearly originated in his decided and faithful opposition to the unsound doctrines sought to be introduced among us, although ostensibly based upon a frivolous and unfounded charge of improper behaviour under the ministry of public friends. He is an exemplary and consistent friend, and united with the Society about seven or eight years ago.

The names of three friends who were nominated on this committee, were rejected on the ground that they were not in unity with the doings of the Yearly and Quarterly Meetings.

The enquiry was made, whether the privilege of coming in and objecting to any of the committee would be accorded to the appellant, if he chose to avail himself of it. After some discussion on this question, in which the clerk said he was willing he should come in and hear the names read, but not that he should have the privilege of objection. T. P. N. was called in, and the minute including the names of the committee was read, after which he enquired, whether he was to understand that he had the right of objection to any of the committee, said he did not intend to ask for any unusual privilege, but only for such as he was entitled to by the discipline and usage of the society. This led to some further discussion, and the citing of former cases in favor of allowing the right of objection, as well as the decision of the clerk of the Yearly Meeting last year, that it had in all cases, so far as he knew, been the usage to allow objections. But both the usage and the decision were positively denied by some of the Yearly Meeting's Committee.

The clerk said there was no discipline for it, and J. M., one of the Yearly Meeting's Committee said, he thought it would be best [or safest] *to adhere hereafter to the strict letter of the discipline, and to begin now.* The right of objection was not allowed, and T. P. N. retired.

After he left, E. F., a friend of the late South Kingston Monthly Meeting rose, and in an impressive manner spoke in substance as follows:

"In view of the judgment of the meeting in the two appeal cases which have been before it,—or rather of the record made by the clerk as such, and in view, and in review of what has transpired in this Quarterly and Yearly Meeting, relating to the

affairs of Society for the past two years, I believe it
will be right for me to say something by way of
declaration of my innocency, and the innocency of
those friends with whom it has been my privilege to
act, touching the affairs of Society; reluctant as I
feel, thus to allude to acts of my own, either separately or in connection with my friends, but this at
present seems to be all that is left for us; and I feel
the obligation to perform this duty to be the more
imperious in consequence of what has been so often
said of us.—I will not say abroad, behind our backs,
in the many unfounded reports that had gone out
against us from one end of the land to the other,
and from this side the Atlantic to the other, but it is
well known to most within the hearing of my voice,
that we had been repeatedly spoken of in our meetings for discipline as being insubordinate, as being
disorderly, as being disturbers of the peace of the
church, as having no interest in Society, and de-
serving none of its privileges, as caring for nothing
but to pull down and destroy. These are some of
the epithets which have been applied to us unsparingly by those who occupy the high seats. I
have often thought we were treated either as though
we had no feelings or as though our feelings, and
our rights too, might be trampled upon with impunity; but permit me to tell you, friends, that we have
feelings as well as you, and how often those feelings
have been wounded, how often our hearts have bled
when those severe and unkind accusations have
been made against us, is known only to Him who
sees the secrets of every heart. And let no one
think that we have taken the ground we have from
a love of controversy, or for the gratification of our
own wills and inclinations; neither have we taken
it inconsiderately or rashly, for I can truly say,
(and what I now say I am aware that I say not only
in the presence of the friends assembled, but in the
presence of Him before whom I expect to render

my final account of all these things at a Tribunal
higher than those of earth, and beyond the bounds of
time—a tribunal towards which we are all rapidly
hastening, and before which every one of us must
soon appear.)   I say then, that a consideration of
these things has occupied the attention of my mind
in deep solicitude and anxious thought beyond all
other subjects combined, and that not only when
assembled for the purpose of transacting the affairs
of Society, but when my hands have been engaged
in my lawful and daily avocations, and oft when my
head has been resting on my pillow in the silence of
the night, have I meditated on these things, and reviewed in the most serious manner the course which
I have pursued, nor have I ever been able to see
that I could pursue any other; not that I have never
erred in word or act, for this I am aware that I may
have done, but if so, I have the satisfaction of knowing that it was not wilful error; and that the Searcher
of all hearts knows the sincerity of mine when I
say, that I have desired that I might do nothing to
injure the cause of truth.   And I feel further to say,
that had I assented either directly or indirectly to
the course pursued by the Yearly Meeting's Committee, for effecting their favorite purpose in South
Kingston Monthly Meeting, I did believe, and I do
believe, that I should have been verily guilty, and
that my peace would have departed from me, but
now I rejoice to say, that in these respects it remains
with me.   Ah, friends, for peace of mind—peace of
mind the reward of conscious innocence and faithfulness.—This in the language of a pious writer is
the pearl of great price which rich men cannot buy,
which learning is oft times too proud to gather up,
but which the poor and despised of all, sometimes
seek and obtain; yea, and it is with me to add, and
which the oppressor in the might of his power, whatever else he may do, cannot prevent their receiving,

and when received, cannot take it from them. Thanks be to the Father of Mercies that it is so."

Soon after, this friend sat down the meeting closed.

At the time of the Quarterly Meeting at Greenwich, in the fifth month, 1844—E. F. was visited by the overseers of Greenwich Monthly Meeting, and taken under dealing, on account of these remarks—and was afterwards disowned therefor.

In the treatment of the Committee of Greenwich Monthly Meeting with him, they strongly contended that he had accused those who occupy the high seats with spreading unfounded reports against himself and his friends from one end of the land to the other, &c. And when he gave them the substance of what he did say in writing, as now published,* they still maintained that it would bear that construction! With what justice and for what purpose the reader may be left to judge.

That those alluded to had accused him and those acting with him as stated, with being insubordinate, disorderly, disturbers of the peace, &c.—they did not pretend to gainsay—for it could be easily corroborated by many witnesses.

At the Quarterly Meeting in the 5th month, 1844, the committee in the case of T. P. N. reported in confirmation of the judgment of the Monthly Meeting, which being adopted, he informed the Quarterly Meeting that he should appeal to the Yearly Meeting, and a committee was appointed to represent the Quarter therein.

---

* The foregoing remarks in the Quarterly Meeting were committed to writing immediately after the meeting, by the Friend who made them, from an apprehension, that a wrong version of what was said might be given and insisted on; as had been previously done in some other cases, which apprehension the sequel justified. They were submitted to the examination of other Friends who were present, and are believed to be substantially correct, and nearly in the words spoken.

At New England Yearly Meeting, held on Rhode Island, 6th month, 1844, the account from Rhode Island Quarterly Meeting brought to view the appeals of John Wilbur and T. P. N. against the conclusion of that meeting in confirming the judgment of Greenwich and Rhode Island Monthly Meetings in disowning them. A committee of twenty-one was appointed, to which *both* these cases were referred. In the appointment of this committee, the meeting decided that members of the Standing Committee of the Yearly Meeting, who had heretofore been engaged in the case of J. W.—and those Friends who constituted the committee appointed last year, on the appeal of South Kingston Monthly Meeting, (the two cases being nearly similar) should be excluded. It was further proposed that *those who had openly expressed themselves opposed to the proceedings of the Yearly Meeting should also be excluded.*

To this proposition it was objected, that it would be making an improper distinction, inasmuch as in a case of so much importance and interest, it was probable that most of the members had expressed themselves either for or against—and if those of one class were to be excluded, those of the other should be also; and further, it was feared that this course might tend to *trammel* the committee. The meeting, however, decided in *favor* of the proposition, and when a name was offered, supposed to be of the class alluded to therein, it was rejected.

The right was asked for the appellants to be present and object to a portion of the committee, should they desire it, in conformity with the discipline and usages of the society. This gave rise to considerable discussion, and views of an opposite character were expressed. The clerk said that in our discipline, under the head of Appeals, nothing is said of this right, but under the head of Defamation and Detraction, the right is allowed, provided it do not extend to the major part of the committee. He said if we should turn from our own discipline to those of other Yearly Meetings, we should find different provisions in regard to the right of objection.

To this it was replied, that the decision of the Yearly Meeting last year, in the case of the appeal of South Kingston Monthly Meeting, was undoubtedly correct, that we *must be governed by our own discipline*, and further that the clerk stated last year that in cases of Defamation and Detraction the right of objection is allowed by the discipline, and that *it had been the usage in all other cases;* and that one of the principal charges against J. W. is detraction.

The meeting finally decided that the appellants might state their objections, if they desired, and the meeting would take them into consideration, and decide on their validity. This was objected to on the ground that it would render the right of no value, and that there was neither discipline nor usage for it.

The appellants were separately called into the meeting, and the privilege of objecting proffered to them under this restriction. It was declined by both. J. W. requested to be allowed some one to assist him before the committee, as from his age and infirmity it would be a hard task for him to perform the necessary labor. Many expressed themselves in favor of granting this request, but the meeting decided against it.

The committee having completed the investigation of these cases, reported in favor of confirming the judgment of the Quarterly Meeting in both; one of their number declining to sign the report in the case of J. W.

The reports were adopted by the meeting.

John Wilbur, desiring to be present to hear the report of the committee in his case, and conclusion of the meeting, was called in, and they were read in his hearing. After sitting a short time in silence, he rose, and remarked in substance, that however unjust he believed the decision to be, yet he should entertain no hardness against any concerned in the proceedings against him : that it was his desire that none of our members should depart from the ancient principles or testimonies of the society, nor suffer any innovation upon them ; these had been dear to him from his youth up, and were still dear to him :—he then withdrew.

The subject of more clearly defining and explaining the discipline, in regard to the rights of individuals and meetings,—the proper subordination of inferior meetings,—the mode of proceeding in the execution of the discipline, &c., was taken into consideration by the meeting, and resulted in referring the subject to the Meeting for Sufferings, with instructions for them to make such *explanations, alterations,* and *additions,* as shall meet the concern of the Yearly Meeting, and report next year.

Returning minutes for the ministers from other Yearly Meetings, were prepared and adopted for those in attendance, with the exception of one minister from Ohio Yearly Meeting,—for whom none was prepared.

(The certificate of this beloved and faithful gospel minister, embraced a prospect of further religious service within our limits ;—but he was visited by a deputation from the Yearly Meeting's Committee, who informed him he could not travel here, unless he would unite with their proceedings, and refrain from associating with those known to be dissatisfied therewith ; and advised him to return without accomplishing his prospect !)

MONTHLY MEETING'S APPEAL.

Some account of the Proceedings of the Committee of the Yearly Meeting on the Appeal.

The Committee of the New England Yearly Meeting on the Appeal of South Kingston Monthly Meeting, met at Newport, 3d day, 13th of 6th month, 1843, and appointed John Milton Earle their clerk—and notified the parties that they would meet 4th day morning to hear the case.

Fourth day morning, committee met—and the parties were present. Perez Peck, of the Quarterly Meeting's Committee, said there was a person present who was not a member of society, and that they should object to any such sitting. Some one said there appeared to be several members from South Kingston there, who were not of the committee, and thought they ought not to be allowed to be present. Perez Peck continued to object to John Wilbur upon the ground that he was not a member of society. The clerk said he thought it would be proper first to decide whether any except members of the committees should be present. He said *he* had been enquired of, whether any besides the parties immediately interested could be present— whether the strangers now attending the Yearly Meeting could be admitted. He had been unable to give a decided answer to these enquiries—but his own opinion was, that it would not be proper. Several of the Committee from South Kingston remarked that they were not aware that any not of the committee contemplated attending—and thought as there was objection to it, they would be willing to withdraw ; and they did so accordingly.

The propriety of J. Wilbur's sitting was now further discussed—South Kingston Friends taking the ground that this was not a question proper to

be raised here—that J. W. came before this committe with as good credentials as any of the others,
and they had no right to go back of these to look
for objections. It is claimed that the Quarterly
Meeting had placed J. W. under dealing, at the
same time they dissolved South Kingston Monthly
Meeting,—that Greenwich Monthly Meeting have
since disowned him, and that this disqualifies him
from appearing here on behalf of the Monthly Meeting, as an appellant—upon the same principle all
the other members of the committee on the appeal
might have been disowned, and thus the right of appeal, secured by discipline, would be defeated altogether—besides, this appeal is against the action of
the Quarterly Meeting annulling our records, and
thus placing one of our members under dealing who
had been acquitted by his own Monthly Meeting,
and for which proceeding no discipline could be
produced—that J. Wilbur's interest in this question
was perhaps greater than that of any one besides—
that all the proceedings in his case were involved in
this of the Monthly Meeting, and surely he could
not be debarred from appearing here as an appellant. The Quarterly Meeting's Committee took the
ground that the decision of the Quarterly Meeting
must be binding until it was reversed by the Yearly Meeting. Having heard the parties on this
question—the committee requested them to withdraw while they came to a conclusion thereon. After being by themselves for upwards of an hour,
the committee called the parties in, and the clerk
stated that they decided at present to allow all to
sit who appeared by the record to be of the committee. But if the Quarterly Meeting's Committee
were still dissatisfied, and wished to raise the question again, they could have the privilege of introducing further proof from the records, of this
Friend's disqualification. The appeal was now
read, and the appellants were then asked to pro-

ceed—when a member of the committee, on behalf of the Monthly Meeting, commented upon the great importance of the case, and the necessity of being governed by the discipline in its decision. He had understood the Yearly Meeting to have very fully instructed the committee to that effect. He then stated the order in which we proposed to proceed, beginning with a history of the proceedings which had taken place in South Kingston Monthly Meeting, including the conduct of the Yearly Meeting's Committee, &c. This was objected to by the Quarterly Meeting's Committee, and the clerk said he did not see what relation these matters had to the case; if it could be proved that the Yearly Meeting's Committee *had* done wrong, it would not show that the proceedings of the Quarterly Meeting had been in violation of the discipline; it seemed to him proper that the investigation should be confined to the evidence of the violation of the discipline, as claimed in the appeal. It was replied, that the Monthly Meeting appealed against the dissolution as *not warranted by any of its proceedings,* as well as against the *manner* of it. That the Monthly Meeting was charged with disorder, insubordination and want of unity, and these were claimed to justify the dissolution. They therefore claimed the right to show what the Monthly Meeting had done, as well as the proceedings of the Yearly Meeting's Committee therein, upon whose complaint the Quarterly Meeting had taken the matter up—and besides that, such a statement of facts as we proposed to make, in the order of time as they transpired, was best calculated to give the committee a correct idea of the case, and they would be much better prepared to comprehend and appreciate, whatever might be afterwards said in relation to it.

It was a mere statement of facts, what was said and done, without comment—and if any thing therein was claimed to be incorrect by the Quarterly

Meeting's Committee, we wished them to note it down as the reading progressed, and for which time would be allowed—and at the close we would take up all such contested points, and canvass them, and if necessary introduce proof thereon. That they should remark fully upon the violation of the discipline, in the course of the investigation, but they deemed it important that the committee should first have a history of previous proceedings in the Monthly Meeting, and Rhode Island Quarterly Meeting, which had led to it. The clerk of the committee said he thought this course might be proper, in order to show that the dissolution of the Monthly Meeting was not warranted (in the language of the appeal) by any proceedings of theirs.

The Quarterly Meeting's Committee said if this was allowed, they should not be willing any statement should be made of what took place previous to the appointment of the committee by the Quarterly Meeting in the 8th month to attend South Kingston Monthly Meeting, for they *only* represented the Quarterly Meeting, and that meeting had nothing to do with the case previous to that time. It was replied that the Quarterly Meeting's Committee, in their written advice to South Kingston Monthly Meeting, had condemned its proceedings as far back as the 5th month, and the Quarterly Meeting itself had undertaken to annul and make void those proceedings—and besides, the Quarterly Meeting had taken the case up upon the report and complaint of the Yearly Meeting's Committee, and therefore the right was claimed to investigate the doings of that committee. Perez Peck, on behalf of the Quarterly Meeting's Committee, said if this was to be allowed, they should claim the privilege of having J. Osborne, the clerk of the Yearly Meeting's Committee, present, to correct any misstatements made respecting them. He had full minutes of their proceedings, and they wished to show what the *opinion* of the Yearly Meeting's Committee was, respecting that Monthly Meeting. A member of the Monthly Meeting's Committee said he trusted the *opinions* of the Yearly Meeting's Committee would not be received as evidence before this committee; if any facts were brought forward, they would no doubt be allowed their weight, but with the *opinions* of the Yearly Meeting's Committee we had nothing to do. Some one of the Committee of South Kingston said there were at least two members of the Yearly Meeting's Committee, on this Committee of the Quarterly Meeting, (Perez Peck and Allen Wing,) who were among those who had visited South Kingston Monthly Meeting, and they could no doubt see that no injustice was done to that committee. These members of the Yearly Meeting's Committee said they did not appear there in the capacity of a Yearly Meeting's Committee—they were there only to represent the Quarterly Meeting. The Committee of South Kingston Monthly Meeting declared their willingness to have J. Osborne present, if it was wished; expressing their desire to have the *fullest* investigation. This being decided on, the committee adjourned to meet in the afternoon. 4th day, P. M., committee again met, John Osborne being present, when the Quarterly Meeting's Committee produced the records of South Kingston Monthly Meeting, and extracts from the minutes of the Quarterly Meeting, and also of Greenwich Monthly Meeting, to show that J. W. had been complained of by the Yearly Meeting's Committee, and that although acquitted by South Kingston Monthly Meeting, the Quarterly Meeting had annulled the proceedings by which it was done, and laid down that Monthly Meeting, and that Greenwich Monthly Meeting had since disowned him, upon the original complaint, and the report of two of the committee appointed in the 4th month, which only was recognized as valid—that the other members of the committee declined to meet with them, and that John Wilbur, though requested to meet them, had not done so, &c. At the close of the reading of these documents, J. W. said he felt called upon to notice a misstatement contained in the minutes of Greenwich Monthly Meeting :—it was there stated that he had been requested to meet with those two members of the committee who had reported against him. This was not so, they did not ask him to meet them, he had the letter now which they wrote him, which would show the contrary. The whole of this sitting was occupied in the discussion of the question of J. W.'s sitting, but nothing new either of fact or argument was elicited. At the close of the sitting, the committee were for a short time by themselves in consultation, and then adjourned to meet again in the evening. On coming together again the clerk of the committee informed the appellants that they might proceed with the case, and being about to do so, Perez Peck interrupted them, saying they had not yet had a decision on the question discussed at the previous sitting. The clerk replied that they had concluded to allow J. W. to sit, if he chose to do so. Perez Peck said, that being the case, he must request an adjournment until next morning, in order to consult other members of the Quarterly Meeting—as he was sure they would not be satisfied to proceed under this decision. The clerk said that he hoped this question would not have been further urged by the Quarterly Meeting's Committee, as it seemed to him to be unimportant. The presence of this Friend could do no harm—and as to precedent, (about which much had been said by the Quarterly Meeting's Committee,) it was not probable a like case would soon if ever occur—and no minutes of the trial would be kept. Stephen Jones, jr., one of the committee on the appeal, said, " that he was sorry that the Quarterly Meeting's Committee should continue to press this matter in the manner they did, and thus consume the time, which ought to be occupied in investigating the merits of the case,—he had hoped all would acquiesce in the decision of the committee, and we might proceed at once to the merits of the case,—if time was thus to be taken up, in settling preliminary and unimportant questions, there would not be time to go through with the investigation without detaining the Yearly Meeting. Several of the Quarterly Meeting's Committee had said that *individually* they cared little about this question, but only objected on account of *precedent.* He said he did not apprehend much from this, as it was hardly probable another case like this would happen in the lifetime of any of us, and as no record of this matter would be kept, he did not think future generations would be much troubled by our decision of this question." One of the Monthly Meeting's Committee said that they were very desirous to proceed with the case—that much time would be necessary to a full hearing of it. One whole day had now been consumed with this question, and they feared others would arise which would defeat our having a fair hearing—that the Committees of the Quarterly and Yearly Meetings, had often urged upon *us* the duty of subordination to superior bodies, and by their own rule they were now bound to acquiesce, especially as it was not a very important question. If, however, we could be assured that we should have an opportunity for a full and patient hearing, we had no disposition to oppose any indulgence to the Quarterly Meeting's Committee which the committee on the appeal were disposed to grant. W. A. Robinson said he understood the clerk to say the decision of the committee was, J. W. might sit, "if he chose to"—he wished he would state, whether, the decision was that he had a right to sit, or that he might do so as a matter of indulgence. The clerk made no reply to the question. Arnold Cong-

don said he hoped the committee would adjourn, it
was much more important that this case should be
decided right, than the time when ; it would be better
even to allow it to go to another Yearly Meeting, than
any thing wrong should be done. One of the Monthly Meeting Committee, said that would be a very
great wrong—it would be injustice to the Monthly
Meeting, and subject them to very great inconve-
nieuce, and it was hardly to be expected that this
committee of twenty men would all meet here again
next year. W. A. Robinson said he did not wish
to press his question, but as he thought an answer
to it might settle this difficulty, he would like to have
the clerk say whether the committee intended to
decide that J. W. had a *right* to sit, or was allowed
to as an indulgence granted him. The clerk replied
that he did not know as he had any other answer
to give, than what he had already given as the decision of the committee. Tobias Meader, one of the
committee, said he considered it merely as an indulgence, and so said one or two more. Another
of the committee said he did not consider there had
been any decision come to, the last time they had
taken it up—others made explanations of their
views, &c. One of the Monthly Meeting's Committee said we could have no other means of ascertaining what was the decision of the committee than
what was given by its clerk as such. The clerk had
-stated what was the decision of the committee. We
of course considered him the organ of the committee. The clerk said he did not intend to have done
more than he had in giving the decision of the committee, he thought that sufficient—but as the views
of different members of the committee had been so
much expressed, he now felt it proper to state that
the committee appeared to come to the conclusion
they did with various views,—perhaps no three or
four of them would agree as to the reasons for it;

but the decision he had stated was agreed upon, and he believed he had given it correctly.

Several of the committee said, as the Quarterly Meeting's Committee wished an adjournment, they thought it best to adjourn. Stephen Jones, senior, asked whether John Wilbur would not, for the sake of accommodation, be willing to waive his right, and withdraw; he had said in the morning that he did not regard his presence of much importance to the management of the case. The clerk said if the committee adjourned now, they would be obliged to sit while the Yearly Meeting was sitting, or else the Yearly Meeting must be detained. He was now satisfied that this case was of such importance as to justify them in making all other engagements subordinate to it. He should be sorry to lose any of the sittings of the Yearly Meeting, and he had hoped he should not be obliged to—but he was in favor of *taking time* to hear this case. Several of the committee united in this view, and it was agreed to meet to-morrow, 5th day morning, at half-past 10 o'clock.—(There being a select meeting at an earlier hour, and some of the committee members. The committee also concluded to ask leave of the Yearly Meeting to sit during the sittings of the meeting—several of the members of the committee being representatives.)

5th day morning, again met—John Wilbur not present, having concluded to attend the public meeting. The clerk requested the appellants to proceed with the case. And they commenced reading a statement of facts, embracing the substance of what was said and done in South Kingston Monthly Meeting, and Rhode Island Quarterly Meeting, having relation to this case, from the 4th month to the 11th inclusive, 1842, and also some portion of the minutes of the committee in the case of J. Wilbur; all given in the order of time as they occurred. At this sitting the reading was proceeded with as

far as the Monthly Meeting in the 8th month. When
that part was read relative to the attempt of R. G.
and T. A., prematurely to break up the meeting at
Hopkinton in the 8th month, Perez Peck said he
wanted it to be understood that those Friends did
not acknowledge *that*.   The Monthly Meeting's
Committee replied, they were willing to admit they
did not, but that matter would be gone into at the
proper time—that they had full proof of it.   The
committee adjourned to meet at 2 o'clock, P. M.

The reading was resumed and concluded at this
sitting, after which the appellants laid down twelve
principal positions which they intended to establish,
and upon which they should rest their case.   These
were reduced to writing, and at the request of the
clerk afterwards placed in his hands.   The committee then adjourned to meet again at the rising of the
P. M. sitting of the Yearly Meeting.

5 o'clock, P. M., again met.   The appellants said
they were now through with their statements of
facts, and supposed the regular order of proceeding
would be for the Quarterly Meeting's Committee to
go forward with their part of the case, and when
they were through, for the Monthly Meeting's Committee to make their closing plea.   Perez Peck objected, saying that courts of law made use of these
terms, of opening and closing, &c., he hoped they
would not be introduced here.   *They* should want
the privilege of replying to the Monthly Meeting's
Committee.   The clerk said that he supposed the
next thing in order would be for the Quarterly
Meeting's Committee to say how far they were
willing to admit the statement of facts as given by
the appellants to be true.

The Quarterly Meeting's Committee raised no
specific objections to the statement of facts, but J.
Metcalf said he supposed there were several things
they should not exactly admit—he thought some
things were represented in a different light from

what they should be—that a coloring was given them calculated to produce wrong impressions. The Quarterly Meeting's Committee now commenced by calling upon John Osborne to read his minutes of the proceedings of South Kingston Monthly Meeting, and of the Yearly Meeting's Committee, relating thereto. These minutes contained few specific accusations, and none against the meeting, as such, other than it did not accede to the advice of the Yearly and Quarterly Meeting's Committees. A few expressions of individual members were brought forward as evidence of the bad condition of the meeting, and many assertions unsupported by any proof, of the turbulence and confusion of the meetings in the transaction of the business, laboring to lower the character and standing of the members, representing them as destitute of religious weight of character, &c. But said that amid these scenes of turbulence and excitement, the committee could but notice with satisfaction the quiet conduct and orderly deportment of that portion of the members who disapproved of the proceedings of the meeting, affording evidence that the *true seed there was by no means extinct, though under oppression !*

During the reading, some of the Monthly Meeting's Committee took notes of such passages as they thought would require notice, which at a subsequent sitting were commented on at some length. The committee adjourned to meet again at 8 o'clock in the evening. On coming together, Arnold Congdon commenced by commenting on the authority and powers of the Yearly Meeting's Committee. He said every conclusion of the Yearly Meeting is discipline, just as much so as if it was printed in the book. To illustrate his meaning he referred to the document on doctrines read the day before, where it is said that those wanting religious weight of character, ought not to direct in meetings for discipline.

6*

He said that was now discipline, and as binding as
any former discipline,—that the Yearly Meeting's
Committee being appointed directly by the Yearly
Meeting, any advice coming from them had all the
authority of discipline. He then undertook to explain the discipline relative to laying down a Monthly Meeting. In reading this paragraph he strongly
emphasised the words *ought to submit*, saying that
present submission was the duty of the Monthly
Meeting—they should conform to the judgment of
the Quarterly Meeting, and then appeal. He then
read the succeeding paragraph, saying, it gave the
Quarterly Meeting the right *either* to dissolve the
Monthly Meeting or to bring the matter before the
Yearly Meeting,—and the Quarterly Meeting had
concluded to dissolve the Monthly Meeting. He
said that the next paragraph was involved in some
obscurity, but he thought the Yearly Meeting's
Committee would understand it as they did. It provides for the joining of the members to another
Monthly Meeting, and requires the Quarterly Meeting to take care that no inconvenience thereby ensue to them concerning any branch of our discipline.
He said they had complied with this requirement,
by annexing the members to another Monthly
Meeting. They then proposed to read from the
discipline of Indiana and Baltimore Yearly Meetings. This was objected to by the Monthly Meeting's Committee, on the ground that the Yearly
Meeting had decided that the case must be tried by
the discipline of this Yearly Meeting, and the
Yearly Meeting's Committee decided against the
reading. J. Metcalf said that what they wanted to
read would show that the discipline of those Yearly
Meetings gave superior meetings the right to annul
records. They next proposed to read from Foster's
Reports. This was objected to on the same ground
as the former, and decided against by the committee. A. Congdon then said, that what they proposed

to read was the testimony of Samuel Bettle, Thomas Evans and Samuel Parsons, as to the general usage of the society. Perez Peck said that he had previously objected to the statement in regard to the attempt to break up the Monthly Meeting at Hopkinton, as not being admitted by those Friends, and if insisted on he should introduce evidence showing from what it originated. He said that one of those Friends took hold of the other's arm, and spoke to him on another subject, and this was undoubtedly what was seen; he did not think we meant to make a false statement. Two of the Monthly Meeting's Committee said *that was not what they saw.* They distinctly saw them shake hands, and were prepared to prove it by six credible witnesses. P. Peck said he hoped we would waive this matter—the persons implicated were not present to defend themselves, &c. Several of the Yearly Meeting's Committee also expressed a desire that we would waive it. J. M. Earle said he did not see that it had much bearing on the case if we did prove it.

One of the Monthly Meeting's Committee said that having introduced it, if we should leave it so, it might be construed into an abandonment of the ground we had taken, and thus operate against us. If left so, he wanted an admission from the committee, that we vacated no ground we had taken, and that the omission to read the proof should not be allowed to militate against us. It was stated by another of the committee that they were prepared to produce written testimony, proving most conclusively the fact as here charged;—they were willing, however, to leave the subject here, if there was objection to going further into it, but it must be distinctly understood that we have full proof of the facts stated, and are ready to produce it. Moses Farnum said he had no doubt but the committee of the Monthly Meeting had the testimony they said they had.

With this statement and admission the subject was left. The committee soon after adjourned.

6th day, morning, committee again met. The Quarterly Meeting's Committee proceeded. Perez Peck commented upon the Discipline relative to dissolving Monthly Meetings,—said the first paragraph was not at all applicable to the case—*that* only related to a case of difference in a Monthly Meeting ; this was a difference between the Yearly Meeting's Committee and a Monthly Meeting. In other respects he talked about it much as Arnold Congdon did.

When the committee of South Kingston Monthly Meeting were commenting upon the advice to several of the members of South Kingston Select Preparative Meeting, not to attend that meeting, Beriah Collins said, by way of explanation, that as John Wilbur had been restored against the advice of the Yearly and Quarterly Meeting's Committees, they *had* advised *him* not to attend the select Meeting. One of the Monthly Meeting's Committee enquired of Beriah, whether they advised any others in the same manner, and if so, how many ? Beriah replied with apparent reluctance, that they did so advise *all* who supported John Wilbur.

One of the Monthly Meeting's Committee now proceeded to comment on the power claimed for the Yearly Meeting's Committee, and to trace the consequences to which, if conceded by the Yearly Meeting, it must lead. He showed it would concentrate all power in the hands of such committee, and that as their authority is thus made paramount to every thing else, all pretensions of a co-ordinate branch of the Society to move in the transaction of business under the guidance of the Head of the Church must be vain and futile, that the right of appeal would afford no protection to the appellant against injustice or abuse of power, for an individual appealing from the judgment of a Monthly Meeting acting under the control of such a committee, would appeal to same body, at whose bidding he was disowned in the first instance. If it be argued that such a committee, composed of ministers, and elders, &c., would do no wrong, he thought it would savor rather too strongly of the Papal doctrine of the infallibility of the church, with further remarks in illustration of these positions. He then proceeded to review such portion of John Osborne's minutes as had been noted during the reading. Among other things he said he was surprised that J. Osborne should labor as he had done in those minutes, to give the impression to this committee, that three-fourths of the members of South Kingston Monthly Meeting are devoid of religious or even moral weight of character. But what evidence had he adduced to sustain his position? Surely nothing better than assertion. He maintained that general charges and broad assertions, unsupported by proof, ought to weigh nothing, and he trusted would weigh nothing with this committee. That no charge had been brought against the Monthly Meeting save that it had refused to take the advice of the Yearly and Quarterly Meeting's Committees, (which had been answered) and very few specific charges against individual members, and those related only to improper expressions said to have been uttered by them in Monthly Meeting. He said a meeting could not justly be held responsible for the unguarded expressions of one or two of its members, that aside from a few expressions of two members of the South Kingston Monthly Meeting, he believed the remarks of those who sustained the course pursued by the Monthly Meeting were as free from excitement and no more objectionable than those of the Yearly Meeting's Committee. John Osborne in order to strengthen his position had highly extolled the small number in that Monthly Meeting who sustained the Yearly Meeting's Committee, representing them as the seed, &c. He said he could name from those who sustained the Monthly Meeting a larger number than the whole of these who would not only outweigh them in point of character, moral or religious, but whose characters had not been and he trusted could not be impeached, some of whom are now present,—does their deportment here bespeak for them the character which has been given them? He left the committee to decide this question. As to the minority who had been so highly eulogized, he was not disposed to do them the least injustice, but thought they would by no means bear the exalted character which had been awarded to them, for he believed it must be admitted by all who were acquainted in that Monthly Meeting, that *some of them at least did not stand remarkably high for religious weight of character*. J. Osborne had spoken of the great improbability of the clerk long remaining a member, giving it as a reason for advising the former clerk to retain the records; he was greatly surprised at the expression. What he had seen in Samuel Sheffield to lead him to such a conclusion, he knew not, his character as a man and as a Friend was above reproach, he was a Friend in principle, and had acknowledged it in the presence of the Yearly Meeting's Committee, and he was a consistent friend in practice, he was then present sustaining, by his deportment, (as he trusted) the character he had given him. Why then the Yearly Meeting's Committee should come to the conclusion that he would not long remain a member, he could not conceive, unless they designed to disown him, in the exercise of the high authority they had assumed.

Another of the appellants followed with some additional remarks and strictures upon John Osborne's minutes. He remarked, in the first place, that in his view, the minutes of John Osborne were not calculated to give a correct impression of the state of things in South Kingston Monthly Meeting. A

stranger, he said, having no other means of information, would certainly get a very erroneous idea from
them. These minutes were of a very general and
indefinite character, specifying but little, whereas our
statement gave an account of what was said and
done, and furnished, he thought, a much clearer and
more correct idea of the actual state of things. We
had taken down what could be recollected, and were
of course most likely to recollect expressions of an
improper character when they occurred, that we
were not disposed to say there had been none such—
it would have been strange indeed if there had not
been, considering all we had been obliged to pass
through, but nothing of this kind had at all affected
any of the decisions of the meeting. In our statement we had made no comment and expressed no
opinions, while J. O.'s minutes are very much an
expression of the opinions of the Yearly Meeting's
Committee. These minutes also gave a statement
from T. C. Collins, of his opinion of the condition of
the Monthly Meeting at the time the clerk was
changed, and this is adopted by the Yearly Meeting's Committee. By this authority they say the
clerk was not removed by the sound and weighty
part of the meeting. He tells them that when he
left the table, he declared it as his judgment, it was
not the sense of the meeting that Samuel Sheffield
should act as clerk. This he said was very improba-
ble, it was not recollected by any of the Monthly
Meeting's Committee, and he thought the fact of his
leaving the table, was a sufficient refutation of it. If
this was his judgment, then it was his duty to remain
at the table ; why did he leave it? Besides, it had
been acknowledged here by one of the Quarterly
Meeting's Committee, that T. C. Collins' excitement
and confusion of mind was such that he scarcely
knew what he did say at that time. J. M. Earle
said, you have the fact of his leaving, which seems
to me to be sufficient.

The appellant continued :—the Yearly Meeting's Committee say of the Monthly Meeting's Committee, in the case of J. W., that all their decisions were approved by him. If by this they mean to say there was any understanding between them and John Wilbur about these decisions, we deny that it was so, for the committee in every instance came to its decisions without the presence or interference of any other person. If J. W. was satisfied with what we believed to be *right*, it was not our fault. These decisions are recorded, and will show for themselves whether they were unreasonable. The Yearly Meeting's Committee justify their refusal to allow J. W. to have any one with him, before the Monthly Meeting's Committee, by instancing the former example of a larger body of the same Committee, who to the number of about thirty had an interview with him, and did not then allow any to be present, not even his wife. This was but an illustration of the great injustice which had been practiced towards him. This committee can judge of the character of such an act. The Discipline of the Society provides that an accused person may have the privilege of taking one or two with him, and this right was then plead for by J. W., but denied.

One of the Quarterly Meeting's Committee here said, that case did not come under this provision of the Discipline; no disciplinary proceedings had then been had against J. W. It was replied, that in addition to the injustice of such denial, this only proves that the authority cited by the Yearly Meeting's Committee to justify them now, does not all apply,—for J. W. was before the committee of South Kingston Monthly Meeting, under disciplinary proceedings. It was also said that John Osborne in his minutes had given a version of the Monthly Meeting's Committee's decision, as to the matter which might be introduced by J. W. in his defence, which was very erroneous ; that decision was given in writing and will show for itself. John Osborne was called upon again to read that portion of his minutes relating to this decision. He then read from his minutes, by which it appeared that the decision was to allow J. W. to introduce *any matter having, in his opinion, any bearing on the case.*

The decision, as recorded, was read, which allowed John Wilbur " to introduce such evidence and documents on these subjects (doctrines) as shall appear *essentially* to relate to his defence." It was remarked this was very short of allowing him to introduce any matter he chose to ; this was but one instance of the incorrectness of those minutes ; in this case there can be no mistake, as the decision of the committee was at the time given in writing.

It was stated in John Osborne's minutes, that at the time of the investigation of the case of J. W. at Hopkinton, one of the Monthly Meeting's Committee rose, and pointing to the door, said to the Yearly Meeting's Committee, " there is the door, you can go out or stay, as you please." An explanation was made by one of the Monthly Meeting's Committee, of the circumstances under which something like this was said, by one of the committee. At the time referred to, the Yearly Meeting's Committee had for the *third* time threatened to leave the investigation, unless the course pointed out by them was pursued. In the first instance, after submitting to the Monthly Meeting's Committee, whether J. W. should have assistance, and it was decided without a dissenting voice, that he might, they said, unless this decision was reversed they should leave. Although the committee could not do this, yet J. W. consented to proceed without assistance ; afterwards, upon the introduction of a pamphlet he was charged with circulating, they again threatened to leave if it was all read, instead of the extracts they produced ; yet it was read, and they did not leave. Afterwards J. W. proposed to enter upon his de-

fence by introducing the matter of Doctrines, and
they again threatened to leave if *this* was allowed.
At this time it was that one of the committee used
the expression alluded to. Several of the other
members of the committee checked him, and expressed regret that he should have so spoken; and
such an unguarded expression being condemned by
the committee at the time, they cannot be held responsible for it.

In John Osborne's minutes mention is made of
scenes of turbulence and confusion, clamor, &c. A
member of the Monthly Meeting's Committee said
he had never, at any time, witnessed so great a degree of excitement and violent feelings on the part
of *any* members of the Monthly Meeting, as was
exhibited by one of the Yearly Meeting's Committee on the occasion above referred to.

The reading of the argument on the appeal, was
then commenced by the Monthly Meeting's Committee, in the early part of which was introduced an
extract from R. Barclay, containing general remarks on the administration of the Discipline, and
going to show that the basis of good and right government, is an adherence to the genuine doctrines
of the Society.

When the extract was about half read, Arnold
Congdon said he thought the reading of this extract
ought not to be allowed, as *they* had not been permitted to quote authorities beyond our own Discipline. It was replied, that this was not authority
on which the Monthly Meeting relied to sustain
their case, but general remarks on the administration of the Discipline, thrown in as an introduction
to their appeal; but if the Yearly Meeting's Committee thought it improper, they would not read the
residue. One or two others of the Monthly Meeting's Committee said they were willing to dispense
with the remainder if it was thought best. The
clerk said he had anticipated this objection, but

thought *himself* there was a distinction between referring to authorities to substantiate particular positions, and general remarks like these ; he thought, as the reading had continued thus far, it had better be concluded. Two or three others expressed themselves to the same effect. The reading then proceeded without further interruption, and concluded about 12 o'clock.

Some remarks and explanations of minor importance having been made, both parties here rested the case, and the committee adjourned to meet again at 2 o'clock, P. M., at which hour they met, and continued together until 7 o'clock, when, not being ready to report, and the Yearly Meeting having adjourned to meet at 8 o'clock seventh day, morning, the committee also adjourned to an earlier hour.

At the gathering of the Yearly Meeting, 7th day morning, the committee being through, attended and presented two reports, one signed by thirteen of their number, in favor of confirming ; the other signed by six of them, in favor of reversing the judgment of the Quarterly Meeting.

Two of the committee did not sign either report. That signed by the thirteen was adopted by the Yearly Meeting.

APPEAL OF SOUTH KINGSTON MONTHLY MEETING.

The following positions, which the Monthly Meeting's Committee proposed to established, were reduced to writing at the request of the clerk of the committee on the Appeal, after the investigation commenced, and placed in his hands.

It is proper here to state in addition to the following argument in defence of the Monthly Meeting, there was read a statement embracing a particular account of what was said and done in the various meetings and Committees in relation to the case, and that whatever is not brought to view in the argument, was fully shown by the facts contained in that statement.

(For the document of Appeal, signed by the clerk, and also by individual members, see preceding Narrative, page 93.)

The appellants intend to establish the following positions:

First, that in the manner of bringing and urging the complaint against John Wilbur by the Yearly Meeting's Committee, in the 4th month, 1842, they disregarded the proper business and labor of overseers and Preparative Meetings, as well as the plain order of proceedings laid down in our Discipline (founded upon the precepts of the Saviour) in regard to detraction, a prominent feature in that complaint, and very improperly threatened if the Monthly Meeting did not comply with their requirement for immediate proceedings, to complain of it to the Quarterly Meeting.

Second, that they interfered with the rights of the Monthly Meeting in the election of its officers, by attempting to remove its rightful clerk from the table, and to place another person there in his room.

Third, that both the Yearly and Quarterly Meeting's Committees have interfered with our right of property, having withheld and even taken away from us our records *before* the Monthly Meeting was dissolved, or in any form compatible with the Discipline, deprived of any of its rightful authority.

Fourth, that they, the Yearly Meeting's Committee, charged South Kingston Monthly Meeting with an intention to effect a separation in Society, without evidence and against the fact.

Fifth, that they themselves gave their countenance and encouragement to the proposition of a disaffected member for a division in our Monthly Meeting.

Sixth, that two of the Yearly Meeting's Committee attempted to break up our Monthly Meeting in the 8th month, while the report in John Wilbur's case was yet in the women's meeting, and other business remained upon the table; that this was afterwards denied by them, but fully proved to be true.

Seventh, that the Yearly Meeting's Committee attempted to dictate to a committee of the Monthly Meeting, the course of its proceedings in the investigation of a case submitted to it by the Monthly Meeting, a case too, in which themselves were parties, and failing in this attempt they precipitately left, while the trial was still in progress, taking with them all the papers and documents which they had introduced to sustain their charges.

Eighth, that the Quarterly Meeting's Committee assumed the right to cancel our proceedings and records at pleasure, and to sit in judgment upon a case which the Yearly Meeting's Committee had brought to South Kingston Monthly Meeting for its decision, and which properly appertained to it alone in that stage of the proceedings. And they further ventured to attempt a division in our select meeting by advising one half of its members not to attend that meeting.

Ninth, that the advice of the Quarterly Meeting's Committee to the South Kingston Monthly Meeting in the 10th month, 1842, is absurd and improper, incompatible with the Discipline and the rights of the Monthly Meeting and individuals.

Tenth, that the dissolution of the South Kingston Monthly Meeting is against the Discipline, and in violation of its plainest provisions, in the following particulars, viz :—

1st. We have not received the judgment of the Quarterly Meeting in writing.

2d. We have not been allowed the right of appeal against such judgment.

3d. We have not been allowed the right of appeal against the dissolution, according to the due order of proceeding laid down in the Discipline, *before* the annexation of our members to another Monthly Meeting.

4th. In that there is no Discipline to warrant the annulling of our records.

Eleventh, That the Quarterly Meeting has deliberately denied us all access to their records, in violation of our rights, secured by Discipline, thus as far as possible denying us information important to us in conducting this appeal.—Even the minutes of the Quarterly Meeting. decreeing the dissolution of our Monthly Meeting, has been withheld from us.

Twelfth, that the proceedings against our Monthly Meeting throughout, were not on the ground alleged, or for the reasons assigned, but the measures taken were for the purpose of disowning John Wilbur, and always directed to that object.

Argument on the Appeal to the Yearly Meeting, sixth month, 1843, (by the Committee thereon appointed by South Kingston Monthly Meeting.)

If order and Discipline were needful in the days of George Fox and his cotemporaries, for the due administration of justice, and a correct management of the affairs of Truth, by rules and regulations, instituted, established and recorded, even in those purer days of the Society, when the Divine will, guidance and presence, were so remarkably known and witnessed among them, how much more essential in this our day, under an obvious declension from the Life and Power and Wisdom with which *they* were endued, that the order and discipline which they introduced, not merely for their own times, but for the succeeding times, should be sustained and scrupulously regarded, seeing the liability of a departure which might take place under a lapsed condition of the church in after times; the same as did occur and fall upon the Christian Church in her early days; to be as a hedge about her, lest the same might again befall her with whom the Lord was mindful to place his name to the latest generations.

And inasmuch as the leaders of his people caused them to err in the primitive church, by lording it over the heritage of God, making their own wills and the authority with which they had vested themselves, the supreme law of the church, George Fox, from whose penetrating eye, things past, present or to come, relative to the church, could scarcely be concealed, who in order to avoid the like again, labored with great assiduity and zeal, and as we may well believe, under the dictates of best Wisdom, to guard and fortify the church as much as might be, against the *like* as well as other departures or infringements upon her Rights, her Doctrines or her Discipline; so that whosoever, whether among the leaders, or among the people at large, should unhappily be left to disregard, abuse or violate that system of order, whether in the spirit or in the letter of it, there should be plain and tangible rules agreed upon by all, directing the course to be taken, both in matters of the greater and smaller consequences.

And Robert Barclay was not only a beholder of that admirable order of Discipline and church government, suggested by George Fox, but a fellow-helper in its furtherance and ultimate establishment. In his treatise upon the subject he points out the ground of union, and prescribes a remedy for such defects as may occur in the body. The following is extracted from the first volume of his works, beginning on page 512.

After speaking of the papists and others placing conscience in things that are absolutely wrong, goes on, "now say we, being gathered together into the

belief of certain principles and doctrines without
any constraint or wordly respect, but by the mere
force of truth upon our understanding, and its power
and influence upon our hearts; these principles and
doctrines, and the practices necessarily depending
upon them are, as it were, the terms that have
drawn us together, and the bond by which we became centered into one body and fellowship, and
distinguished from others. Now, if any one or more
so engaged with us should arise to teach any other
doctrine, or doctrines, contrary to these which are
the grounds of our being one, who can deny but
the body hath power in such a case to declare, this
is not according to the truth we profess; and therefore we pronounce such and such doctrines to be
wrong, with which we cannot have unity ; nor yet
any more spiritual fellowship with those that hold
them : and so such cut themselves off from being
members by dissolving the very bond by which
they were linked to the body.   Now, this cannot
be accounted tyranny and oppression no more than
in a civil society, if one of the society shall contradict one or more of the fundamental articles upon
which the society was contracted, it cannot be reck-
oned a breach or iniquity in the whole society to
declare, that such contradictors have done wrong,
and forfeited their right in that society; in case, by
the original constitution, the nature of the contradiction implies such a forfeiture as usually it is, and
will no doubt hold in religious matters. As if a body
be gathered into one fellowship by the belief of
certain principles, he that comes to believe otherwise naturally scattereth himself; for that the
cause that gathered him is taken away, and so
those that abide constant in declaring the thing to
be so as it is, and in looking upon him and witness-
ing of him to others (if need be) to be such, as he
has made himself, *do him no injury.*   I shall make
the supposition in the general, and let every people

make the application to themselves, abstracting from us, and then let conscience and reason in every impartial reader declare, whether or not it doth not hold? Suppose a people really gathered unto the belief of the true and certain principles of the gospel, if any of these people shall arise and contradict any of these fundamental truths, whether has not such as stand, good right to cast such an one out from among them, and to pronounce positively this is contrary to the truth we profess and own, and therefore ought to be resisted and not received, nor yet he that asserts it as one of us? And is not this *obligatory upon all the members*; seeing all are concerned in the like care as to themselves to hold the right and shut out the wrong? I cannot tell if any man of reason can well deny this, however, I shall prove it next by the testimony of the Scriptures." [Here he extracts Gal. 1: 8. 1 Tim. 1: 19, 20. 2 John 10.] And says, "These Scriptures are so plain and clear in themselves as to this purpose, that they need no great exposition to the unbiassed and unprejudiced reader, for seeing it is so, that in the true church there may men arise and speak perverse things contrary to the doctrine and gospel already received; what is to be the place of those that hold the pure and ancient truth? Must they look upon these perverse men still as their brethren? Must they cherish them as fellow-members, or must they judge, condemn and deny them? We must not think the apostle wanted charity, who will have them accursed; and that gave Hymanæus and Alexander over to satan after that they had departed from the true faith, that they might learn not to blaspheme. In short, if we must (as our opposers herein acknowledge) keep those that are come to own the truth by the same means that they were gathered and brought into it; we must not cease to be plain with them and tell them when they are wrong; and by sound doctrine, both exhort and

7

convince gainsayers. If the apostles of Christ of old, and the preachers of the everlasting gospel in this day had told all people, however wrong they found them in their faith and principles, *our charity and love is such we dare not judge you, nor separate from you; but let us all live in love together, and every one enjoy his own opinion, and all will be well,* how should the nations have been? Or what way now can they be brought to truth and righteousness? Would not the devil love this doctrine well, by which darkness and ignorance, error and confusion, might still continue in the earth, unreproved and uncondemned." Again, p. 554: " That this infallible judgment is only and unalterably annexed and seated in the power of God, not to any particular person or persons, meeting or assembly, by virtue of any settled ordination, office, place or station, that such may have, or have had in the church; no man, men or meeting, standing or being invested with any authority in the church of Christ upon other terms than so long as he or they abide in the living sense and unity of the life in their own particulars," &c.

And the ministration of these rules of Discipline which those who have gone before us laid down, under the guidance and superintendency of His spirit, who is the head of the church, is indeed one of the greatest outward blessings that has been vouchsafed to her, all along from the early days of the Society of Friends to the present time. But however good and wholesome this discipline is to the body, yet if it should unhappily be wrested or perverted from its original intention, by unskilful or unhallowed hands, it will scatter instead of gathering, it will wound instead of healing, it will destroy instead of restoring to life."

The appeal which is now offered for the consideration and determination of the Yearly Meeting from South Kingston Monthly Meeting, probably involves the deepest interest, and most important and serious consideration of any case that has ever occurred in the Society in New England; without a precedent and without an example; we trust, therefore that the Yearly Meeting or its committee, will give it such patient and careful attention, as will be commensurate with its importance. And we think it proper to state in the first place, that we are not aware that South Kingston Monthly Meeting has violated our discipline during the course of its late proceedings, complained of by the committees, although as has heretofore happened in many meetings for discipline, in the discussion of subjects of an exciteable cast, undesirable expressions have escaped some of those who have taken part therein; so with us, in the late very important transactions, the *manner* of speaking has in a few instances been undesirable, and which we regret, not effecting, however, any decision. But we now inform the committee on this appeal, that we feel ourselves aggrieved, and our rights, (delegated to us by the Yearly Meeting,) as also the Discipline, to have been violated, as we shall make appear in the following statement: First, by the Yearly Meeting's Committee; second, by the Quarterly Meeting's Committee, and third, by the Quarterly Meeting itself.

1st. By the Yearly Meeting's Committee the rights of South Kingston Monthly Meeting and the order of our Discipline were violated by their compelling said Monthly Meeting to act immediately upon their complaint against one of its members, without suffering it to go first to the overseers, and to come up to the Monthly Meeting through the Preparative Meeting, agreeable to all the order of disciplinary proceedings; and at the same time threatened the Monthly Meeting, that if it did refer it to the overseers, and thus avoid immediate action upon it, by the appointment of a committee at that time, that they would complain of South Kingston Monthly Meeting to the Quarterly Meeting ; averring that as they were appointed by the Yearly Meeting, they were clothed with the authority of the Yearly Meeting, and therefore had a right to make this requirement of the Monthly Meeting, the order of the society to the contrary notwithstanding, a power which we conceive the Yearly Meeting itself has no right to exercise against its own order, and especially when the rights of meetings or individuals are affected by it. Neither South Kingston Monthly Meeting nor any of its members felt a disposition to avoid a due examination of the case, thinking it quite time that the reproaches which the committee had been, in a manner, publicly heaping upon one of our members, should be wiped away, if without cause, and if with just cause, an early investigation was certainly needful—and the Monthly Meeting were desirous of no more delay than was requisite for regular proceedings, agreeable to Discipline and usages of the Society.

2nd. The Yearly Meeting's Committee, soon after our last Yearly Meeting, attended South Kingston Monthly Meeting, and then and there made an effort to remove our clerk from the table for the purpose of placing another person there, a measure which they proposed under the profession of restoring unity ; but they were told that the present clerk was chosen but the month before, by the expression of three-fourths of the meeting. And the committee was also reminded, that it would seem to be a very singular way of restoring unity, (if wanting,) thus to remove a clerk who was appointed by three-fourths of the meeting ; to displease three-fourths of a meeting for the sake of pleasing one-fourth, upon the plea of restoring unity, would be contrary to the plainest dictates of reason. Moreover, for a committee of a superior meeting to attempt the removal of a good clerk from the table of a subordinate meeting, in order to bring in one of their own choice, would be a precedent, if yielded to, tending to consequences destructive to the safety of society. This proposition being closely pressed by the committee, was considered by the Monthly Meeting too great a depredation upon their rights, to be acceded to, seeing that no good cause could be assigned for it.

3rd. And a still greater depredation, upon both the rights and property of South Kingston Monthly Meeting was the frank acknowledgment of the committee in that Monthly Meeting, that they had advised the former clerk to withhold the books and papers from it. And whilst speaking of this property, we will mention, that a committee, subsequently appointed by the Quarterly Meeting, not only gave the same advice to our former clerk, but actually came themselves, and without our leave, took away our books and papers out of our limits, from a constituted and legally authorised body and branch of New England Yearly Meeting. And their plea for this outrage was, that they were afraid of a separation, but the sequel will show whether they and their adherents, or we, were readiest for, or most rightfully chargeable with an intention of a separation, whereby the fallacy of such a plea will appear, unless indeed, they then intended themselves to bring it about. But suppose a man *should* conclude to dissolve fellowship with a society, or a community, does that conclusion vest that society, or that community, with authority to seize on his property, and to take it from him without his knowledge or liberty? 11 Can a man be found that will answer this question in the affirmative? And can a man be found, who will say that any man, or body of men, without incurring both guilt and dishonor, can come into our enclosure and take away, without liberty, books that we had purchased with our money, and therein recorded our marriages and the births of

our children, and by such evidence established the
certainty of those marriages, and consequently the
legitimacy of our children? No! nor have we any
conception how any man, or body of men, scrupulous of regarding even moral integrity, can sanction
such a procedure.

At the same time they unjustly charged South
Kingston Monthly Meeting with doing its business
out of doors, which was not true, and therefore could
not be proved.

4th. At the close of the business in South Kingston Monthly Meeting in the 7th month last, W. S.
P., one of the members, devoted to the Yearly Meeting's Committee, proposed that those who were in
unity with the Yearly Meeting and its committee,
and the *proceedings* of that committee, should remain in the house, with which proposition T. C. C.,
another member in like circumstances, expressed
unity, and proposed that the women should be informed of it. With which proposition the Yearly
Meeting's Committee united, but a friend objected
to the proposition as looking like a plan for separation—he was opposed to any scheme for a separation, and hoped the proposition would be rejected,
and several other friends spoke to the same effect,
approving of the stand that had been made against
this extraordinary proposition, &c. ; and it was said,
if we are about to commit ourselves, let it be to principles, and not to men. And another friend said, he
was surprised at this attempt to draw lines of division among us by the introduction of this extraordinary test ; he considered it a very improper test,
and one which he thought ought never to be applied,—he could not conceal his surprise that the Yearly Meeting's Committee, professing to come to restore unity and harmony, should give this scheme
the countenance they had done—he viewed the
proposition as very objectionable, and hoped it
would not receive any encouragement from the

meeting. We were ready to say, that we had full
unity with the well known principles of friends, and
no more ought to be required. T. A., one of the
committee, said that a man might be *entirely sound*
in doctrine and yet be *very far* from being in unity
with the Yearly Meeting.

And more fully to show, that both the Yearly
Meeting's Committee and some of our members who
adhered to them, intended to bring about a separation, we need but notice, in addition to the above,
that when it was desired that the women's meeting
might be notified of the proposition, some one said,
that the women had risen. R. G., one of the Yearly Meeting's Committee, replied, "they can easily
be collected again." The same Friend had previously commended the proposition, because he said
W. S. P. made it in so weighty a manner. And
furthermore, during the discussion, when the proposition was repeatedly spoken of as *a scheme for a
separation*, the committee did not disclaim it as such,
nor make any attempt to clear themselves from
such an intention. And moreover, T. C. C. afterwards acknowledged, that his expectation was that
the proposition would result in a separation. And
W. S. P., who introduced the proposition, on being
asked if he anticipated that a separation would
thereby be effected, replied, " *What use in remaining together when so much disunity exists ?*"

Here it seems necessary again to refer to their
reason, the month before, for advising our former
clerk to refuse our books and papers, to wit, *the apprehension of a separation.* When this reason was
rendered, the idea was entertained, that *they* suspected the three-fourths, who thought best for Samuel Sheffield to be clerk, would separate themselves
from the one-fourth, who favored T. C. C. for that
service; groundless was that apprehension, as in
the sequel is abundantly proved. Little did we then
think that their determination was such to choose

a clerk to South Kingston Monthly Meeting, as to resort to such a measure as this; to divide asunder a Monthly Meeting, and to take its property, and give it to such as they should succeed in drawing from it, although it might be but a fourth part. Than which, if greater disorder was ever practiced by a Committee of a Yearly Meeting, appointed to promote unity, or if greater abuse was ever inflicted upon a Monthly Meeting and its rights, we must say that we have never been made acquainted with it.

And our astonishment was greatly increased to see, that even after they had had some days to reflect upon it, they should make complaint to the Quarterly Meeting the following week, charging South Kingston Monthly Meeting with disorder, a want of unity, and insubordination !! As to disorder, the committee we are now addressing will be able, from the foregoing, to judge to whom the charge belongs. And as to *unity*, they will see who it was that attempted a breach, so unlikely ever to be healed, if that attempt had been successful. And our insubordination consisted in our standing for our rights which the discipline had dictated and guaranteed to us as a Monthly Meeting, in choosing our officers. When the Yearly Meeting's Committee complained of South Kingston Monthly Meeting for disorder, insubordination, &c., no judgment, or decision of the case, which they brought, had been come to, it being yet in the hands of the committee unreported to the Monthly Meeting.

5th. Divers overt acts of the Yearly Meeting's Committee, manifest in their attempts to coerce John Wilbur and the Committee of our Monthly Meeting, when their case was on trial, to an unreasonable conformity to their wishes, are proper in this place to be noticed. They threatened to leave on several occasions: 1st. If the Monthly Meeting's Committee suffered J. W. to have any friend to assist him; 2d. If they admitted his request, to have read the anonymous pamphlet, which they accused him with spreading; 3d. They threatened to leave if they allowed him the right of alluding to the doctrines of the society in his defence before the committee. And when the committee decided that he should be so heard, they *did leave;* which was after they had stated the case, and plead on their part, taking with them their own complaint, and papers, including several which were essential for his examination, in making his defence: and were reprehensible, as we think, (such of them as had offered themselves as witnesses in the case under investigation,) in refusing to answer questions that were propounded to them, such as in the judgment of the committee were proper in the case.

In remarking upon the argument of the Yearly Meeting's Committee, that a *recurrence to the doctrines of Friends* was irrelevant to the case, it is proper for us to state, that in their complaint they had charged one of our members with circulating a pamphlet which went to reproach our *doctrines* and tended to close up the way of a minister in this country with a certificate, and with writing and circulating letters which had the same tendency, now produced by themselves, which letters contained his remarks upon, and extracts from the printed doctrines of J. J. Gurney, the Friend alluded to. And John Wilbur made it appear that the first intimation of the committee's uneasiness with him, was his writing letters to his friends ; and that those letters, as now brought and made to appear by the Yearly Meeting's Committee themselves, had little or no allusion to that author's personal character, but rested upon his doctrines. And J. W. did then and there ask for an opportunity of showing that the doctrines thus alluded to, were the root and ground of this difficulty ; and were so palpably at variance with the fundamental and well known doctrines of the society, as to warrant, and even to require, in

7*

conformity with our discipline, his applying, in the first place to the author, and subsequently, as that labor proved ineffectual, to inform divers ministers and elders of his exercise relative to those objectionable doctrines. And J. W. did call on the committee to prove that any proceedings of his, aside from his recurrence to, and exposure of, the doctrines of J. J. Gurney, had any tendency to close up his way, whilst travelling in this country with a certificate,—as charged in the complaint, but without success. And it is too obvious to admit of dispute, that the Yearly Meeting's Committee did come forward in a *defence* and *support* of J. J. G., as clearly proved by their own document of complaint against J. W., attested by their own signatures,—hence they have thereby, as clearly identified themselves with *his* doctrines as did the *defenders* of Elias Hicks identify themselves with *his* doctrines ; and perhaps with about as much justice, claim to hold to our original principles ; unless they will yet redeem the time, and acquit themselves by a formal and designate condemnation of such of his sentiments as are at variance with the doctrines of Friends. Hence we can but see their unfairness, not to say equivocation, in refusing to hear the case argued in a doctrinal point of view.

The Quarterly Meeting having appointed a committee in the 8th month last, to join the Yearly Meeting's Committee, and to render advice and assistance, &c., they attended our ensuing Monthly Meeting, when the report of our committee in the well known case was to be acted upon, and there claimed the right of being incorporated and embodied, and declared that they were incorporated and embodied with the Monthly Meeting, in judging upon such matters as should come before it ; and even went further, and claimed the right and prerogative to dictate to the Monthly Meeting all its proceedings, and even to abolish its recorded acts

for months past. But South Kingston Monthly
Meeting saw things differently, under an apprehension that our discipline makes Monthly Meetings the
sole judges of all complaints against their own members, until appealed from to a superior meeting, and
did not admit the assumption of the Committee of
the Quarterly Meeting, as being thus incorporated
and clothed with such powers, knowing of no discipline, good reason, or former usage that would
justify or sustain such an assumption ; and least of
all, to abolish records of former proceedings. Furthermore, this Committee of the Quarterly Meeting
for discipline assumed the right and authority of
dictation to the meeting of ministers and eiders, and
exercised that right and authority, so far as to attempt to divide asunder the select preparative meeting of South Kingston, by gravely and earnestly
advising one half of its members not to attend it.

That such committees are and can be commission-
ed to advise and explain, will be agreed, but cannot
be clothed with judiciary powers, in a subordinate
meeting, because such, if attempted, would be an
infraction upon the plain and practical provisions of
our discipline, in the travel of cases from the lower
to the higher tribunal, wisely ordained for the avoid-
ing of all abuse or imposition, not only by us in our
excellent order of church government, but also of
the highest importance in the civil department of
proceedings amongst men.

Therefore, when such a committee has advised
and explained, there its mission terminates. If such
an interference be proposed for adoption, in points
purely judicial, or in the determination of alleged offences, we would say, better far to constitute one
body the sole tribunal of all offences. And in concluding this paragraph, we would notice an assumption of the Yearly Meeting's Committee, viz., that
the Quarterly Meeting had disqualified from acting,
one of the committee appointed by South Kingston

Monthly Meeting on its appeal, *by placing him under dealing !*   But we would ask, whence does the Quarterly Meeting derive its authority for placing any member of Society under dealing? If it can place one member of that committee, appointed to prosecute an appeal against its own acts, under dealing, and thereby disqualify him from attending to the duties of his appointment, then, forsooth, it can place every member of that committee under dealing, and thus, of their own power, foreclose an investigation of their own proceedings !

At South Kingston Monthly Meeting, held at Hopkinton, 10th month, 1842, a few of the Quarterly Meeting's Committee attended, and presented a document of advice, purporting to have been drawn up at Hopkinton that morning, signed by four out of a committee of fifteen, and will be found at page ·· .

And the committee seemed disposed to call on the Monthly Meeting for immediate action on their advice.   But inasmuch as they informed the meeting that all the committee had not seen it, as was indicated by the time and place of its execution, and inasmuch, too, as it contained things altogether new and unexampled, and of a serious and doubtful nature, involving in its consideration and decision, as might be, the very existence of the Monthly Meeting, it was therefore concluded to be referred, and the committee were informed that the meeting felt itself unequal, at once to decide upon questions of such magnitude without further consideration, and that it would therefore be referred for one month.

This committee however reported to the Quarterly Meeting, (which occurred on the week following,) recommending a dissolution of South Kingston Monthly Meeting, and the annexation of its members to Greenwich Monthly Meeting.

Review of a document presented to South Kingston Monthly Meeting by Rhode Island Quarterly Meeting's Committee, dated 10th month 24th, 1842, containing objections to the proceedings of said Monthly Meeting, when held in the 5th and 8th months preceding, with their advice and requirements that said Monthly Meeting should disannul and reverse divers of their transactions and conclusions therein.*

First,—They say, "that the placing of Samuel Sheffield at the table to act as clerk, was irregular and disorderly, and by which the feelings and views of many of its members were wholly disregarded." Replied to as follows : The number of those Friends whose feelings and views they say were wholly disregarded, was very small, at most not a fourth part of those who spoke to the case. And would it most harmonize with the committee's views, in relation to *regularity* and *order*, for the *feelings* and *views* of three-fourths of a meeting (and that number containing the most weighty Friends,) to be wholly disregarded, in order that those of one-fourth should be sustained ?

If this committee had been present, they must have seen that if there was any-thing "irregular or disorderly" in that transaction, it was chargeable upon T. C. C., and those few who supported him, by their long resistance to the voice and general sense of the meeting.

It had been the practice for some time in our *men's* meeting, at the time for the appointment of clerks and other officers, for the representatives of the preparative meetings, to meet previously and propose names to the Monthly Meeting. On this

---

* For the document here reviewed see page 83.

occasion, the representatives met and were not able to agree on names for clerks, which was reported to the meeting,—viz., that they were equally divided. Now, no one will pretend to say that the bare nomination of an officer, by the representatives of inferior meetings, is conclusive on the superior meeting, even if there was no discrepancy of opinion among them. The nomination of an officer is one thing, and his appointment and installation is another thing, and ought to be so, because many other members of such meeting *may* have better knowledge of some disqualifying trait in a man's character and conduct than any of those representatives. But the actual transaction was this,—the time for which the former clerk was appointed had expired; the *usual time for making the appointment had come*, and the Monthly Meeting must have a clerk, either by the continuance of the former, or by the appointment of a new one; and the representatives had not reconciled their views in relation to it; whereupon the meeting, not giving the preference to either of those talked of in the representatives' meeting, agreed upon a third person, and him it appointed for its clerk, and that without any expressed objection to the individual by any one present. And this practice of *naming* as well as of appointing a clerk immediately by the meeting has been the ancient usage and practice of South Kingston Monthly Meeting from its first organization until within a few years; and the same practice has prevailed in the preparative meetings, and in our women's meeting up to this time. Nor can there be found any conclusion on our records cancelling that practice, or establishing any other to the forfeiture of the right vested in our Monthly Meeting, of naming its own officers.

Second,—The committee further state, "that they are satisfied that Samuel Sheffield took his seat at the table, and made the minute appointing himself, out of the usual and long established order of said meeting in the appointment of its clerk." To which we remark as follows : That T. C. C. having served this meeting as clerk for many years, has, as we believe, in every case of his re-appointment, that is every year, (to use the committee's own words,) " made the minute appointing himself." And the same has been the case under similar circumstances, in relation both to Quarterly and Yearly Meeting's clerks, if not in all business meetings in New England. But that it is usual, where a new selection is made, for the former clerk to make the minute of the appointment of the new one, we shall not pretend to gainsay ; but do subscribe freely to the propriety of such a usage ;—but we would ask, who was in fault that it was not so done on the occasion in question ? T. C. C. was requested to make the minute of Samuel Sheffield's appointment, but refused doing so, and left the table saying, " that it was not customary."

Who then will say that it was improper or indecorous for the new clerk to go to the table and make the minute of his own appointment, when the table *was vacated*, and the meeting requested him to do so? And if any indecorum was manifested on the occasion, was it not on the part of T. C. C., by remaining long at the table and advocating his own claims, after the question had been fully decided by the meeting; as well as by the *manner* of his leaving the table?

Third,—They object to the addition made at this time to the committee appointed the month before, pronouncing it " *contrary to the general usage of our Society.*"

To prove that such has been the *frequent* usage of the Society, we need but refer to the recollection of every intelligent member of it. But we might refer to our own records for proof of such practice, if indeed this committee had not taken them from us ! and all access to them since been denied us !

We would call the attention of Friends particularly to the usage of both our Quarterly Meeting, and our Select Quarterly Meeting, within the last two or three years, in relation to additions to committees.

But if any thing were needed to show the utter inconsistency of this charge, we have it in the fact, that at the time when the first four were appointed, in the 4th month, the Yearly Meeting's Committee, (while urging the immediate appointment of a committee on the case,) *themselves* suggested to South Kingston Monthly Meeting that they could make an addition at their next meeting, if desirable, on account of the smallness of the meeting at that time !! And they afterwards, in the 7th month, consented to an addition to another committee in our meeting !

Besides, the Yearly Meeting's Committee acknowledged the *whole* of the committee of the Monthly Meeting, by proceeding with their case against John Wilbur before them,—and refusing to proceed with any one present but *the committee* and John Wilbur; threatening to leave if the committee was not *select.* When it was so, they produced their documents, and proceeded with the case, without objecting to any of the committee, upon any ground whatever.

Fourth.—They say that they "have *cause* to apprehend from the manner in which the committee was selected, and from their relationship to the individual under care, it was *with a view to prevent an impartial exercise of our Christian discipline.*"

This high charge and accusation of *design* in South Kingston Monthly Meeting to prevent an impartial exercise of our Discipline, is well known, as we trust, by all who took a part in that nomination, to be equally unfounded and unjust !

But inasmuch as we have no discipline which excludes or exempts relations from such service in the church, it has with us always been considered to be discretionary with Monthly Meetings to appoint such as are thought most suitable for the service, as was done in the present case. It is true that several of the committee are distantly related to John Wilbur, but not one of them stands within the line prescribed by our Discipline, as being a relationship unsuitable for the marriage connexion. Besides, two of those appointed without objection in the fourth month, when the Yearly Meeting's Committee were present—-were relations of John Wilbur.

It is remarkable that the Quarterly Meeting's Committee, at this late period, should have come forward with objection to the addition, as well as the relationship of the Monthly Meeting's Committee, where no objection on this ground, or indeed any other, was made at the time of its appointment, nor afterwards, by the Yearly Meeting's Committee before the trial, or while it was in progress, but they brought forward all their charges and went through with their evidence, and it was only after the report was made, and found to be in favor of John Wilbur that this singular objection was urged.

And but for the unjust act of our former clerk, endorsed by this Quarterly Meeting's Committee in withholding from us our Records, we should have been able to make it appear thereby, that in cases of dealing, much nearer relatives to the party have often been appointed to treat with him, a usage which we not only claim as having been long practiced in this meeting, but also in others.

But it seems proper under this head to state, inasmuch as the Quarterly Meeting's Committee have charged us with deviation from our former practice, that in addition to their advising and endorsing our former clerk's *breach of trust*, they had at the time gone so far themselves, as to have sent, a few days previous to making this grave charge, and *taken away* our books of records, papers, &c., and

conveyed them to some place not within our bor-
ders, and unknown to us! and then, after this *trespass* upon our rights of property, they challenge
our late practice as not being in accordance with
our former, whilst they themselves are thus *surrep-
titiously* withholding from us the only *legal* evidence whereby our former practice can be proved,
and by which most easily done, but for this their
conduct, so foreign from the Christian rule and precept.

And we may further say, that one of this *very*
committee appointed by Rhode Island Quarterly
Meeting, to advise and assist in the disposition of
the case of John Wilbur, is *more nearly* allied to
him by blood than either of those in his own Monthly Meeting's Committee; and shall we, for that reason, charge the Quarterly Meeting as they have
South Kingston Monthly Meeting, "that they have
acted with a view to prevent an impartial exercise
of our Christian discipline?" If *they* have cause for
such charge, therefore, on the ground of relationship, *we* more.

The circumstance that the Quarterly Meeting's
Committee did not *attend* our Monthly Meeting in
the 5th month, and consequently their knowledge of
its proceedings was only through the reports abroad,
and those reports, as it would seem, by their effects
on the minds of the committee, must have been of
a very deceptive and partial character, and hence
forming premises insufficient and unsafe whereon
to predicate a complaint, and to form a judgment
without hearing both sides of the case, in matters of
so serious a nature as contained in their document,
now under consideration. And it is a circumstance
greatly to be regretted and lamented, that a committee from a Quarterly Meeting of Friends, entrusted with affairs of great moment to the peace and
well being of Society, should have been so credulous
and unguarded, as well as so adventurous as thus

to have condemned a Monthly Meeting upon vague report, and *without a hearing !* and upon such ground to attempt to break up its doings for near half a year back, is a matter of no small surprise to us. Hence we are persuaded that all impartial friends must see that the advice of the Quarterly Meeting's Committee, in relation to the transactions in the 5th month, if accepted and drawn into precedent, would tend to break up and lay waste the order of Society, and lead to an overthrow of the rights which our Yearly Meeting has conferred upon our subordinate branches, as set forth in our Discipline.

Moreover, any attempt by a Quarterly Meeting, or by a deputation from it to interfere with the disciplinary proceedings of a Monthly Meeting, acting with and under the provisions of our Discipline ; or to arrest it in its usual progress, we must say would be an abuse of the superior authority of a Quarterly Meeting, which like that of a Monthly Meeting, has but a derived authority, and both from the same source, to wit, from the Yearly Meeting. And the subordinate is as equally entitled to its *rights* as the superior, and, moreover, ought to stand as independent in its judgment in the concerns properly belonging to it, as the superior, being the only body authorized by the Yearly Meeting to deal with and disown offenders. But the Quarterly Meeting (if applied to and not otherwise) has the right to reverse the judgment of a Monthly Meeting, but not to coerce a Monthly Meeting, nor to arrest its proceedings, nor to reverse them until the case be brought through the prescribed channel. And the Quarterly Meeting is subject to a similar reversal of *its* judgment by the Yearly Meeting, (when properly applied to and not otherwise.)

And who would expect the Yearly Meeting, having been informed that a case of judicature was pending before a Quarterly Meeting, and likely to result either in the confirming or the revoking of the disownment of an individual by a Monthly Meeting, we say, who would expect the Yearly Meeting to interfere with the case until it be brought to that body in the manner which itself has ordained and prescribed? Surely no one. Nor has the Yearly Meeting, in the nature of things, any right, either religious or moral, to act contrary to its own laws and regulations; and especially where it affects the rights of either individuals or of Monthly or Quarterly Meetings. No more has a Quarterly Meeting any right at all to infringe upon those rights of a Monthly Meeting, which the Yearly Meeting has given it and guaranteed to it. But the Monthly Meeting is to be left to act conscientiously and freely, so long as it remains sound in our doctrine, and faithful to our Discipline; and that without the coercive interference of any other body. But if a Monthly Meeting become apostate in principle, it is then consequently unfit to exercise the concerns of a Monthly Meeting, and if it act contrary to the doctrines and Discipline and constitution of a Monthly Meeting, then the course to be taken with it is obvious, being plainly pointed out by the Discipline.

And by the tenor of our Discipline in providing for appeals from the judgment of all subordinate meetings, it would appear that the Yearly Meeting supposed it altogether possible, that each of those bodies might be or become disqualified in relation to either principle or judgment. And, however capacitated and honestly disposed any Monthly Meeting may be, with a desire to act sincerely and correctly, agreeably to the mind of truth, and in conformity with the Discipline, yet without the *rights and independency* which it gives us, our meetings for the ordering of the affairs of truth, will at best be but merely nugatory, and the authority which they are designed by our excellent system of

Church government, to extend over the members thereof, will be lost, and any pretensions to such authority will be in vain.

The proceedings which have been resorted to, in order to coerce South Kingston Monthly Meeting to a conformity with the views of others in authority, brings to mind the trial of William Penn and William Mead, before the Court of Oyer and Terminer, in London ; the judges whereof derived their authority from the highest source in the kingdom. These judges by the exercise of their power, or rather the abuse of it, attempted repeatedly to coerce the jury to a conformity to their own wills. But William Penn clearly set forth that the jurors in *their department*, ought to be as independent as those in any other department, though never so high, under the great charter of England, and were to act according to the testimony adduced and their own consciences. And who will venture to say that the jury alluded to, went beyond their right of authority in giving in their opinion, though contrary to the advices and menaces of the higher power, or in their disobedience to its commands ? If a jury must do just as the court shall say, then what use in juries ? And who will say that any of the requirements of men, (let them assume whatever authority they may,) directed to a Monthly Meeting, or to an individual, if that requirement is unauthorized by our Discipline and usages, and contrary to a sense of duty, on the part of those to whom it is offered, we ask who will say that a disobedience to it is reprehensible, or an offence against society ?

And now in relation to the concluding portion of the document of the Quarterly Meeting's Committee under review,—embracing their *requirements* of us :—We believe that no candid and impartial man need do more than read it, to be convinced of the magnitude and danger of the authority there claimed, and attempted to be exercised.

The requirement of the immediate removal of the clerk, duly appointed by the meeting, and recognized as our rightful clerk by the Committees of both the Yearly and Quarterly Meetings, and by the Quarterly Meeting itself;—and the *selection and naming by them*, of a successor, without allowing the Monthly Meeting any voice in the matter, strikes us as a most extraordinary and dangerous assumption of power. And no less surprising is their advice to annul and make void our records.

To discharge an individual from under dealing who had committed a high offence against his Monthly Meeting, by withholding from it its rightful property,—it is true with the advice and consent of this Quarterly Meeting's Committee ;—but no less an offence and breach of trust for that ;—and one which the Monthly Meeting was not at liberty to pass over, while it was in the exercise of its just rights, and authority granted and secured to it, and enjoined upon it, by the Yearly Meeting for the government of its members.

In addition to this is the direction " that the decision in the 8th month last, as entered on our minutes in relation to John Wilbur, be set aside and be made void and of no effect."

The disownment of this Friend, we would have the committee bear in mind, was the great object sought to be attained by all these extraordinary movements,—the great end, which all the means put in requisition from the beginning were aimed at.

It was because South Kingston Monthly Meeting could not be brought to condemn and disown a member, whose offence consisted in his *faithful testimony* against those things which were calculated to lay waste and desolate, the only true bond of Christian union among us ; namely, an agreement, and unity in those doctrines and testimonies, revived and promulgated by our worthy predecessors, and still held dear by all true Friends ;—we say it was because South Kingston Monthly Meeting could not be induced by all the influences which had been brought to bear upon it, to disown this Friend against its own judgment, that that Monthly Meeting was dissolved, and done too as we verily believe, not by the Quarterly Meeting, really and truly as such, but by a few leading men therein, the very *same* who had in an unauthorized and improper manner, taken up J. W. in the first instance, and all along pursued their object with a zeal worthy of a better cause.

In the introduction of this case to our Monthly Meeting, it was called upon by the Yearly Meeting's Committee, as the legitimate body, to give its judgment upon an alleged offence of one of its members. Whereupon a large committee was appointed by South Kingston Monthly Meeting in the order of society, and much time was allowed by them for deliberation previously to the interview with the parties ; and when met, a patient investigation of the case was had, and the evidences and allegations in relation to it were heard, occupying the space of four days ; and the committee reported at the time alluded to, that the complaint in their judgment, was *not sustained ;* with which report the meeting being satisfied, it consequently adopted it, a very large proportion of the meeting uniting therein. And, inasmuch as these proceedings were not precipitate, but very deliberate, and in the order of our Discipline, we see no reason nor *right* we have to reverse that decision, affecting as it would the rights of an individual, whose case had been once decided by the proper tribunal and he acquitted. (And seeing that the committee who brought the complaint, had previously made so light of the alleged offence as to assure him *that they were disposed to require but a very little concession from him,*) we think it truly remarkable that such unprecedented advice should have been given ; and that such great efforts should be made for the expulsion of a member whose offence appears only to have been found in the exercise of a concern to sustain our doctrines, testimonies, and Discipline.

(The record giving an account of divers interviews which the Yearly Meeting's and select Quarterly Meeting's Committees had with John Wilbur, evinces his importunities with them for a plain statement in writing, of the ground of their uneasiness with him, in order and preparatory to a deliberate vindication of the course he had taken :— and this record at the same time shows their refusal, as well as the shifts and evasions to which they resorted, to prevent him from having an opportunity for a fair and full hearing before them ; a refusal which they continued, until they brought a complaint against him to his own Monthly Meeting.) And subsequently, in carrying out the same determination not to hear his defence, when the case was investigated by the committee of South Kingston Monthly Meeting, the Yearly Meeting's Committee, after their own efforts adducing evidence, and after pleading for the sustainment of their charges, refused and *would not,* and *did not* stay to hear J. Wilbur's defence, and consequently did not know, and do not know what it was. And these remarks are adduced, not so much in this place to show their ostensible abandonment of the case, by withdrawing themselves, and taking the complaint and all the papers with them, as they are to show that they *never had, nor ever would allow themselves* an official hearing of J. Wilbur's vindication of his proceedings and of the course which he had taken.

Hence, we see how absurd and arbitrary were the proceedings of this Committee of the Yearly Meeting, in their attempts to coerce South Kingston

Monthly Meeting in the 8th month last, to refuse the acceptance of the report of its own committee, who *had* patiently heard and examined the evidences brought on *both* sides.

Again, it becomes us to say, that the Quarterly Meeting's Committee (who also attempted at the time alluded to, to press South Kingston Monthly Meeting to a rejection of the report aforesaid,) were so entirely uninformed of the merits of the case, as never to have heard J. Wilbur's vindication and defence from the charges preferred against him!

Therefore, they, the Quarterly Meeting's Committee, are justly chargeable with attempting to compel South Kingston Monthly Meeting to a measure in the decision of a case, which themselves, had not the legitimate means of understanding!! Furthermore the same Committee of Rhode Island Quarterly Meeting, labored under the same disqualification and want of the requisite understanding of the case, when they so gravely advised South Kingston Monthly Meeting, at a subsequent sitting, at once to cancel and annul their decision therein!

These proceedings of the Quarterly Meeting's Committee must, as we conceive, be considered, by all judicious men, regardful of the welfare of society, to be in no small degree, rash and adventurous; and if sustained, of dangerous consequence, as well in relation to the establishment of so hurtful a precedent, as the direct and serious effects of a violation and disregard of the *rights* of a Monthly Meeting and of individuals, directly tending and leading as an example to the trifling with Friend's records, and rendering them precarious and void at the pleasure of superior bodies. And should the authority claimed in the document before us, be sustained and established by the Yearly Meeting, it will be seen that not only the right of membership, but our property and the line of inheritance, will be jeoparded and made to lie at the will of such, as

8

may in the lapse of things clothe themselves with such authority as is assumed by this Committee !

Upon a review of the proceedings of the Quarterly Meeting in dissolving our Monthly Meeting, we submit to the committee the following remarks.*

And although modesty and civility combined, with the deference usually paid to persons of standing and influence, would suggest a forbearance of expression, yet those leading essentials, *Truth* and *Justice*, hold a superior claim that cannot be denied, in the judicial department especially, when the character and rights of individuals are in question, when the rights and existence of delegated bodies, instituted by the highest authority and for indispensable purposes, are in great jeopardy. Then it is that even charity itself cannot exclude the rights and demands of these arbiters, the umpire of Truth and Justice. We therefore feel bound to say,

1st. That the principal actors in this Quarterly Meeting, against South Kingston Monthly Meeting are recognized among the members of the committee which first complained of that Monthly Meeting to the Quarterly Meeting; thus assuming the seat of judgment on the decision of a complaint first brought by themselves.

2d. That those friends and such others as were determined to dissolve South Kingston Monthly Meeting, were exceedingly unwilling, and long and strenuously opposed and resisted the reading of the Discipline and Law of the Society, (in such cases provided) in the hearing of the Quarterly Meeting, as ordained by the Yearly Meeting as a Rule of decision in such cases as was then before the meeting.

3d. That when, after a long struggle, the propo-

---

* For the proceedings of the Quarterly Meeting, here remarked upon, see preceding Narrative, page 85.

sal for reading the Discipline, did prevail, no one of these persons attempted in any way whatever to reconcile this proposed measure to that Discipline by an exposition of its several items, nor to show the adaptation of their proceedings to it; but only claimed its authority in the gross, for which omission the reasons must be obvious.

4th. That the representatives and members of South Kingston Monthly Meeting, and many others on their behalf, earnestly solicited an appeal to the Discipline on the subject then in discussion, and were willing to rest their whole case upon its premises.

5th. That one of the representatives from South Kingston Monthly Meeting, did in this Quarterly Meeting challenge the authority and explain that Discipline, and exemplified the bearing of its several items, showing the gradation and deliberation therein clearly premised in the management of such cases; and that such usage had not been regarded in the travel of this case.

6th. That these complainants were not only disposed themselves to decide this case against the Monthly Meeting without a hearing, but most cruelly striving to *deprive and debar its members from being heard in any way, even as suppliants pleading for their rights,* and peremptorily forbidding their representative giving an account even of some of the most prominent facts and circumstances that had transpired in the Monthly Meeting.

Now let it be enquired,

1st. Who were they that plead for their case to be first investigated, and then judged by the Law of the Society?

2d. Who were they that strenuously resisted the light, *by refusing* to hear the case in any way, and chose to judge it without Law or Rule of Discipline?

3d. What penalty would the law of the land inflict upon that tribunal, which should have judged and condemned a man for a crime, and shall have executed that judgment upon him, without allowing him any hearing upon his indictment?

As directed, several of the Quarterly Meeting's Committee attended South Kingston Monthly Meeting in the 11th month, and after the meeting was opened as usual, they declared the object of their mission, and then read the doings of the Quarterly Meeting, comprehending its decree as heretofore noticed, and then called on the members quietly to separate. But friends of this Monthly Meeting having from the first acted sincerely in pursuing what they believed to be the mind of Truth and the order of Society; and clearly seeing, as they thought, that the Quarterly Meeting had violated the plain provisions which were made for Monthly Meetings in such cases, concluded to appeal to the Yearly Meeting for a redress of their grievances, and informed the committee that they were minded to remain together a sufficient length of time to make suitable arrangements for that purpose. And as it was the doings of the Quarterly Meeting which they had just read to us, that we only had to appeal from, they were requested to furnish us with a copy thereof, but they refused to do so!

Nevertheless, an appeal was drawn up in a summary way, and we, the undersigned, were appointed to represent South Kingston Monthly Meeting, and to act on its behalf in the prosecution of it. And subsequently we applied to the clerk of Rhode Island Quarterly Meeting for a copy of the minutes dissolving our Monthly Meeting, but were refused by a reference to the Quarterly Meeting itself; therefore, verbal application was made to the Quarterly Meeting in the second month last, for the necessary copies, but which copies that meeting refused to grant.

Again, as an access to the records was very essential to us in preparing our case, and such was also our right by Discipline, and in order that no informality should be alleged as an excuse, the committee at large made a written application to both the Quarterly Meeting and the Select Quarterly Meeting, for the liberty of access to the records of both meetings, but were refused by both!—Were refused such rights as the law of the land has guaranteed even to criminals, and which is never refused them, and such too, as our Yearly Meeting has guaranteed to all its members. And whilst we are referring to usages, we feel it our duty further to inform the committee that on divers occasions in meetings for business, when a recurrence to discipline, in things relating to this case, has been asked for, the reading has been waived and declined.

DISCIPLINE,

Authorising the dissolution of Monthly Meetings, &c.

(From Book of Discipline, pages 118–119.)

" When a Quarterly Meeting hath come to a judgment respecting any difference, relative to any Monthly Meeting belonging to them, and notified the same in writing to such Monthly Meeting, the said Monthly Meeting ought to submit to the judgment of the Quarterly Meeting; but if such Monthly Meeting shall not be satisfied therewith, then the Monthly Meeting may appeal to the Yearly Meeting, against the judgment and determination of the Quarterly Meeting.

"And if a Monthly Meeting shall refuse to take the advice and submit to the judgment of the Quarterly Meeting, and notwithstanding will not appeal against the determination of the said meeting to the Yearly Meeting; in such case the Quarterly Meeting shall be at liberty either to dissolve such Monthly Meeting, or bring the affair before the next or succeeding Yearly Meeting.

" And in case a Quarterly Meeting shall dissolve a Monthly Meeting, the dissolved Monthly Meeting or any part thereof, in the name of the said meeting, shall be at liberty to appeal to the next or succeeding Yearly Meeting, against such dissolution ; but if the dissolved Monthly Meeting, or a part thereof in its behalf, shall not appeal to the Yearly Meeting, the Quarterly Meeting shall join the members of the said late Monthly Meeting, to such other Monthly Meeting as they may think most convenient ; and until such time,* shall take care that no inconvenience doth thereby ensue to the members of such dissolved meeting, respecting any branch of our Discipline.

" And if any of the Monthly Meeting, to which the Quarterly Meeting shall join the whole or a part of the late Monthly Meeting, do think themselves aggrieved, they shall be at liberty to appeal against the Quarterly Meeting to the Yearly Meeting, and until such appeal is heard and determined, the friends added by the Quarterly Meeting to them, shall be deemed their members." 1743.

DISCIPLINE ON THIS CASE CONSIDERED.

When a Quarterly Meeting hath come to a judgment respecting any difference relative to any Monthly Meeting belonging to them—

Now, whether this difference relates to a misunderstanding among the members of a Monthly Meeting, or whether it relate to a dispute with another Monthly Meeting, in relation to the settlement of those who are needy ; or whether it relate to rights of membership, or whatever—this discipline

---

* This portion of Discipline was transcribed from that of London Yearly Meeting, and adopted here. In the original the words 'until such junction" were used instead of " until such time."

does not define, neither does it matter what it is, if the Quarterly Meeting has come to a judgment: it is the Quarterly Meeting that must first come to a judgment: and whether that judgment is grounded upon the report of a committee, made in open session, or whether the parties had been fully heard in the Quarterly Meeting itself, it matters not, provided the Quarterly Meeting itself "had come to a judgment;" which point arrived at, the rule goes on and says—*and notified the same in writing to such Monthly Meeting.*

Question.—Who is to notify the Monthly Meeting in writing?

Answer.—The Quarterly Meeting.

Question.—But where and how is that writing to be agreed upon and executed?

Answer.—In the Quarterly Meeting, and signed by the clerk: and any paper whatever, which is not there openly agreed upon, and so signed, cannot be accredited any where as the judgment of the Quarterly Meeting: a position which no person will gainsay.

Well, when such writing arrives, the rule says or continues to say, *The said Monthly Meeting ought to submit to the judgment of the Quarterly Meeting.*

Here the order, or relative standing of the two bodies is alluded to;—the Quarterly Meeting the superior, and the Monthly Meeting the inferior. But what follows shows that the judgment of the Quarterly Meeting is not imperious and final upon the Monthly Meeting, for it further says, *But if such Monthly Meeting shall not be satisfied therewith, then the Monthly Meeting may appeal to the Yearly Meeting, against the judgment and determination of the Quarterly Meeting.*

Here we find no requisition laid upon the Monthly Meeting to decide immediately upon that document, (or at the same sitting,) whether it will abide the decision or not; consequently, this discipline,

good reason, and Christian usage, all agree in allowing time for due deliberation, inasmuch as questions
of great importance may demand and require it.

And when, on due consideration, such Monthly
Meeting feels itself dissatisfied, then it has the right,
by the above, to appeal to a body of higher authority than the Quarterly Meeting—to the ultimate umpire of the Yearly Meeting.

Now, in the above recited provision, as compre-
hended in the first paragraph, we see that there is
not the least mention made of laying down the
Monthly Meeting.

But the next paragraph, in an extension of the
subject, provides as follows:

*And if a Monthly Meeting shall refuse to take the ad-
vice, and submit to the judgment of the Quarterly Meeting, and notwithstanding will not appeal against the determination of the said meeting to the Yearly Meeting;
in such case the Quarterly Meeting shall be at liberty either
to dissolve such Monthly Meeting, or to bring the affair before the next or succeeding Yearly Meeting.**

Here in this second paragraph it is provided and
decided beyond all disputation, that a Quarterly
Meeting shall have no authority to lay down a
Monthly Meeting, until the Quarterly Meeting's
advice is resisted by a two-fold refusal—first, if
the Monthly Meeting refuse to accept of the Quarterly Meeting's advice, or to abide its judgment;
and secondly, if it refuse to appeal therefrom, then
the Quarterly Meeting may lay it down, or consult
the Yearly Meeting in the case: evidently making
it a serious matter to take from a Monthly Meeting
its charter, as evinced by this whole paragraph,
and more especially by the last sentence of it. And
no mention is yet made, nor liberty given for the
annexation of the members to another Monthly

---

* In which see how much time is allowed.

Meeting, nor subsequently until the members thereof have time more fully to consider the case, and have opportunity the second time for appealing now against the *dissolution* of the Monthly Meeting, as set forth in the first part of the third paragraph, which is as follows :

And in case a Quarterly Meeting shall dissolve a Monthly Meeting, the dissolved Monthly Meeting, or any part thereof, in the name of said Monthly Meeting, shall be at liberty to appeal to the next or succeeding Yearly Meeting against such dissolution.*

And here no construction is wanting to make it plainly appear that this second provision and liberty for appealing, is against the *dissolution*, not against the *annexation ;* for no annexation is as yet provided for, unless such second opportunity of appealing is refused or neglected, as set forth in the latter part of this third paragraph, to wit,

But if the dissolved Monthly Meeting, or part thereof, in its behalf, shall not appeal to the Yearly Meeting, the Quarterly Meeting shall join the members of said late Monthly Meeting to such other Monthly Meeting as they may think most convenient ; and until such time, (the time of annexation) *shall take care that no inconvenience doth thereby ensue to the members of such dissolved Monthly Meeting respecting any branch of our discipline.*

Here, again, in this last part of the 3d paragraph is further and incontrovertible evidence, that the enactors of this law of Society, designed that the annexation should be subsequent, and to follow, and only to follow, the refusal or neglect of appealing against the act of the Quarterly Meeting in dissolving the Monthly Meeting.

And the latter clause, " until such time, shall take care," &c., if it has any meaning at all, it means that there will have been a space of time between the *dissolution* of the Monthly Meeting

---

* Here again, see how much time is allowed

and the *annexation* of its members to another, as
indeed does the whole section on this subject, clearly demonstrate by the gradations therein premised,
that it was the design of the framers of that discipline,* that in so serious a matter as the dismem-
bering of a Monthly Meeting, (like that of dismem-
bering the human body,) that great deliberation,
caution, and care should be observed, lest a rash
procedure should be cause of sorrow.   Finally, we
see that in considering this discipline that there are
prominent and governing features which stand forth
in full view, to wit :

First,—The Quarterly Meeting must be informed
that a difference exists in a Monthly Meeting, and
secondly, the Quarterly Meeting must in some way
become ascertained of the true merits of that difference, and by means of that knowledge come to a
judgment in relation to it ; and when the Quarterly
Meeting has thus come to a judgment, then the
course to be pursued is to send that decision, (relative to the proper disposition and settlement of the
case,) in writing, signed by the clerk, and directed
to that Monthly Meeting.   And if that Monthly
Meeting is not satisfied therewith, it has the right
allowed it, after mature consideration, to appeal
from that judgment of the Quarterly Meeting, in relation to the existing difficulty, to the Yearly Meeting.   But when the Quarterly Meeting has had time
to ascertain, and has ascertained, which cannot, of
course, be less than three months after the issuing of
its judgment; and peradventure it may be six
months, (the time which discipline provides for the
limit of appeals) before the Quarterly Meeting can
be informed.   And if such Monthly Meeting decline the acceptance of the Quarterly Meeting's
judgment, and also decline appealing, then the

---

* First agreed on in London Yearly Meeting, in earlier times.

Quarterly Meeting is authorized, after due consideration, either to dissolve the Monthly Meeting or to apply to the Yearly Meeting for advice. But if it decide to dissolve it, then, of course, that decision goes to the Monthly Meeting, in writing, again as before, signed by the clerk; and then again the prescribed time for appeals is to be allowed for the Monthly Meeting to come to a conclusion whether it will abide that decision, and to get the result of their deliberations to the Quarterly Meeting: and if not to appeal, then it is, and not till then, that the Quarterly Meeting is authorized by our discipline to annex its members to another Monthly Meeting. And then also it is, when a Monthly Meeting has twice refused the decision of the Quarterly Meeting, and twice declined to appeal, and not until then, if the Monthly Meeting remain dissatisfied, that our discipline ordains that the members of that Monthly Meeting shall become members of such other Monthly Meeting, as the Quarterly Meeting may direct, and from which afterward there is no appeal, on the part of the dissolved Monthly Meeting.

And here we would call the attention of the committee to another very important consideration, viz., that the Monthly Meeting was not laid down on account of any disorderly proceedings therein as was professed to be the case; but that these extraordinary and high handed measures of the Quarterly Meeting leading to and resulting in its formal dissolution were evidently elicited by the Quarterly Meeting's Committee, for the reason that said Monthly Meeting, as was feared, would find no cause of disownment against one of its members whom they, the Yearly Meeting's Committee, wished, and were apparently determined should be disowned: a desire and determination evinced by the precipitation and recklessness with which they hurried forward towards the consummation of this darling purpose, prostrating every obstacle which interposed; even the discipline itself: and still further evinced by the reports of *extermination* which went abroad, viz., that if South Kingston Monthly Meeting refused to disown that member, it *must be put down*, and *it would be put down ;* and this reported, and apparent determination of the Yearly Meeting's Committee was openly and widely spread, even beyond the limits of New England Yearly Meeting.

That they would proceed to this extremity of destroying a Monthly Meeting, not the least among the tribes, nor yet the least in weight of character or concern for the right management of the affairs of a Monthly Meeting. And all this for the sake of exterminating from the Society one individual ! for the sake of driving from the church an approved minister of the Society, whose guide in the proceedings complained of, were the impressions of apprehended religious duty, and the requirement of our discipline. And when, too, this committee, in a collective capacity, had given him the assurance that " they would be satisfied with a *very little* concession," and during their urgent entreaties for this kind of satisfaction, no mention was made of sincerity. And subsequently the committee sent to him a deputation of four of their number, proposing that he should say, " If I have done wrong, I am sorry for it," and thus voluntarily reducing their uneasiness and claim for concession to a " very little thing"—nay, to what we consider nothing at all : and to which form he might safely have subscribed, but for the *version* which he suspected they would give it, and send abroad. And no complaint was made to South Kingston Monthly Meeting of any thing as having transpired since those interviews with the Yearly Meeting's Committe, above alluded to. And the aid of the Quarterly Meeting was evidently invoked for the purpose of effecting the object of the Yearly Meeting's Committee, to wit : the disownment of this Friend ; which object could not be consummated without the instrumentality of the Quarterly Meeting, in either compelling the Monthly Meeting to a nullification of its records, or a reversal of its proceedings in regard to that individual ; or on failure of *that*, to dissolve the Monthly Meeting ; and to place that member within the reach of their power, in another Monthly Meeting, which might be expected to be more obedient to their mandate. And when there placed, the object of his disownment, so desirable to them, was effected, by the personal presence, dictation and control of at least seven of that committee, who were the complainants against the individual, and against the Monthly Meeting, and one of the Quarterly Meeting's Committee : and barely two members of that Monthly Meeting, who were not included in those appointments, that agreed to J. Wilbur's disownment : and of these two, one was a son and the other a brother of the two most active members of the Yearly Meeting's Committee, who brought the complaint against our member. And the great unreasonableness of the Yearly Meeting's Committee is further apparent in thus acting, and thus judging and thus carrying over the heads of the great body of that Monthly Meeting, the denial of an honest Friend, upon the report of a small fraction of a committee consisting of only two out of nine.

RECAPITULATION.

In order for a summary and more concise view of the cardinal and most essential features in this important case, we have again brought them to view as follows :—

1st. We have shown that the Yearly Meeting's Committee, by threatenings and other means, coerced South Kingston Monthly Meeting into measures prematurely, and aside from the usages of our Discipline.

2d. That the same committee interfered with the local and private concerns of South Kingston Monthly Meeting, and attempted to interrupt the free action of that meeting in the appointment of its officers.

3d. We have shown that the same committee attempted, by menaces to coerce the committee of South Kingston Monthly Meeting to a compliance with their own unreasonable requirements ; and that they refused to testify as witnesses, in which capacity they had offered themselves : and finally, left in the middle of the examination in a disorderly manner.

4th. Again we have shown, that instead of laboring to promote unity and harmony agreeably to their instructions, the Yearly Meeting's Committee did actually give their strength and support to two or three restless persons, who attempted at once to produce a schism in our Monthly Meeting.

5th. We have shown that this same committee, not long after this palpable disorder of their own, complained of South Kingston Monthly Meeting to the Quarterly Meeting for disorder !

6th. We have shown the disorderly proceedings of the Yearly Meeting's Committee, in attempting to break up our Monthly Meeting, whilst the report in that well known case was in the women's meeting for adjudication, and other business unfinished.

7th. We have shown that the Committee of Rhode Island Quarterly Meeting, on their first attendance, assumed the authority of cancelling our records at pleasure, and of setting in judgment upon a case which the Yearly Meeting's Committee had submitted to South Kingston Monthly Meeting to decide ; and we have also shown that this committee assumed the authority and right of dictation, (beyond the bounds of their appointment or of the Quarterly Meeting's authority,) to South Kingston Meeting of ministers and elders, by an exercise of such assumption, so far as to attempt a division or separation of that meeting, by gravely and earnestly advising one-half of its members, "Not to attend that meeting."

8th. We have shown that both the Yearly and Quarterly Meeting's Committee have wronged us, in advising our former Clerk to withhold from us our property contained in our books and papers; and the latter still more flagrantly in coming themselves and taking them away out of our limits.

9th. We have shown by their own document that the same Quarterly Meeting's Committee proffered to us their advise, requiring the nullification of divers portions of our records for nearly half a year then passed over—to release an offender from dealing, incured by the withholding from us our property,— and that they also declined to allow us reasonable time for our consideration of these advices, as their report to the Quarterly Meeting a few days after clearly showeth.

10th. We have shown, that not only their Committee as above, but the Quarterly Meeting itself, has condemned and deprived us of our rights, prematurely and unjustly, as well as contrary to our discipline; and without the opportunity of a hearing and circumstantial representation of our case. We have also shown its long resistance to the reading of our discipline in relation to laying down Monthly Meetings: and when read, declining any exposition of it, or to compare their proceedings with it. But we have shown you as above, the plain and clear exposition of that discipline, (easily understood by the most ordinary reader,) and how palpably discordant therewith the Quarterly Meeting's proceedings have been.

11th. We have shown the invalidity of the objections to our proceedings, and the absurdity of the advice contained in the written document, presented to us by the Committee of that Quarterly Meeting in the 10th month.

12th. We have shown that the Monthly Meeting was not laid down as was pretended on account of disorder, &c., but because it did not, and could not be induced to disown one of its members, whose only offence, on a careful and deliberate investigation of the case, appeared to consist in his having faithfully, and in compliance with the requirements of discipline, borne testimony against the promulgation of unsound and defective doctrines in the Society. And, that after the Monthly Meeting was thus illegally dissolved, and just enough of its recorded proceedings nullified, to place this, our friend, again within their power in another Monthly Meeting, he was *there* disowned by those very men who first brought the complaint against him, and that on the report of but two out of nine of a committee who had investigated the case.

13th. And furthermore, we have shown that the Yearly Meeting's Committee complained of South Kingston Monthly Meeting, upon a charge of insubordination, when as yet, it had not decided, nor given judgment upon the complaint which they had brought; it being yet in the hands of the committee unreported. And that the Quarterly Meeting's Committee appointed upon this representation, reported in favor of the summary dissolution of the Monthly Meeting, and its annexation to another, while as yet, it had not been allowed time to consider and investigate, but had referred only one month for consideration, their written advice. And that the Quarterly Meeting did adopt their report, and *at once* consummated the dissolution and annexation therein recommended.

Hence we say, and in saying, are not afraid of

being contradicted, that the course of proceedings which have been taken, and pursued by the Yearly Meeting's Committee, and by the Quarterly Meeting s Committee, and by the Quarterly Meeting itself, have not been in conformity with our discipline, but plainly an infraction upon it, and upon its order and usages ; and we do therefore ask, and expect redress at the hands and by the decision of that body, which made and ordained that discipline, and enjoined its observance upon all its subordinate branches ; and in *conformity* to which, as its own rule of action, the Yearly Meeting can only be the umpire for the termination of all controversies in the Society. And we apprehend there can be no sensible, candid mind, possessed of the knowledge of this case, and of the usages of our discipline, but must admit that there are in the foregoing, innumerated diverse measures resorted to by the committees, and by the Quarterly Meeting, *any one of which* would be sufficient to reverse the proceedings of these bodies in this unhappy case ; and we are therefore assured, that the Yearly Meeting cannot confirm the judgment of Rhode Island Quarterly Meeting against South Kingston Monthly Meeting, and yet maintain its reputation as the righteous supporter and faithful upholder of the truth, and its own rules and regulations.

OTHNIEL FOSTER,
JOHN WILBUR,
JOHN FOSTER,
CHARLES PERRY,
ISAAC COLLINS,
JOHN FOSTER, of Hopkinton,
ETHAN FOSTER,
SAMUEL SHEFFIELD,
ELISHA KENYON.

Newport, 6th Mo. 13th, 1843.

JOHN WILBUR'S APPEAL,

Against the proceedings of Greenwich Monthly Meeting, in their assumption of disowning him; as also against the proceedings of Rhode Island Quarterly Meeting, in confirming the doings of Greenwich Monthly Meeting, in which the complaint is referred to and answered; the erroneous proceedings of said Monthly Meeting refuted, and his own course vindicated. Substantially the same before the Yearly Meeting's Committee as before that of the Quarterly Meeting.

His first exception against any disciplinary proceedings over, or dealing with any of the members of South Kingston Monthly Meeting by Greenwich Monthly Meeting, rests in their want of jurisdiction over those members, for the reason that Rhode Island Quarterly Meeting did not proceed in manner and form prescribed by Discipline, in essaying to lay down said Monthly Meeting, that there was no cause for laying down said Monthly Meeting; but if such had been the case, their manner of proceedings was arbitrary and palpably at variance with and in direct violation of the Discipline, made and provided for laying down Monthly Meetings when the case required it, as will most plainly appear by a recurrence to the Appeal of South Kingston Monthly Meeting to the Yearly Meeting.

But Greenwich Monthly Meeting professed, by the rules of subordination, to be under an obligation, (or more truly the Yearly Meeting's Committee professed it for them,) to disown the appellant; alleging that the Quarterly Meeting put him under dealing, and required of them the consummation thereof.

But Greenwich Monthly Meeting was officially informed that South Kingston Monthly Meeting,

and its members on its behalf, had appealed to the
Yearly Meeting against the proceedings of Rhode
Island Quarterly Meeting in the assumption of laying it down, and of annexing its members to that
of Greenwich, whereon is grounded his

2d Exception.—That appeals from lower to
higher courts or tribunals in all cases, are a bar to
all executive proceedings thereafter, until that appeal is decided by the superior authority. A suspension of action which is scrupulously observed,
and was never violated, (so far as he knows,) in
any civil or religious proceedings heretofore.

And the possibility, or even the probability that
the judgment of the superior body may coincide
with that of the inferior, is no license at all for executive proceedings, until the final issue, inasmuch as
such overt proceedings may lead to great injustice,
both in relation to civil and religious rights, and
would also be an impeachment upon the wise and
necessary provisions for a careful review of cases,
for the safety of the community. And furthermore,
such irrational and rash proceedings bespeak disloyalty, or a want of deference to the supreme body,
(the Yearly Meeting,) on the one hand, and on the
other, a disregard of the rights of individuals, if not
a betrayal of some personal grudge, rather than a
desire to do by him as they would that others should
do by them in such cases.

Hence we see not only the justice but the obligation of all judiciary bodies, carefully and conscientiously to observe those laws provided for appeals,
in order for fuller hearing, and staying their hands
from all further proceedings after an appeal is made
to a higher tribunal, agreeable to the wholesome
provisions made by constituted authority.

If a law can be disregarded in one instance with
impunity, it can be disregarded in any number of
instances that might occur. And in all such pro-

ceedings the merits of cases have nothing to do with
the course to be taken.

3rd Exception.—After a case of an alleged offence has been duly tried, and decided in one Monthly Meeting, and the accused acquitted, can that
same case afterwards be tried and decided in
another Monthly Meeting, agreeable to any discipline to be found in our books ?   Or, can a precedent of such case, or such usage be produced as
having ever transpired in the Yearly Meeting since .
its first establishment ?   The appellant thinks not.

4th Exception.—That a Monthly Meeting cannot
at once judge of a case, which has not been examined by itself or by persons of its own appointment.

And seeing that the investigation and opinion of
deputed persons, is the lowest evidence upon which
a Monthly Meeting can safely decide a case of personal rights, how can it safely decide upon the opinion of those whom it never deputed, and especially upon the judgment of only two of a committee of
nine, appointed, not by itself, but by another Monthly Meeting.

5th Exception.—The complaint was never read
in Greenwich Monthly Meeting until a few minutes
before that meeting was called upon to disown the
appellant.   And what a claim to divining must a
meeting make, to determine, under such circumstances, that the report of *two* out of a committe of
nine was *right*, and the seven more intelligent
members were wrong, seeing that not one then
present had ever heard the vindication and defence
of the accused individual, except those two.

Therefore the appellant thinks such measures
contrary to all usage and discipline in the Society
of Friends, and for that reason considers the proceedings of Greenwich Monthly Meeting to have
been, in his case, disorderly, precipitant and arbitrary, if indeed it was in the abstract an act of

Greenwich Monthly Meeting, a thing very doubtful if not unsupportable, even if no appeal, as above, had been pending ; and because the question of disownment was carried by the voice of seven of the complainants, there collected to all appearance for the purpose, with one of the Quarterly Meeting's Committee, and only two others, common members of the Monthly Meeting, who favored the motion, the one a brother and the other a son of two of the complainants; in whom could but be seen the greatest anxiety that this work should be accomplished, [and by whose bidding, and by whose assistance, sitting in judgment, it was effected.]

Hence the Yearly Meeting's Committee, who brought this complaint against the appellant with two of their near relatives and one other, who had claimed to be embodied with the members of South Kingston Monthly Meeting, and had there acted on the case, were exclusively the body which disowned him from the Society, though in the name of Greenwich Monthly Meeting, and on their book the assumption was recorded by the willing hand of one of the complainants above referred to ; as also was recorded the report of the two of South Kingston Committee, and all with the appearance of solemnity, as though it had been the act of Greenwich Monthly Meeting, although divers of its members objected thereto. And which report, thus recorded on the book, contained an assertion, " that John Wilbur refused to meet with the committee on the occasion when desired." But the true state of the case was, *they never requested him to meet with them, nor did he ever refuse to do so.*

6th Exception.—In justification of these precipitant proceedings, the Monthly Meeting at Greenwich, or some of its members, professed to be bound by the direction of the Quarterly Meeting to take up all *unfinished* business which they found with the records of South Kingston Monthly Meeting.

One of the items was a complaint against a member
for marrying out of the Society.   Another was an
account of a widow woman for a debt due her for
keeping the poor, just presented, and which remained unpaid.   And although Greenwich Monthly
Meeting was twice applied to for payment, they
utterly refused to acknowledge the claim or to make
payment !   The former was not taken up until after
the appeal was decided, and the latter never was
paid by them, they taking the ground, she might as
well apply to another Monthly Meeting as to them,
so that Friends in the neighborhood felt themselves,
by the obligations of humanity, bound to remune-
rate the widow woman.

So it seems that Greenwich Monthly Meeting felt
so independent of the Quarterly Meeting's directions
as to take up only such things as they inclined to
do, or rather such things as the Yearly Meeting's
Committee inclined they should do, and to defer and
refuse such as they inclined to defer and refuse ;
howbeit, the business which they did take up had
been *finished* by South Kingston Monthly Meeting
in a most deliberate manner. '

*Consideration of the complaint of the Yearly
Meeting's Committee, to South Kingston Monthly
Meeting against John Wilbur : brought to view by
quotations and replies.*

They say, " John Wilbur has departed from the
good order of our society, in the disrequard of our
Christian Discipline."

This general and leading charge does, and if it
had been correct, might properly have stood fore-
most in a complaint to be tried and decided by the
rules and provisions of the discipline of New England Yearly Meeting, of which the complainants in
this case are members, and to which discipline they
also are amenable as well as he, as are all others in

whatever capacity they stand ; whether individual
or official ; whether Quarterly or Monthly Meetings ; or whether committees or other officers appointed by Quarterly or Monthly Meetings, are all
equally bound to adhere unequivocally to the usage
and authority of this discipline;—yes, even the
Yearly Meeting itself is bound by considerations
and consequences still more sacred, involving re-
sponsibilities of a much higher order than those
which rest upon single individuals, in the keeping
inviolate its own laws and testimonies, and itself
faithfully exemplifying, as well as ordering justice
and judgment to others; for if the Yearly Meeting
violate its own laws, and continue to do so, the consequence must be a state of anarchy and confusion,
unless there be more virtue in the members than in
the body.

Nor can the Yearly Meeting itself invest with
any authority whatever any special body, committee, or deputation, with power to act or to proceed
in any manner at all, (as has been vainly assumed
by the Yearly Meeting's Committee,) touching the
rights and privileges, or duties of those subordinate
meetings, or members, in any way or manner not
strictly in conformity with that discipline, or the
rights thereby guaranteed to them, or the duties
thereby enjoined upon them. And when the superior meeting, or its deputation attempt more, it will
directly tend to destroy the compact.

For in direct proportion to the superiority of
order in which the different bodies stand, in that
same proportion will a violation of the usages of the
discipline tend to mar, if not to destroy, the ground
work, union, and authority of such religious compact.

Hence, we see the responsibility which the complainants, to wit, the Yearly Meeting's Committee,
were under, to make the discipline and its usages,
their *guide and rule of action,* that they mete out such

measure to others as they are disposed to exact of
them. Otherwise, even if the supposed offender
were guilty of a breach of discipline, those who
attempted to deal with him, would labor but in vain ;
because he would be likely to say unto them, first
pull the beam out of thine own eye, &c.

By the sequel is brought to view an enquiry,
whether this and other committees and meetings,
touching the management of this case, and its
inseparable dependencies, have been careful to
adhere to our discipline as the conscientious admin-
istrators of it ?

And seeing the committee assume for their first
premises, "Our Christian Discipline," and have
promptly appealed to it, in condemnation of the
appellant, peradventure it may not be amiss for him,
in the outset to introduce and bring to view, some
of *their* acts and proceedings in this very case, and
to compare them with that excellent system of
Church Government.

1st.—Did the Yearly Meeting's Committee pursue the course pointed out and required by discipline on pages 33 to 37, previously to entering a
complaint of detraction against him ?

2nd.—Did they act in conformity with our rules
and Christian justice, in withholding from him a
knowledge of the whole complaint, as they ought to
have done, agreeable to Christ's directions, before
telling it to the church ?

3rd.—Did they not compel South Kingston
Monthly Meeting to an immediate process of dealing, contrary to the order of our discipline, and the
rights of individuals, in having a hearing by overseers, and the concurrent voice and help of a preparative meeting, previous to bringing the complaint to a Monthly Meeting ?

4th.—Did not that committee attempt to cramp
and coerce the Monthly Meeting, by threatening to
complain of it to the Quarter, if it did not *immedi-*

ately, and without further time for consideration, proceed to dealing?

5th.—Did they not assume to themselves the right and authority of thus ordering such proceedings, the Discipline to the contrary notwithstanding?

6th.—Did they not afterwards attempt to interfere with the rights of South Kingston Monthly Meeting in the appointment of its officers?

7th.—Did they not join with two disaffected members in attempting to bring about a separation in that meeting?

8th.—Did they not attempt the breaking up of South Kingston Monthly Meeting, for the purpose of perverting judgment?

9th.—Did they not advise a member of South Kingston Monthly Meeting to withhold from it its property?

10th.—And are not the Qarterly Meeting's Committee chargeable with the same offence in a still more aggravated form, by coming themselves and taking our records, and removing them out of our limits, to a place unknown to us?

11th.—Did not the two committees in conjunction strive to coerce South Kingston Monthly Meeting to disown one of its members contrary to the report of its committee of seven Friends, and contrary to its own judgment?

12th.—Did not the Quarterly Meeting's Committee require South Kingston Monthly Meeting, immediately to remove a suitable clerk from the table, and to place there one of their own choice?

13th.—And to cancel and undo some of its proceedings for near half a year past?

14th.—And did they not require of that meeting immediately to annul and make void an act thereof recorded two months previous?—a measure that would seriously affect the rights of an individual?

15th.—Did they not, because the Monthly Meeting was not prepared to adopt a measure so strange

9

and unprecedented, without a day's consideration, report to the Quarterly Meeting the next week their advice to dissolve said Monthly Meeting?

16th. Did not the Quarterly Meeting adopt that report and lay down that Monthly Meeting, and annex its members to another, and that without a hearing, and to the great abuse of the discipline, as well as of the Monthly Meeting thus laid down?

17.—Did not the Committee of the Yearly Meeting on the appeal of South Kingston Monthly Meeting against that judgment, acknowledge, in open Yearly Meeting, when they brought in their report, *that the proceedings of the Quarterly Meeting were not conformable to our discipline?* Nevertheless, did not that committee report it as their judgment that the doings of Rhode Island Quarterly Meeting ought to be confirmed ; and rendered as a reason for it that the Yearly Meeting's Committee, by whose advise South Kingston Monthly Meeting was laid down, *ought to be sustained?* Hence this appeal was not decided by rules of discipline, but by rules of subordination. And the Yearly Meeting, by the acceptance of that report, and upon the ground premised by the committee, have adopted a precedent or rule, that the authority of the Yearly Meeting's Committee shall be paramount to the discipline, and to the authority of all subordinate meetings. So that no appeal in future can go contrary to the will of that committee. Nor has the Society any reason, as we conceive, to expect them to go back, and hereafter to concede any of their powers.

Which of these acts enquired after, if so, was not contrary to the spirit and letter of all Christian discipline?

First item in the complaint, (viz:) "*He has circulated an anonymous pamphlet which impeaches the character of our Society, and in which some of its important doctrines, as exemplified in the*

*religious engagements of some of its faithful minis-
ters are reproachfully held up to view,"* &c.

Reply. The pamphlet alluded to, by the request
of M. and B. Purinton, who were at the appellant's
house, was sent by them to J. M, a minister at Providence, with the injunction *not to spread it,* as
proved by the committee's own witness.

And the person to whom it was sent, never made
any comments upon it, good or bad, in relation to
its exposure or merits—it came directly home.

If such be the *circulating* of that pamphlet, then
the appellant circulated it ; and then the committee
are chargeable with circulating it, by handing it
from one to another. But their motives for doing
so may possibly have been as pure as his—theirs
might have been for the purpose of obtaining their
friends views upon it, and no harm came of it neither, as he knows of, although it is evident they put
it into many more hands than he did,—hence we
see an entire failure in this charge, as they could
prove no more than his sending of it to one of their
own number.*

The appellant does freely acknowledge that some
portions of the pamphlet alluded to, are of an improper character, as will more fully appear from
the following note, placed by him upon one of its
pages in writing, before letting it go out of his
hands.

" The paragraph thus concluded, appears to have
been supposed by the writer to be a conclusive argument against immediate revelation in the present
day, to wit: that persons professing to have the
mind of the good Spirit, should entertain contradictory views in relation to a proposition. But we

---

* This pamphlet consisted principally of an account of the proceedings of the Yearly Meeting and the Select Yearly Meeting of
London, in the year 1837—giving a detailed account of the latter in
its liberation of J. J. Gurney to visit America.

should have supposed that, *reason, his* governing
rule, would have dictated his conclusion, that if one
was right the other must be wrong, as both could
not be right nor both wrong ; as in case of the prophets who were consulted in the question whether
the two kings should go to battle against the Assy-
rians. Ahab's Prophets told him that he should
prevail ; but Micaiah, the Prophet of the Lord, spoke
in direct contradiction ; and the result of the expe-
dition proved who was the true Prophet. Not
that both were wrong ; nor will it be plead that the
mere pretensions of the false prophets in that day,
should destroy our faith in the true, nor in the revelation of the counsel of God to his faithful ministers
and servants in any day. See account of London
Yearly Meeting, 1837, pages 76—77."

And I would ask if the Yearly Meeting's Committee placed upon that book any written marks of
their disapprobation of any passage in it before handing it from one to another? The appellant conceives
it unnecessary to follow any further, the committee's complaint as to this pamphlet, or upon its
bearing upon the character of any Friend, inasmuch
as he has not circulated it, and acknowledges parts
of it to be unsound, and certified it therein.

Second item in the complaint, viz :

" *The object of which, together with sundry letters which
he has circulated, appears to be to induce the belief that
the concern (the liberation of a minister from England to
visit this country,) did not receive the unity of the meeting;
and that the clerk did not act in conformity with the true
sense and judgment of the meeting in signing the certificate.*"

The letters alluded to, when brought forward,
speak for themselves, and no one has ventured to
call in question the truth of any account of that
meeting, that has been produced : but both the
pamphlet and letters from correspondents, certify
us that the concern did receive the full approbation

of a part of the meeting; and probably the clerk
was correct when he said he thought that the
greater number of those who had spoken were in
favor of granting the certificate; which J. W. does
not recollect to have seen disputed in any letter.
Nor has he ever to his recollection represented the
case differently. But he has seen it expressed in a
letter "that the parties were believed to be nearly
balanced."

And whether the reasons rendered by some of
those who objected, for the view which they took
of it, to wit: *the defective character of his doctrines*
was a sufficient reason for the knowledge of that
dissension reaching America, the appellant will
leave for those who are concerned for the safety of
the Society to judge. But he knows it to be the
opinion of these that the denial of so many of our
fundamental doctrines by that Friend, is not only
sufficient cause for the Society at large to know that
many faithful Friends in that meeting did remon-
strate against his going abroad, and rendered good
reasons for it, and did not concede their views from
first to last.

And the appellant still deems J. J. Gurney's denial of our early standard writers, to be a sufficient
reason for whatever himself has said or done, tending as is alleged in this complaint, to close up the
way of the individual alluded to: and all relating,
originally and principally, if not exclusively, to his
defections in doctrine.

The appellant claims, and has the right to make
apparent what the ground of his objections to J. J.
G. really is, and the reasons for the course he has
taken, and to prove by a reference to his writings,
that he had good cause for such a course. And this
committee being bound by our discipline, by our
doctrines and our testimonies, cannot deny him the
good right of making his defence of that course, by
showing that he had sufficient reason for it; and

whether those reasons rest upon the personal character of the man or upon his doctrines, the result will determine.

When Elias Hicks applied for certificates to travel in the latter part of his time, had those Friends who felt dissatisfied with him and his religious opinions a right to object to his liberation on that account; and had Friends where he went a right to know of that objection, and the ground of it?

And had they a right to inform one another of the unsoundness of his doctrines by way of caution against the imbibing of them? If we have no such *right* now, our case is precarious and alarming. Was E. H.'s certificate a protection or foreclosure against all inquiries or information in relation to the state of his views, which were the same after as they were before his liberation? And were not his letter to Phœbe Willis and his printed sermons a sufficient warrantee for an exposure of his views when abroad, though written and printed previous to his liberation?

Now, if it be the case that the corresponding framework of the Society, throughout all the Yearly Meetings and their dependencies is so delicate and fragile; or if it be the case with any one of them, that its travelling ministers cannot be called upon to give account of their unsound books which they had written before their liberation, or for unsound doctrines which they held, and continue to hold, without an interruption of good faith and a good understanding; then our situation is unpropitious and forlorn indeed, and our continuance on the primitive foundation precarious and uncertain; and especially now, seeing a disposition prevails among us to *uphold and defend* those persons who do not hesitate to deny the soundness of Robert Barclay and other standard writers in defence of our fundamental doctrines.

Similar charges to those last noticed are reiterated through this protracted paragraph, avouching the credibility of the person and the authority of his credentials and accusing the appellant with *want of abidance in the truth*, &c. But does the credence given to the certificates in question, by New England and most other Yearly Meetings in America, as in the complaint set forth, any more prove the doctrines of the bearer to be sound, than did the credence given to the certificates of Hannah Barnard in the Yearly Meetings of London and Dublin, and their subordinate meetings, prove her to have been sound in doctrine?

And were not those who were so adventurous in London under those circumstances, as to call in question the standing of Hannah Barnard, probably as chargeable with *a want of abiding in the truth* as he who questions the soundness of J. J. G., if the accrediting of certificates is to be esteemed as a test? And are not " all faithful Friends" so earnestly called upon and enjoined by our discipline, (see Book of Discipline, page 74,) to bear testimony against those who entertain unsound doctrines, (if obedient to that injunction,) just as chargeable with *a want of abidance in the truth*, because they have done so, as is the appellant for the same thing? It is evident by the discipline alluded to, that if any one, no matter who, advances unsound doctrines, it is only to be made to appear, to entitle him who conscientiously testifies against them, to justification; and not only by the discipline but by its author, the truth itself: for the truth always stands opposed and always bears witness against false doctrines, as abundantly appears in the holy Scriptures.

The great object of guarding the Society of Friends against false doctrines stands over and above all other considerations relative to the compact, because false doctrines make way for and have always been succeeded by bad conduct and pernicious consequences; whilst a sound faith holds together all the members in one, and guards them against deviations from Christian rectitude.

And it is a fact that cannot be disproved; nor, can any one rightfully gainsay it, that the late introduction of unsound views into the Society have been the occasion of the doctrinal dissensions now existing in almost all parts of it.

The Discipline referred to speaks of " the importance of steadfastly maintaining our ancient principles respecting the doctrines of the gospel, and *earnestly recommends and enjoins* upon Quarterly and Monthly Meetings, and upon all *faithful friends*, to be watchful over our members as regards the profession of their faith, &c., and if in any instance there should be manifest *any deviation from our Christian priciples*, in these respects, that they proceed to labor, &c." [But according to the reasoning of the Yearly Meeting's Committee, and some others, this discipline is in full force upon all, except ministers travelling with certificates, and them it does not reach, having a license embodied in their credentials, which no Discipline can reach, however impartial in its operations, or binding upon all in its conclusions. Nay, if they have good credentials from abroad, they may record their denial of Fox, Penn and Barclay, and spread it over the whole society, and yet neither Quarterly or Monthly Meeting, nor any faithful friend can take cognizance of the case ! Old fashioned Quakers had never before known snch economy as this, *that there are some who have an exclusive right to hold and publish such sentiments as they choose,* and that without remedy !]

The respondents are called upon to prove that the appellant has said or written any thing which was not applicable to the one great object of dissuading the society from imbibing those dividing and degenerating sentiments.

And he is not disappointed that the respondents do suppose it to be for their interest, and should therefore strive to avoid, if possible, any allusion to *doctrines*, because primarily the alleged offence of the appellant rested upon the stand which he made against those doctrines; hence the obtaining of his rights hinges upon the exposition of them, and therefore it would be great injustice to him and to the cause, to debar him from canvassing those doctrines, inasmuch as the Yearly Meeting's Committee in their complaint have taken up the case of J. J. Gurney, and have defended him, and in which, if his doctrines be fundamentally *right*, then the committee have certainly done *right* in upholding and defending him, and John Wilbur has certainly done wrong, and ought to condemn his course. But on the contrary, if on a careful investigation of those doctrines, and a comparison of them with those of R. Barclay, they are found to be fundamentally *wrong*, then of course the committee are *wrong* in taking up his, J. J. Gurney's cause, and in defending him against those who are honestly concerned for the honor of Truth; and the readiest way, if not the only way, to convince these concerned friends that they are mistaken, is to go into a deliberate examination of the doctrines in question.

If the Yearly Meeting's Committee do believe, as they say, that J. J. G. is *a sound friend*, with their ability to explain and define sound doctrines, and the object of reconciliation upon sound principles being so exceedingly desirable, why object, why not at once accomplish a thing so highly important?

And if the Yearly Meeting's Committee will show him, and prove to him that those doctrines are separately and collectively in accordance with our standard writers, then, and under that proviso, the appellant will acknowledge the course which he has taken to be wrong and reprehensible, and will

9

pursue his appeal no further, because the whole course of his proceedings in this case was under an apprehension of their unsoundness.

But on the contrary, if it is clearly proveable that the writings of J. J. G., on some of the fundamental points of our principles, are unsound, and such as our discipline enjoins on all faithful friends to testify against, then it will and must be agreed, that his concern in testifying against them is justifiable.

Now, therefore, let the meeting for Sufferings, or the Yearly Meeting's Committee, officially decide the question, as they have heretofore been desired to do, whether these specified doctrines are in conformity with the doctrines of Fox, Barclay, Penn and Penington, and if they do officially and candidly decide that they *are*, then I will prosecute my appeal no further. But if they find themselves under the necessity to decide, that some of his doctrines are fundamentally at variance with the doctrines of Friends, and as in duty bound by the Discipline, report them so, as a caution to Friends against imbibing them, then they will have done the same that the appellant has done, and will feel honestly bound and disposed, as he trusts, to advise the restoration of his right of membership in the Society.

So this committee, appointed by the Yearly Meeting, now sitting to decide upon this appeal, if they find, by a full and impartial examination that these doctrines are radically defective, then the course which the appellant has taken (in all sincerity,) with an eye to the safety of our principles and testimonies, will be justified in conformity with our Discipline, which is decidedly and scrupulously to be the rule and guide of all committees entrusted with the society's concerns. They are to judge with a righteous judgment, as I trust they are aware, and to be tender of the rights and religious concerns of individuals, as well as to guard the society against any infraction upon its discipline or testimonies.

But the Yearly Meeting's Committee themselves, in their complaint, as it has been seen, refer to *doctrines*, to what they justly call *some of the important doctrines of the Society*, charging the appellant with having reproached those doctrines, and some who hold them, and were fully allowed before the committee of South Kingston Mo. Meeting to do what they could to substantiate that charge, a privilege which the appellant now in turn asks for, for they were not only allowed to exhibit their evidence, but to plead in support of their complaint in relation to doctrines.*

Third item.—† "*That for the want of maintaining his integrity in that dependence upon the Holy Spirit, which would have preserved him in unity with Friends, he has indulged in a spirit of detraction,*

---

* Here the respondents strongly remonstrated against allowing the appellant to represent his case upon doctrinal premises, and considerable time was taken up in debating upon the question of Right before the Yearly Meeting's Committee on the appeal. The committee did not finally decide it as a question of *rights*, but of expediency, to let the appellant proceed on doctrines, without interruption, as a saving of time.

The Yearly Meeting's Committee not only referred to doctrines in their complaint, but did, on all the occasions of the investigation before committees, adduce as evidence against him, a letter previously written to J. M., one of their number, which was grounded almost exclusively on doctrines. The producing of this letter was truly satisfactory to the appellant, as thereby the complainants brought to view, in part at least, the doctrinal ground desired. But the advantage which they at first appeared to expect to derive from it was this:—The receiver of it appeared to have kept it pretty close, and the writer being desirous that another friend should be put in possession of similar information, sent him a copy of it as "*a copy of a letter from one friend to another in his possession*," and inasmuch as the writer did not inform the second recipient that himself was its author, it was inferred by the committee that he had intended the receiver should think that others had such views as well as himself, but the reader may judge whether this *manner* was pursued by the writer of that letter, to avoid the appearance of self-estimation, or to encompass the judgment of another. Be that decision as it may, the letter he believes has been in the right place and there put by the right hands.

† No small thing to make so many and such heavy charges against a friend unjustly.

*in speaking and writing, by which the religious
character of divers friends in our own and other
Yearly Meetings, has been much misrepresented.*

Some strangers, (and one of them a minister)
travelling with certificates, fell in at the house of
John Wilbur, and introduced much conversation on
doctrines as well as on men and their religious opinions, making remarks, and in a manner calculated
to draw conversation from J. W., and as it afterwards appeared, with an *intention* to do so, and to
make use of it to his disadvantage. They also enquired, as he remembers, as to the soundness of
some Friends here; and as one or two of those enquired after, were known to have changed their
views, and strongly to have sustained Joseph John
Gurney, these questions were answered conformably to those circumstances, and allusion was made
to the influence which large gratuitous donations
had produced, as it appeared, on some who had received those gratuities. Before these Friends left
New England, John Wilbur found that their sympathies were with Elisha Bates, lamenting as they
did, the step which he had taken, viz: *being bap-
tized* with water, inasmuch as it led to his being
separated from Friends, and at the same time strongly advocated his opinion of the resurrection of *the*
body. And one of them finally betrayed his own
agreement with the Beaconites in their opinion of
the *paramount* authority and standing of the Holy
Scriptures.

Those men, it seems, in a most dishonorable and
unchristian manner, carried what they had gathered (though one of them says, they were almost com-
pelled to do it) to members of the Quarterly and
Yearly Meeting's Committees, (in full tale if not
more than measure,) and that without letting J.
W. know of their intentions, or of suggesting to
him the least dissatisfaction with any thing he had
said to them; so unlike the ambassadors of Him who

said, "If thy brother trespass against thee, go and tell him his fault between thee and him alone," &c. And if there had been *cause* for complaint would they not have done it?

Now, inasmuch as this last mentioned course, as directed by the Saviour, was not taken either by the strangers, or by the members of the committees, nor yet the course pursued, so clearly and fully enjoined and required by our discipline to be pursued, before a complaint can be brought to a Monthly Meeting for detraction or defamation, and inasmuch, too, as the words spoken were true, (unless J. J. Gurney's doctrines are sound Quaker doctrines) no such complaint can be sustained by our rulers.

And how consistent with good practical experience is the course pointed out by the Saviour and by the framers of our Discipline. A mode by which, it is probable, most of such conversations might be amicably understood to the removal of all unpleasant feelings. And if the right course in this case had been taken at first, if any uneasiness was really felt, J. W. has no doubt that such feelings might have been removed, if others had no more disposition for controversy than himself, or to propagate unsound principles.

When the complaint was first acted upon in Rhode Island Quarterly Meeting, and the right of objecting to a portion of the committee was claimed on behalf of the appellant, *the complainants did disclaim all charge of detraction in their complaint against him, and declared that if the word detraction was therein contained, it was incidental.*

However it may be with this last declaration, they might well relinquish this charge. 1st. Because neither themselves nor the witnesses they relied upon had proceeded in the matter according to the Christian rule of our Discipline, and 2d. Because it was unfounded; they were unable to disprove the words spoken, for the reason that they were true.

The apparent object of this disclaimer of the charge of detraction, was to give a pretext for denying the appellant his right of objection to any part of the committee.*

Fourth item.—"*That he has made divers assertions tending to induce dissatisfaction among Friends, and with the proceedings of our Yearly Meeting in various particulars, and calculated to produce division therein, and also to disturb the unity of different Yearly Meetings, and to alienate the feelings of their members from each other.*

In answer to this it is only necessary now to say, that the appellant has no knowledge of giving any just cause for such charges, and that he recollects no attempt on the part of the complainants, to prove them to the committees on the case, appointed by the meetings below†.

It may be asked, whether the well grounded uneasiness which the appellant felt with the published and unretracted doctrinal sentiments of "the Friend" to whom the committee have so frequently alluded in their complaint against him, (and upon which indeed it seems to be principally founded) *was* more likely to "induce dissatisfaction with the proceedings of this Yearly Meeting, to produce division therein" or "to disturb the unity of different Yearly Meetings, and to alienate the feelings of their members from each other, than was the conduct of

---

* On the trial before the committee of the Yearly Meeting, the appellant took the ground that the complainants had relinquished their charge of detraction, as above, and the respondents did not attempt to gainsay it.

† This was stated to the committee of the Yearly Meeting on the Appeal to remind the respondents that they now had an opportunity to prove those charges, if able to do so, but they made no reply.

the members of this same committee who preferred
these charges; in assuming the control of the Yearly Meeting, and so overruling its proceedings as to
send back without certificates in the year 1843,
three ministers in attendance from Philadelphia
Yearly Meeting, and one from Ohio, as well as their
companions respectively, all of whom were in the
station of elders except one; and with the like exceptions all were *as* duly furnished with the necessary credentials, which were also as " duly presented, received and accredited" as those of "the Friend"
first mentioned, thus setting them at liberty for religious service therein, " in the full and acknowledged
character of approved and authenticated ministers"
and elders " of the Society of Friends?" And
whether the conduct of the same committee, subsequently, has not been eminently calculated to produce the very result which they have unjustly
charged upon John Wilbur? In the year 1844, a
deputation from the same or of the Select Yearly
Meeting's Committee, mostly composed of the same
individuals, called on another minister in attendance
from Ohio Yearly Meeting, also with as full certificates from his Monthly and Quarterly Meeting,
which had been as duly received and accredited,
and which embraced a prospect of religious service
within our limits, beyond the mere attendance of
the Yearly Meeting, and informed him that he could
not travel here unless he would unite with their
proceeding and comply with their advice to refrain
from associating with those who were known to be
dissatisfied with the unsound doctrines of Joseph
John Gurney, ["the Friend" to whom allusion is
made in their complaint against J. W.] He too,
was turned back without being allowed to perform
the visit he had in prospect, and without the usual
returning credentials! But these ministers and
their companions *were known* to have maintained
their integrity and allegiance to the *original prin-*

ciples, order and Discipline of the Society of Friends, and *to be opposed to the change* attempted therein, and to the disorder and misrule which followed that attempt, on the part of the adherents of Joseph John Gurney, the members of this committee and many others.

Fifth and last item in the complaint.—*That he wrote a letter to one of the committee, in which he made unjust insinuations, and preferred charges against them, which they deny in point of fact.*

The letter here alluded to, written to the Select Quarterly Meeting's Committee, is as follows, being now prefaced by a few introductory remarks.

When sentiments are spread in the Society by any of its members, which strike at the root of its fundamental doctrines, and properly coming under the character of "pernicious books," how important that all into whose hands these works may be likely to come, should be told of the dangerous tendency of the views therein contained. And what minister or elder, overseer or parent, concerned for the safety of the flock, can feel himself, (*as one that is to give account*,) acquitted from the blood of the innocent, without faithfully detecting the evil which he is given to see, and warning them against receiving the misleading sentiments as well as against reading the books which contain them.

It was under impressions like these that the writer of the following letter consulted, by way of correspondence, divers ministers and elders on the subject, and endeavored to discourage others from adhering to doctrines of this description, now spread abroad among us.

This testimony, he believed it to be his religious duty to bear, and in doing which his peace, as he apprehended, was concerned, " as one that is set for a defence of the gospel," however unworthy, and did on many occasions, though not so faithfully as the truth dictated, point out to his friends some of the errors to be found in certain books purporting to be Friend's doctrine, but tending to lead them astray, and to warn them against the adoption of such opinions, a course which it seems, gave offence to some of the Friends of the author of those books.

And of a committee appointed in Rhode Island Select Quarterly Meeting in the 5th month, 1840, most of the number proved themselves to be of this description. And, however, the committee was appointed professedly for the purpose of restoring unity in one or two select meetings, whose account expressed a want of it. Yet this committee, going entirely in another direction from the business of their appointment, as well as beyond any authority with which our discipline clothes them, they arrested the writer, relative to his proceedings touching those unsound doctrines, entered into judgment and attempted to lay the restraint of their advice upon him, to wit : " To stay at home and to be quiet," and that without allowing him to exhibit evidence to show that he had *good cause* for the course he had taken !

This unauthorised injunction of the committee, and their refusal to hear evidence which he offered, sufficient to exculpate him from all blame, gave occasion to him to address to them the following letter, a few weeks afterwards, directed to the first named on that committee :

LETTER.

HOPKINTON, the 30th of 5th mo., 1840.

To my dear friend T. A. :

After thus allowing time for solid deliberation on the subject of discussion with friends at thy daughter's, it seems right for me to address a few lines to thee in relation thereto, inasmuch as I had not full opportunity in the end to speak for myself, by reason of the claims of others on the time, as well as the *want* of time ; thou wilt, I apprehend, allow me the opportunity of reviewing it in this way, and to remark further upon the charges brought against me, and as I trust, will hear me patiently, seeing that vastly more is involved in the consideration of the question than merely the exculpation or condemnation of an individual, without allowing him the right, both civil and religious, of a defence, not only of himself, but of the testimonies and usages of the society, such as truth and justice call for.

Thou art well aware that even in the civil department the laws of the land allow the accused a defence of himself in all the bearings of his case, and not only so, they premise if need be, that he should be provided with counsel, lest unhappily the innocent should be adjudged guilty. And in the religious department thou wilt agree that a still higher and purer order of justice and righteousness is contemplated, for beyond all controversy, such is the true character of Christianity, and its superiority over every other system of moral or civil order instituted by the children of men.

But when we become acquainted with the history of ecclesiastical transactions since the Christian era, we are bound to acknowledge that the civil has never been more abused than the religious, under the dominion of power.

But to come directly to the question, and the capacity in which friends acted, I deem it right for me to remark, that I might suppose they acted as individuals under an apprehension of the necessity of the case, and not as a committee of the Select Quarterly Meeting, for the appointment of the committee was *grounded, and only grounded*, (if I understand it,) upon deficiencies represented in the answers to the queries from the subordinate meetings, and consequently, friends could not as a committee of that meeting, extend care to any meeting, or to a member of it, which gave no account of deficiencies in relation to things queried after ; and no tangible inference can be drawn from that of South Kingston, (however it may be in others,) that there does any want of harmony or unity exist in that meeting; and which I esteem as a favor, for which we are bound to be thankful. But I am entirely prepared to say, that I ever hope to be willing to receive advice either from committees or individuals, acting conformably to the mind of truth, and the order established in our society.

But are friends now prepared to evacuate the ground which has been taken, viz., that a certificate for a man to travel as a minister is a full defence to him, against all comers in relation to whatever may have transpired previous to the issuing of that certificate ? Or will they say that the deputed right of one body shall be regarded, and that of another may be disregarded and contemned ? And does it rest with committees or others not delegated *for that special purpose*, by the Yearly Meeting itself, to arrest the established right and order which that body has conferred upon its subordinate branches ? Or shall these things yet rest upon their ancient foundation and usage, that when a minister, though liberated by an authorized body, is found defective either in *faith or conduct*, and for which satisfaction has not been made, that he shall be liable to be called to an account, by those whose constituted duty it is, under whatsoever circumstance he may have placed himself, or others may have placed him ?

By this rule, my dear friend, I am entirely willing to be tried and judged, but not upon mere hearsay, or vague allegations and reports—not for the alleged faults or imprudence of others ; nor yet without a hearing upon the great point and premises of the case, to wit : the stand which I have taken against the erroneous doctrines which are spread

abroad among us by their author, both before and
since his liberation for our land.   And whatever I
have said or done in the case, relates unequivocally
to those doctrines ; and consequently, the *merits or
demerits* of that course rests upon the *soundness or
unsoundness* of those doctrines, as will be shown
further on : and I hesitate not to say, that the present
dissension in the society at large, is the legitimate
fruits of the circulation, and the Author's continued
adherence to the doctrines alluded to.   And my
concern has been (as I told Friends when together,)
that those sentiments might be clearly developed
and faithfully reprobated, so that the fearful consequences of such dissension might be obviated.

But if these baneful doctrines, or their unrelenting
Author, which is the same thing, are continued to
be advocated and defended, we have reason to fear
that serious difficulties will ensue ; because there is
no doubt there are some, and perhaps not a few in
this Yearly Meeting, who cannot be brought to the
adoption of such sentiments, come what may come.
And inasmuch, as great wrong has been inflicted
upon the truth, and its principles, who, thinkest thou,
my dear friend, will find the most peace of mind in
the result of things ?   Will it be those, who out of a
good conscience have withstood those innovations,
(though perhaps not always in the most perfect line
of Divine wisdom,) or those who have defended
such views by strenuously advocating and warmly
defending, and thereby giving strength to their
Author ; and by endeavoring to put down those
who have honestly withstood his sentiments ?

How any can defend an *unsound man,* at the
expense and rejection of those who are sound, and
yet be acting upon sound principles, is a problem
which I very much desire to see demonstrated, if
demonstrated it can be.

I will now remark upon the charges brought
against me, and however so trivial as some of them

are, and so unreasonable as others appear to me, yet as they have been deemed by ministers and elders to be worth naming, they will be recognized by way of a defence and apology, for the course I have taken.

1st. That I have frequently in conversation and in writing, reprobated some of the statements of J. J. Gurney, and even on some occasions when abroad in the ministry. To this charge, so worded, I confess guilty, if guilt is attached thereto, and in remarking upon it, I will first ask thee Thomas, whether thou will admit that a professed minister abroad, could be chargeable with doctrines so dangerous as to warrant such procedure?

2d. Whether the doctrines of Hannah Bernard and Elias Hicks, were so exceptionable as to warrant a watchword to the churches under similar circumstances?

3d. Whether Moses and the Prophets were warranted, in so full and so public a manner, as they often did, in testifying against the abuses of the doctrines and commandments of the former covenant?

4th. Whether the apostle Paul and George Fox did right in publicly withstanding and *marking* those, who caused divisions by introducing doctrines contrary to the doctrines of Christ?

The Apostle, it seems, in his public epistle, entreated his brethren, without distinction of age or standing, and without exception to any circumstance to *mark* those which cause divisions and offences, contrary to the doctrines which they have learned, and to avoid them. Rom. 16: 17. And so we shall find if we examine the Holy Scriptures, that both prophets and apostles were prompt and vigilant, in detecting and exposing, as well as in exterminating every thing which stood at variance with the Lord's doctrines and testimonies, whether seen in kings, princes, or prophets, (however reprehensible such

detection was deemed by those in power,) a procedure led to by the inspiration and commands of
God. For it was seen then as it in some degree is
seen now, that human nature is so propense to ease,
and to overlook the needful restraints of true religion, that a guard against the inlet of evil was continually needful.

But one of our Friends said, that he acknowledged
the doctrines in question were *very unsound*, but
afterwards said he thought we ought to give a pass
to their Author. But truly he could not have meant
to have been understood to say, that the Yearly Meeting ought to give him a certificate of unity, for in so
saying, he would exhibit an opinion different from
that of the Apostle, when he was speaking of those
who brought in doctrines contrary to the doctrines
of Christ; for, said he, " He that biddeth him God
speed, is a partaker of his deeds."

2d charge. That I knew the Yearly Meeting's
Committee were unwilling that I should travel in
the ministry, therefore, I ought not to have gone to
Philadelphia. To which I need to say no more
than to refer to thy expression to a friend—to Thos.
Howland's own hand-writing, and to J. M.'s to me
at Dover Quarterly Meeting, all amounting to this,
that the committee had no desire to stop my going
on the proposed visit; besides which, I had never
heard from them—how then could R. say so?

3d charge. That they understood that I had favored the idea of a division of the Yearly Meeting,
and which was so fully answered at thy daughter's,
viz.: That no one among us, to my knowledge, had
labored more to keep Friends in New England to the
one faith, even to that alone which would keep us
together, and prevent our being scattered; [show-
ing] that a disagreement in principle is the root of
schism.

4th charge. That I have companied with some
young men, who have made a stand against the

unsound sentiments of J. J. Gurney, and to which
I confess judgment; and that I have also companied
with some who are not young, but have the same
opinions of the same man. But I would say, that I
believe these with whom I have companied, and
who have taken the same ground would not suffer
in point of character in a comparison with others.

5th charge. That I suffered T. B. G. to go with
me, as companion, to Philadelphia. That he went
in company with me, as did divers other Friends, I
acknowledge, but that he went with me as a *companion*, in the way that this phrase is understood by
Friends, is altogether unfounded.; nor did he pass
for such at any place where we were; nor G. F.
R. neither, though he lodged with me every night
at Philadelphia, and is also a sound Friend : nor am
I ashamed to be in company with either of them,
although neither of them may be without his faults
—nor yet myself—did not think of its being any
disgrace to be seen with them.

6th charge. " That I suffered letters and extracts
from John Barclay and Ann Jones, to pass through
my hands to others." In answer to this, I would ask,
whether it would be more harm to quote English
authority against *very unsound* doctrines, or to quote
English authority in defence of *very unsound doctrines?* And I would ask again, whether there has
not been a great deal done throughout our settle-
ments in America, in spreading English and other
letters in commendation of this *very unsound man?*
I say *unsound man,* for he yet adheres to his unsound
doctrines. Again, whether thy colleagues are so
much dissatisfied, and do find as much fault with
letters which go to give currency to the Author of
these *very sound doctrines*, as they do with letters
which go to expose and detect them?

7th charge. " That I said to N. M., that J. J. Gurney, would not dare to come to New England."
Now we know the difficulty always attending that

of proving a negative:—but I will say, that I was at M.'s, and probably said something in relation to the man ; but in how many and what kind of words, I cannot now recollect ; however, as I know that I never had the least expectation of our escaping a visit from him, it looks so altogether unlikely that I used that *form of words*, that I feel safe in demurring to the charge, however little or nothing could be made of it, if I had so spoken, more than that I was mistaken.

Now if we take all these accusations into view, my dear Thomas, which of the things complained of, would not be effected in point of right or wrong, either by the soundness or unsoundness of the doctrines of J. J. Gurney? When you say that I have spoken against his *doctrines*—that I have written against his *doctrines*—that I have suffered to pass through my hands, letters which go to discourage the imbibing of his *doctrines*, and to warn of the consequences of doing so—that I have companied with others who protest against his *doctrines*, you say truly, and yet wonderful it is to hear you further say, that *his unsoundness of doctrine has nothing to do with my defence for doing so ! ! !* And as wonderful that pertinent evidence offered in defence of the rectitude of the course taken, sufficient to exculpate from blame, thy correspondent should be refused ! ! ! I say sufficient, because the refusal of hearing that evidence, probo factum, gives to me the right of this assumption.

But you seem inclined to resort to the abstract doctrine, that a certificate from a corresponding body or Yearly Meeting, ought to defend him against all charges for wrongs done previous to the date of that document. For a full refutation of which position I refer to my letter to John Meader.

But inasmuch as some continue to advance, an abstract proposition, you will admit an abstract solution.

In the civil department we are an independent nation, yet are on good corresponding and commercial terms with Great Britain : and let us suppose that one of their trading vessels, had heretofore, by means of an inclination thereto, and a strong armory, made many captures, and had committed many wrongs upon the rights and property of the American people.

However, in process of time, the same vessel, having escaped retribution, obtains regular papers for a general trading voyage to our land. And now I would enquire, whether it would be any breach of good faith towards Great Britain, civilly to ask the commander of this vessel to make reparation for the wrongs which he had done us ? Or whether it would be reprehensible in any of our citizens, to speak of the wrongs which that vessel had committed upon us, when those wrongs were clearly proveable by the register of the vessel, and had been fearlessly published by the commander throughout all the trading companies in the country? Or whether it be a breach of faith for our government to refuse to give her returning papers, and a protection upon the high seas, until she would make reparation for the wrongs which she had done us ? And inasmuch as worldly property and civil rights bear no proportion to religious principles and Christian rights, the civil department could not possibly sustain an equal loss by means of the strongest ship upon the high seas, as would be incurred by our society in the striking out of even but two or three of the fundamental and distinguishing articles from our confession of faith, as apparently aimed at by the person alluded to. But let us stop a moment, and enquire whether there have not been some depredations committed during the present visit.

First, he justifies his former wrongs which revives
10

and restores them to the present tense, and refuses to make the least concession of them.

2nd. And further, has himself been spreading defective books since his arrival in America. I saw one which he presented to a friend, with a note desiring his acceptance of it, dated Philadelphia, 8th month, 1837, and signed with his own hand—a book recommending a *form of prayer*, and that of public discoursing upon Christianity, distinct from the ministry. And this is said not to be a solitary instance. And besides his spreading unsound books since his arrival, many defective ideas of doctrine have escaped him in the Gallery; the which if collected with the like industry, as has been obvious in some other instances, the catalogue would be very considerable.

Now, my dear friend, pause for a moment, and see; one man can write, and preach, and spread, very unsound doctrines, and still receive the warm support, or defence of both ministers and elders among us; whilst another, who is afflicted because of the jeopardy which awaits our society, by means of the spreading of these unsound sentiments, and ventures to bear witness against them, is consigned to reproach! However, this case is not entirely new; there have been honest friends heretofore, and undoubtedly, better than thy correspondent, greatly reproached and defamed for withstanding unsound doctrines, and even disowned; and to what extremity this may come, the Lord only knows. But there is one thing which I desire, and another which I lament. The former is, that I may be reconciled to whatever sufferings may be permitted to fall to my lot, in the discharge of duty, and myself made to profit by it. The latter is, that I am not more worthy to suffer for the truth, and for its doctrines, and testimonies. But I might well say, that a releasement from labor, if the enjoyment of

peace and quietness were bestowed, must be esteemed a great favor.

To be released from the labors and dangers of
the field, and yet be permitted to divide the spoil, is
a privilege of God's own conferring. That precious peace and quietness, which is the reward of
honest labor in the field, is nevertheless the fruit of
his abundant grace : how much more then, that
which fills the heart with peace and joy in its private exercise and retirement in the house of prayer,
and under its own vine and fig-tree, must be of
unutterable love.

And, however, he who serveth at the altar, receives his portion of the gift, yet if God be pleased
to release, from the service for a time, as he often
did our first friends ; and though it were by means
of the secular power ; yet it undoubtedly contribut-
ed to their furtherance, and greater depth in the
power of the cross of Christ—his name be praised !
And my confidence in thee is such, that it will not
be periling the pearl to acknowledge to the un-
bounded grace of a good and merciful God, through
Christ Jesus, in vouchsafing to his weak and unworthy messenger in his late journies, a greater
fullness of strength and understanding in speaking
of the things of his own kingdom, and power, and
glory, than he ever saw mete to bestow before :
and my enjoyment subsequent to many of these
seasons was inexpressible. And the praise and the
glory was and is, as I trust, wholly rendered unto
him, for I clearly saw that it was entirely of him
and to him, it was rendered, in language both utter-
able and unutterable. And it has been, and remains
to be, to me an evidence, not to be despised, that
my good God has owned and does own my sincerity in bearing a faithful testimony against " every
appearance of evil," and innovation, upon our
inestimable testimonies, both in the times of our

former,* and our present troubles and dangers,
And that it is his will that I should do so, does
not rest [wholly] upon his unmerited favors abroad,
(as evidence) but peace and quietness have succeeded to the fulfillment of apprehended duty in
that respect at home.

Nor was I ever more clearly instructed, than in
these late journies, in relation to the opening and
shutting of the fresh springs of the Gospel ministry.
In one large public Quarterly Meeting, and in
several other large meetings, the ministry was to
me "as a spring shut up and a fountain sealed,"
and for which I could assign no other reason, than
that *the good master would have it so.* But in the
same Quarterly Meeting for business, which was
held the next day, a very unusual flow of the Gospel life and power (for me) was witnessed in both
the men's and women's meeting.

The two or three exceptionable doctrines of J. J.
Gurney, alluded to above, might be selected from
the many, under the following heads :

1st. That the Gospel of Christ, is not *in itself* the
power of God unto salvation.

2nd. That men are justified by faith without regard to obedience.

3rd. That was the true light which lighteth every
man that cometh into the world, he construes to
mean no more than Christ incarnate, " the enlightener." Let all imbibe these three items of doctrine
and Quakerism would be no more.

Having a little room yet left upon this sheet, I
will occupy it with a few extracts from a piece in
my possession on Church order, as followeth :

" It would appear to be at variance with the very
nature of things, as well as the right order of Church
government, and the spirit of Christian discipline,

---

* Hicksite troubles.

to suppose that a person can *place himself,* or that others *can place him* under such circumstances, as that he cannot be reprehended for a breach of faith in the promulgation of sentiments, perversive of the established and fundamental doctrines of a religious society to which he belongs.

" If a way has been found in which a person can be securely sheltered and protected, under an obvious and public violation of the doctrines of his own Society, (without concessions) then, indeed, it would seem that innovation upon its principles may be considered inevitable, and without a remedy.

" And if a religious body has no alternative, but to unite with and to give currency to the religious and official standing of such person, then would it be in vain to hope for the preservation of the purest system of Christianity, or the best confessions of faith.

" But the truth itself, it is presumed, has never placed a man in such a condition that his misgivings, whether doctrinal or practical, could not be rightly recognized and reprobated, so long as they remain unretracted.

" Hence, it cannot be supposed that any body, acting in conformity to the truth, should be understood intentionally to approve, or give currency to doctrines which are at variance *with* the truth ; nor that any rightly qualified person can be reprehensible for detecting wrongs which have been inflicted upon the truth, and its principles, and doctrines, as exemplified in the Holy Scriptures from the beginning to the end ; nor do we find in those sacred records, that the names of those who had committed depredations upon the truth, are spared.

" By the exercise and dictates of truth's principles, it was that good order and wholesome regulations were originally instituted and established in the society of Friends, for the protection and security of its doctrines, as well as for the support of its moral economy : hence it is not to be believed, that a wise and discreet exercise of that order, can ever lead to the strengthening or upholding of error, or the justification of wrongs committed against the *author of that order*, to wit : the principle of Christianity.

"Therefore any proceedings under a profession of sustaining that order, if their tendency is to strengthen the wrongs done to that principle which brought all good order into existence ; then such proceedings, so far from being the right support of *good order*, are but the abuse of order, and can be accounted of no better than an attempt to support order at the expense of Principle, the parent of order.

"I am thy Friend, &c."

A short time previous to an interview with the committee, (to whom the foregoing letter was addressed,) in the 8th month, 1840, the receiver of it took him aside and repeated or read to him the following sentences, which he said he had endorsed on that letter ; but before that interview terminated, the same Friend acknowledged that he did not think John Wilbur meant to write anything in that letter which was not true.

The endorsement, he believes was this, "I feel it incumbent upon me to say, that the premises taken in this letter are false, and therefore the conclusions are false and unsound."   T. A.

DEFENCE OF LETTER.

The following extracts from passages in the foregoing letter have been referred to by the complainants, as objectionable ; and are the same designated by their pencil marks thereon, and testified by themselves to be untrue : referred to in the complaint as "being *not true in point of fact, and as containing un'ust insinuations.*"

But on the several trials of the case before committees, they have not proved those assertions otherwise than by themselves—by a reiteration of the same assertions : and when the following defence of those passages has been read to the committees, the respondents have never replied thereto.

1st. " But if these baneful doctrines, or their unrelenting author, (which is the same thing) are continued to be advocated and defended, we have reason to fear that serious difficulties will arise."

2d. " And by endeavoring to put down those who honestly withstand his sentiments."

3d. " I will now remark upon the charges brought against me ; and however so trivial as some of them are, and so unreasonable as others appear to me ; yet as they have been deemed by ministers and elders to be worth naming, they will be recognized here by way of defence and apology for the course I have taken : first, that I had frequently in conversation and in writing reprobated some of the doctrines of J. J. Gurney, and even on some occasions have spoken against them when abroad in the ministry."

4th. " But one of our Friends said, he acknowledged that the doctrines in question *were very unsound ;* but afterwards said he thought we ought to give a pass to their author."

5th. " That they understood that I had favored the idea of a separation."

6th. " That I had companied with some young men, who have made a stand against the unsound doctrines of J. J. Gurney."

7th. " When you say that I have spoken against his *doctrines*—that I have written against his *doctrines*—that I have suffered to pass through my hands, letters which go to discourage the imbibing of his *doctrines*, and to warn of the consequences of doing so—that I have companied with others who protest against his doctrines—you say truly, and yet wonderful it is to hear you further say, that his unsoundness of doctrines has nothing to do with my defence ! !"

8th. "One man can write, and preach, and spread *very unsound doctrines*, and still receive the warm support or defence of both ministers and elders among us, whilst another who is afflicted because of the jeopardy which awaits our society, by means of the spreading of those unsound sentiments, and ventures to bear witness against them, is consigned to reproach."

These extracts are considered as follows :

1. *Baneful doctrines.* They are thought to be so, because directly at variance with Quakerism ; and divers of them contradictory to our fundamental principles. And being written by a member of our Society, held in high estimation by many; are therefore liable to lead away our members unawares from the true faith. And if our faith leads to life and salvation, that which goes to destroy it, must be of a baneful tendency.

Unrelenting Author. To support the justness of this expression, we have no real necessity of doing more than to refer to his own, yet unretracted expressions on the third page of his "Brief Remarks," to wit: "That a few conventional misinterpretations have arisen, [among Friends,] and that he has a conviction that the sooner such errors are rectified the better ; that he believes these mistakes are often found to spread their influence to a great extent; and that they are stepping-stones by which many persons may be, in no small degree, assisted in an actual descent *into Heresy.*" These errors, he describes, as being conventional or stipulated interpretations ; not merely as a slip of the pen or tongue of individuals; and that they remained uncorrected errors at the time of this publication, viz., 1836. And he clears none of our writers from this impeachment of error, either ancient or modern : but further on, seems to cast the like imputations upon Barclay, Penn, and Penington, as he there plainly declares that all these authors have their *defects* as well as their *excellencies;* and that he should not describe Quakerism as the system so elaborately wrought out by a Barclay, or as the doctrines and maxims of a Penn, or as the deep and refined views of a Penington ; charging *their* Quakerism with being defective, and not of an approved description ; and by his mode of expression, denies their Quakerism to be in accordance with the New Testament.

He thus implicates our early writers as being accessory to *heresy,* and in a former passage makes them chargeable with *Hicksism :* and thus not only betrays unjust but unrelenting feelings towards those dignified servants of Christ. To say nothing of his vanity, in supposing he understands Quakerism better than the founders of it, I would observe that his use of the word " *conventional*" makes the whole Society accountable as having stipulated the errors alluded to.

Which is the same thing. To advocate a noted public doctrinal character, whose views are well known, whether he be a Christian or an infidel, is, in the common understanding of things, to advocate and defend his opinions. He that advocated and defended the early Friends, identified himself in their opinions, and he that advocated and defended Hannah Barnard and Elias Hicks, did, in the eyes of mankind, identify himself in their opinions : which opinions, very few if any of their advocates, at the time, escaped.

But the expressions, "Advocated and defended," were not intended to apply to one set of men more than another, but only to those who do advocate and defend J. J. G. and his doctrines, or any other unsound writer.

2. *And by endeavoring to put down, &c.* This sentence alluded to the injunction laid by the committee upon the writer of the letter, viz., *to stay at home and to be quiet,* which injunction was responded to by every member of the committee present except Andrew Nichols; and if the meaning was not designed to tally with the *expressions,* he is willing the committee should explain and interpret their own words.

3. *Trivial and unreasonable.* The multiplicity of the charges evince a disposition in the committee to pick up and to bring forward all that could be made to look like a fault, (by a good deal of shaping) against him. But it will be allowed, that if it be so, that J. J. G. is sound in the Quaker's faith, then truly there would have been some importance in one or two charges which they preferred against him at our first interviews, (and this is not denied in the letter,) whilst the rest would have been of little importance, if not very trifling.

But inasmuch as such premises were wanting, the most considerable of those charges were altogether uncalled for if not groundless, and the rest either trivial or unreasonable. And seeing the writer of that letter did therein spare them, by omitting some of the most minute charges which they brought against him in that company of ministers and elders, he thinks they might have been satisfied on that score.

But now, on account of those objections, he seems obliged to bring forward a specimen. One of those trivial charges which he omitted (through deference to their standing,) to introduce in his letter to them, was this, they accused him of sleeping with a young man in New York on his way to Philadelphia, to which he confessed guilty, if guilt be attached to such a deed, but it was by the desire of the woman Friend, of high respectability, who owned the bed, and for the reason that she could not then so conveniently furnish another; and never having refused in case of necessity, and the young Friend being as worthy of my company as I was of his, we did in truth, both lodge in the same bed at the same time!

And truly he did think this was making a great deal out of a little, for so grave a company. Another charge was, (and *unreasonable* because it was not true,) that he had written to a Friend at Scipio, conveying (as they said) a long list of extracts from Gurney's doctrines, and seemed greatly disposed to make a crime of both—the writing to that Friend and the sending of extracts. But he had never written to that Friend any thing at all, however fair his standing was; still they insisted that he had, and disputed him in a manner not very polite nor very civil: and altogether, he thought the charge, being untrue, was *unreasonable*.

That he had frequently, in conversation and in writing, reprobated some of the doctrines of J. J. Gurney, and even on some occasions when abroad in the ministry.

They say that this statement is incorrect, because their complaint against him was for speaking and writing against J. J. G., but not for speaking and writing against his doctrines. A distinction, (as nice as it is,) which J. W. admits was attempted, *after* he proposed to prove the good cause which he had, for the course he had taken, by reading extracts from his doctrines, *but not before*. They had previously accused him of "*spreading long lists of extracts*" from his writings through the medium of letters to divers Friends, &c., which letters he willingly refers to, to decide the question in controversy, whether it was the *person* or his *doctrine* that was spoken of to others.

These letters, (see Appendix,) being matter of record, are the evidence which the nature of the case calls for, to prove the truth of the things complained of, whether it is for speaking against the man or his doctrines.

The letters themselves were emphatically charged upon him as subjects of complaint, and happily they are in being and will decide the question.

That the writer did ever speak to the disadvantage of J. J. G., distinct from his doctrines, and distinct from the right to dissent from them, yet remains to be proved. So that if the committee will relinquish their complaint against the liberty he has taken in dissenting from some of those doctrines, and the right of doing so, then they liberate him from their complaint of every thing relative to J. J. G., which took place previous to their interview with him at Greenwich. And so he feels willing they should be at liberty to insist on the distinction, or not, as they think best, inasmuch as his language now under consideration, correctly defines and applies to facts which previously transpired; that is to say, the doctrine, (though not distinct from the man,) yet not of the man distinct from the doctrines.

4th.—*Very unsound.* At the first interview with the Quarterly Meeting's Committee, at Greenwich, when they had accused J. W. of speaking and writing against J. J. G., or more truly against his doctrines, he proposed reading some extracts from his works, to show that his views were unsound, and that himself therefore had good reason for speaking and writing. To this reading of extracts they objected, and said, there may possibly be some expressions in his writings which might be deemed objectionable; and in reply to which he said, " but I want to show you *how unsound* his doctrines are," when D. B—m replied, (apparently to obviate the reading,) "I acknowledge that some of his doctrines are *very unsound.*" J. M., (then sitting between J. W. and D. B—m,) gave the latter a jog, and in another low tone of voice said, "*I* should not have said so." These expressions of D. B—m being recognized in this letter, written a few days afterwards, were denied by him at our next meeting at Newport, and several others of the committee endorsed that denial. Here follows G. C. Kenyon's testimony:

"EAST GREENWICH, 10th month 9th, 1842.
" I hereby certify that I was in company with T. A., a few days after the interview of the Select Quarterly Meeting's Committee with John Wilbur, at this place, in the 5th month, 1840, and he said to me that D. B. did acknowledge, during that interview, that some of the writings, or doctrines of Joseph John Gurney were unsound.

GEORGE C. KENYON."

Now, at Newport, D. B. said, J. W. is an old man and very forgetful, inasmuch as I did not say any such thing. And at a meeting at Portsmouth, shortly afterwards, the subject so rested on D.'s mind that he revived it himself, and explained himself to have spoken at Greenwich on this wise, viz: " For argument's sake, I will admit that some of the doctrines of J. J. G. are *very unsound.*" And to this version of it J. M. responded and said, " that he recollected that this was the way in which D. expressed himself." Why then, said J. W., did thou jog D. at the time and say, " I should not have said so?" To which enquiry J. M. made no answer ! Andrew Nichols was then called upon to inform what D. B. did say at Greenwich ; and testified unreservedly that D.'s expressions at Greenwich were the same as inserted in the letter,—that the clause, " for argument's sake," which D. had now prefixed to it, were not prefixed to it in the first place. The subject was then left.

In the fifth month following, at Greenwich, the Yearly Meeting's Committee brought against J. W. on behalf of the Quarterly Meeting's Committee an objection to the same expression in the letter, as being untrue, but no mention was then made of the prelude, " for argument's sake." And now again the same Friend, Andrew Nichols, so well known for truth and veracity, and who had testified so clearly to the Quarterly Meeting's Committee, was desired to state to the Yearly Meeting's Committee what words he heard D. B. express a year ago before the Quarterly Meeting's Committee, touching the point in question ? He then stated, in the same clear and unequivocal manner as before, that D.'s words were these, to wit: " I acknowledge that some of the doctrines of J. J. G. are *very unsound.*" This objection was then immediately abandoned. But subsequently, after some years had elapsed, three of the Quarterly Meeting's Committee, (if he rightly remember the number) have been so adventurous, and so regardless of a scrupulous care, as relates to moral, not to say religious integrity or veracity, as to come forward and positively to say, that J. W.'s assertion of the words " very unsound" was *untrue !** By which avowal they also condemn Geo. C. Kenyon and Andrew Nichols' affirmative testimonies. Had those three negative witnesses stated, as all careful, conscientious persons ought to do, if so, that they did not *recollect or notice* such expressions at the time, they would have done

---

* D. B. was invited to state the conversation before the Committee of Appeal at Yearly Meeting. But appeared to have lost his recollection almost entirely about it,—said he had kept no record of it at any time—rather thought he might say, in the first place at Greenwich, that it was probable *some would say* that J. J. Gurney's doctrines were *very unsound*—could not remember of saying any thing about the subject at Newport or Portsmouth.

more honor to themselves and to their cause, and
would have obtained more credence from others.

5th.—*That they understood he had said, there
would be a separation in the Society.* Such was
one of the many accusations brought against him at
the first interview, and words to that import, amidst
his fears of the consequences of the sentiments
abroad among us, have undoubtedly escaped him,
but upon no other consideration than the apprehension of a palpable departure from our doctrines or
discipline.

Schisms have heretofore been occasioned by the
promulgation of unsound sentiments, and by the
support which has been given to the authors of those
sentiments. And if the like should occur again, the
responsibility must rest, as it ever has done, upon
the heads of those who have denied the faith of our
fathers, and upon the heads of those who have supported and defended such, to the abuse of the discipline and good order of the Society.

Within the ranks of this very committee, who have
been seeking to make the intimation of a separation,
a crime in John Wilbur, there is to be found, at
least one, who has, on several occasions, and in religious meetings too, spoken in strong terms of a
sifting time and separation to be looked for in this
Society, and this since the Hicksite schism.

Those whose living concern is, for sustaining our
primitive doctrines and testimonies, could have no
greater joy than to see the whole number disposed
to refuse and reject all other doctrines and opinions,
with the holders of them ; and unreservedly to hold
fast those which can only stand in the one spirit ;
and therein to abide ; and then there would be no
rents or divisions among us ; and in this oneness
would be their rejoicing.

But on the other hand, as painful as the consideration is, those who are disposed to lean towards a
relaxation from first principles; and to walk with

and to support those who are inclined to let down primitive Quakerism, and to make the way more easy to flesh and blood; these would fain have *the whole body go with them,*—would encompass *all* without exception—are not willing there should be any testimony bearers left to witness against them, or to awaken any trouble or guilt in their consciences.

6th.—*That he has companied with some young men who have made a stand against the unsound views of J. J. Gurney.* The writer of the letter understands that the dissatisfaction of the committee in relation to this passage, consists in the *manner* of designating the persons alluded to, but not in the identity of them. It is true that his *manner of designation* was different from theirs, yet plainly distinctive of those alluded to. *They* call them, if his memory serves, as he supposes they have called *him,* "opposers of good order," or, "the order of Society," whilst he alludes to them as those who have made a stand against the doctrines of J. J. Gurney—that they have made such stand no one will deny, and that the making of that stand has drawn down this reproach upon them is equally true. Nor can the author of the letter, on that account, be readily made to call them *disorganizers ;* for our rules require such a stand.

7th.—*When you say that I have spoken against his doctrines, &c.* This passage recapitulates the principal heads of the charges noticed in the letter, and recognizes the substance of the writer's proceedings most complained of by the committee in language applicable to the state of the case. The description of the letters referred to, from John Barclay and Ann Jones, being in his own language, as they were not described by the committee, as he recollects ; and for the correctness of that description the letters themselves are appealed to, and if desired will be produced.

And here he would ask, *what it was for*, that the committee in the first place arrested and reprehend- ed the writer of that letter, and essayed to lay a prohibition upon him? Was it for speaking against J. J. G., distinct from his doctrines? No—certainly it was not; for they had never any evidence of his doing so, nor claimed any; for when impressively importuned to advance evidence of such expres- sion, if known to them, they have not at any time made such attempt. But nevertheless, when they say in an unqualified manner, that he has spoken and written against J. J. G., he does not charge them with being incorrect, because then he under- stands the manner of expression to refer to J. J. Gurney's whole public character, including the person with his sentiments. But if his sentiments are not included, then their complaint is without foundation, and the writer's impeachment at an end.

Hence it did seem wonderful to him that the committee could say that the unsoundness of J. J. Gurney's doctrines had nothing to do with J. W.'s defence, and should refuse the introduction of them, as offered for showing his duty, in the course he had taken.

But the complaint of the committee against him was, for saying something—for saying what? Something either in favor of or against a Friend. There has been much said by most Friends concern- ing him. But to ascertain whether for or against, the words spoken must be adduced, and no judg- ment in a court of judicature for defamation, with- out the identical words, either proved by the plain- tiff or acknowledged by the defendant, can be ren- dered.

But when the defendant acknowledges the words charged upon him, and offers sufficient evidence to prove that he had good cause for saying the things complained of, and that they were known by a great number of credible men to be true, and that the divulging of them was needful for the safety of the community. Then, if the court *refuse to hear that evidence*, and proceed to render judgment against him, should we not suppose *that refusal* to be unjust, and the judgment rendered, cruel and arbitrary, and subject to a reversal.

8. *One man can write, and spread and preach very unsound doctrines, &c.* This passage was marked as objectionable, and so testified against; but whether the expression of *unsound doctrine*, alluded to, or whether the expression of warm support and defence by ministers and elders in our Society, or both, is the cause of uneasiness, the writer did not understand. That the person alluded to has promulgated doctrines very much at variance with Quakerism is easily proved, and was offered to be proved to the committee, but they had not ears to hear it. And that he has been warmly supported and defended by ministers and elders in many places in our Society, is too well known to require a proof.* That the writer of the letter under consideration (and as he thinks, because he has borne witness against those doctrines) has been made a subject of censure and reproach, is undeniable.

And in conclusion, and by way of explanation of one point in question, the writer will say, that in the composition of his letter to the committee, he had no intention of *charging them with unsound doctrine,* nor yet to have recognized their having committed *themselves* in any religious sentiments more exceptionable than those of Joseph John Gurney, and to which it appears, by the foregoing record of the proceedings of the Quarterly and Yearly Meeting's Committees, who met at Greenwich 5th month, 4,

---

* R. G. did, before the committee at Greenwich, on the 4th day morning, 5th month 5, 1841, warmly support and defend the character of J. J. Gurney, and unsparingly placed high enconiums upon him.

1841, that they were ready to respond, and did respond to the doctrines in question at that time.

REASONS

Why J. W. wrote the letter to T. A. as one of the Quarterly Meeting's Committee, and why it ought not to be destroyed as desired.

1st. He wrote it because the committee gave him occasion for it by bringing charges against him for things which were not *reprehensible,* and because they refused to hear good and essential reasons in defence and vindication thereof, a resort to pen and paper was necessary to show his reasons for the course he had taken, and to clear himself from unjust imputations which they had cast upon him.

2d. Because they reprehended him for making a stand against J. J. Gurney, or more truly against his doctrines, and which doctrines being perversive of Quakerism, his loyalty to the cause demanded a defence of that cause in exposing those doctrines, as well as for the defence of our principles. And, moreover, the very circumstance of a committee from a Quarterly Meeting of ministers and elders so coming out in defence of a man of such doctrine as to arrest a friend in so formidable a manner for exposing such doctrines, did, in the apprehension of the writer of the letter in question, call for a suitable examination of the subject for the Committee's consideration.

3d. Because, as he conceives, the committee had no authority, by virtue of their appointment, or by virtue of the Discipline, order and usage of the Society to arrest him, and to pursue such measures with him as they did at Greenwich 5th month, 1840, gratuitous and uncalled for. Hence, for one in the station of a minister, bound by his calling to the Law and to the Testimony, silently to submit to such attempts to deprive him, or the Monthly Meeting to which he belonged, of those rights which that order and discipline, as well as the truth itself, has confided and secured to him as a member and minis-ter in the Society of Friends, and to his Monthly Meeting, as authorized judges of such concern. I say, a silent submission to such gratuitous interfe-rence, could be deemed no less than a virtual sur-render and abandonment of the rights of the Disci-pline and usages which the Yearly Meeting itself has ordained and confirmed as a standard of pro-ceeding throughout all its subordinate branches. Of which rights and usages no Friend, or body of Friends, whose authority is inferior to the Yearly Meeting, can deprive them otherwise than by chan-nels prescribed by the Yearly Meeting.

4th. Therefore he ought not to consent to the destruction of it (or the copy in his hands) in con-formity to the wishes of the Committee, because such a step would be deemed not only a concession of the course which he had taken, but also a con-cession of the doctrines which he had thereby been defending. And because he would then be impli-cated, if not reported abroad, as having thus con-ceded the doctrines of ancient Friends, and to have admitted the doctrines of J. J. Gurney.

5th. That he had no occasion in this way to abandon this letter, because the sentiments therein contained are correct and tenable.

6th. It ought not to be destroyed by the writer because the committee have reported abroad that the premises therein taken are "false and unsound," and therefore if destroyed by his consent, it would follow that whenever the writer should be called upon by his friends, either at home or abroad, to give an account of himself in relation to it, the pre-dicament in which he would then be placed would be exceedingly unfavorable, inasmuch as he would thereby, in a very exemplary manner, condemn his own attempt to uphold the usage, order and doc-trines of Friends.

7th. Because the committee, or a member of it, has endorsed the charge of falsehood upon it, therefore to consent to its destruction at any rate, but more especially until that endorsement is removed, would be deemed, (and not very unreasonably) acceding to the infamy thereon unjustly placed. And inasmuch too, as that charge was reiterated and attempted to be enforced by the committee in South Kingston Meeting of ministers and elders, although they utterly failed in the attempt.

8th. Because no one of the committee has attempted to refute it by fair and honorable arguments in the same way, with ink and paper, most easily done, if it be as exceptionable as they affirm it to be, agreeable to the maxim, viz: "The more exceptionable the argument, the more easy and tenable its refutation."

9th. Because, if the letter should become extinct, and therefore could not be appealed to, then those who have a disposition to condemn it, can place their own censures and constructions upon it with impunity, and without fear of detection, because the negative of their assumption could not be proved by oral testimony, nor by any other means, without the letter itself. Hence it was not without cause that the committee was so anxious for this letter to be destroyed.

The committee to whom this letter was written, were, as heretofore stated, ostensibly appointed on another account, to wit: the want of unity apparent from the answers to the queries from Rhode Island and Providence Monthly Meetings, and as from the committee's own confession, they have never attended to those *reported* deficiencies; it is altogether presumable that those answers were so made out at that time, and sent up for the especial purpose of obtaining the appointment of a committee for arraigning John Wilbur; and this is confirmed by the fact, that they did arraign him, and did nothing else but to deal with him!

If those solemnities of ministers and elders, set apart, shall have been perverted by a feigned representation, in order to bring about an unsuspected process for the annoyance of an innocent brother, it speaks both the language of lamentation over the leaders of our Israel, and of warning to the people : Flee to thy tent, O Jacob! and to thy Tabernacle, O Israel!

TRUTH,

Its own defence under all circumstances.

The argument advanced, that a minister travelling with a certificate, however unsound, ought not to be detected in that unsoundness, because such a measure would hurt his service, and be a breach of the order of Society, has already been thrice fairly refuted.

If there is or ever was any discipline, or conclusion of the Society in any part of the world, prohibiting the detection and exposure of doctrines published at large, and fundamentally unsound, the writer of these remarks makes this confession, that he has never seen or heard of it.

If one man is more dangerous than another, on account of the sentiments which he holds, it is he which has the greater intercourse in society and with the world at large.

Although a man may be never so unsound, if a solitary character and stationary in the world, or known only within a limited circle, the amount of evil proceeding from his opinions, is comparatively small.

But if a man is a public character, is a man of influence, is a man of personal endowments and attractive manners, both in the public and private circles, is travelling in the character of an authorized minister, and mingling with the Society generally, what great and powerful advantages for the diffusion of his opinions are in his possession. How easily is his whole character impressed upon the multitude ! And how full the esteem and credence which he easily obtains, insomuch, that notwithstanding he holds doctrines *fundamentally unsound*, great will be the difficulty of convincing his personal admirers of his heterodoxy in principle, and so it will prove too generally, that those who are attracted and drawn to his person, are prepared by degrees to receive his doctrines.

How needful, therefore, if a man of such influence and notoriety in the society, *is known to be unsound*, if it is known by his own unretracted declarations, that his sentiments are perversive of Quakerism ; I say, how needful that those who are called and appointed to watch over the flock, " as they that are to give account," should warn that flock of the dangers which they themselves have seen.

But it has been advanced by some of the members of the meeting for Sufferings, that no one has a right to gainsay the doctrines of such person, however unsound, until that body* has decided them to be at variance with the doctrines of Friends, a rule and assumption which it is believed was never before suggested or claimed by members of a meeting for Sufferings in any part of the world, to the exclusion of other concerned Friends, unless it was so by those who finally seceded from our principles under the apostacy of Elias Hicks.

The overpowering strength of the defective mem-

---

* Subsequently, some of the doctrines published by J. J. G. were laid before the meeting for Sufferings, and that body desired to examine them, and decide upon their orthodoxy, but that body declined such examination, and members of it rendered, as a reason for thus declining, that they were not authorised to determine upon any doctrines already printed.

bers in the meeting for Sufferings in New York, at that time, is well known, and for which reason no strictures upon the unsound doctrines, then making their way in the Society, could be carried through that body. But will any one among us now say, that no individual therefore had a right to gainsay the doctrine of Elias Hicks?

And were Isaac Stephenson and Samuel Wood, while travelling with certificates in New England, chargeable with a breach of order for exposing the doctrines of Elias Hicks, because the latter was at the same time travelling with a certificate to the westward? The same question might also well be asked with relation to George Withy and Thomas Shilletoe, and others, about the same time, for exposing the same doctrines, under the same circumstances.

These arguments are not here advanced by way of charging any one with Hicksism, or any other unsound doctrines, but to evince that such a *rule* would be extremely absurd if ever adopted by the Society, and also contrary to the Apostle's injunction to all the members of the church at Rome, without distinction, " to *mark* them which cause division and offences contrary to the doctrines which they had learned, and to *avoid them.*"

Hence, is not the question well decided, that at the very least, any well concerned, sincere member of the Society, has a right to call in question such doctrines, advanced by any one, provided those doctrines are tangibly unsound, let the circumstances attending the holder of those doctrines, be what they may. I repeat it again, let those circumstances be what they may, because the safety of the whole Society is of immensely greater consequence than the standing or reputation of an individual. And as it has been shown, as above, the greater danger for travelling ministers, to be unsound, than for others, the more necessity therefore arises for their detection, if such be the case with them.

It has been said that to gainsay the doctrines of a travelling minister will hurt his service—hurt his service? But it may be asked, whether any one who is fundamentally unsound in Christian doctrines, can have any requirement from above to perform any religious service in our Society?

And one more question I would ask, whether *any* member of our Society, (no matter who) can be dealt with in the order of our Discipline for dissenting from and protesting against doctrines which are offered to his acceptance, if he can fairly and clearly prove those doctrines to be at variance with the fundamental doctrines of the Society?

Heretofore we have heard of members of our Society being labored with for advocating unsound doctrines, but never till recently for reprobating them! Whence then this change?

Shall those then who publicly do wrong to our principles, and demur to our early writers, be eulogized and commended, whilst those who conscientiously detect and withstand those wrongs, are reproached and condemned?

What a strange paradoxy and inverted state of things has now transpired and become popular. Can our condition now be like those complained of by the prophet, who called evil good and good evil, that put darkness for light and light for darkness?

Do we not know that a fair examination of the principles of an author reflects upon him only in proportion to the amount of good or evil inculcated thereby?

Does he who offers to our acceptance sentiments which are at variance with those heretofore acknowledged by us, at the same time refuse to us the right of dissenting therefrom?

Whether he be so understood or not, this we know, that the Giver of all our rights has not withheld this from any of his rational creatures.

*And other things relative to the controversy con-
sidered.*

It is contemplated by our principles and Discipline, that our ministers should be so careful to wait for the Divine anointing, as that their ministry should be sound and savory.

But if otherwise, and their services should unhappily become burthensome and without life ; or, if they should evince, either by their preaching, conversation or otherwise, that themselves were not sound, either in the gift or in the true faith; or if their life and conversation should not comport with their profession, then, in either of these cases, if at home, they are to be labored with by the elders of the church in a Christian spirit, and if a reformation cannot be effected, to be advised to suspend their public ministry.

And moreover, if such things are discovered in them when abroad, and continued after due caution, it is considered requisite (if the writer of this understands the order and usage of the Society) that the select members do, for the safety of the church, advise such to return home.

But when none of these defects appear, and a minister gives good satisfaction in relation to the requisite qualifications, both at home and abroad ; and on returning from service abroad, brings satisfactory testimonials from those whom he has visited, then let it be asked, what Friend or body of Friends are authorised to interfere with his *RIGHTS,* or with the *RIGHTS* of the Monthly Meeting where he belongs ?

But there is another article of advice in our book of Discipline, and of sterling import too, which should not be overlooked or mistaken, and that is, that ministers be tender of one another, and be careful not to hurt one another's services, whether at home or abroad. But this Discipline evidently contemplates and refers to those that are sound in word and doctrine, by which Discipline great counsel and caution are extended, that ministers should be kept so, for if otherwise than sound, it would plainly appear that such an one could not be a laborer in the field of service, provided the foregoing Discipline had been administered according to its intent and meaning.

Hence it is clear, that the latter paragraph of Discipline has no such meaning as that a minister should not be allowed to recognize and expose the sentiments of one claiming to be a minister—sentiments which he had seen to be fundamentally unsound and dangerous to the body. And for this reason, because the latter can have no legitimate service in the church *to be hurt thereby.*

If the latter paragraph were necessarily to be so construed, as that one minister had no right to detect and expose the unsound doctrines of another minister, so reputed, lest his character or calling should be hurt thereby; then it would seem that the framers of our Discipline had entrapped themselves, and thereby jeopardized the safety of the Society by means of an oversight in relation to a correspondency of its parts, so as that it might be laid hold of by defective individuals or their Friends, in screening them from the due judgment of truth.

A construction which I deem utterly at variance with the meaning of our rules for the preservation of harmonious labor among ministers, as for the protection of the whole Society against unsound and dangerous doctrines, which construction, as well as any mistake in the forming of our Discipline, the writer is altogether unwilling to allow, because he is well assured that the consistency of its provisions are plain and tangible, and clearly to be understood, that those who are not one with us in doctrine, are not contemplated thereby to be countenanced as preachers, or to be abroad as ministers, and therefore our Discipline cannot have provided for the protection of them.

But there is still another paragraph of Discipline of paramount importance in this case, and which settles the question to every intent and purpose, and places it beyond all disputation, that *all faithful Friends*, [whether ministers, elders or others,] are not only allowed to relieve their minds, when they painfully perceive our principles to be invaded, but are *enjoined* and *required* to be watchful over our members who deviate from our Christian principles, and to labor with them, let them be whom they may, not excepting ministers and elders under any circumstances whatever, any more than common members, and that for good reason too, because if they should deviate, the more of course the harm that must come of it.

A short time before the separation of the Hicksites from Friends, a meeting at Purchase, or thereabouts, was said to have been attended by Elias Hicks, Daniel Wood, and Rowland Greene. And immediately thereafter, we were told, that the two latter gave ready information abroad, that Elias Hicks preached very unsound doctrine at that meeting.

Wherefore, let it be asked, whether or not they were chargeable with a breach of Friend's Discipline, as hurting the service or character of Elias Hicks?

To this question, I apprehend, it will be readily answered, that they were not. Why? Because the doctrine of Elias Hicks was believed to be unsound and dangerous doctrine, and that it was therefore the duty of those friends, (though ministers, and out at the same time on religious service,) to testify faithfully, both against him and his doctrine.

But suppose some of the Friends of E. H., under the professed authority of a Quarterly Meeting of ministers and elders, come forward and call on Daniel Wood and Rowland Greene, to give account of their proceedings in that matter. Whereupon they, the said D. W. and R. G., as an apology, advance the above as their plea, to wit: "that the doctrines which E. H. preached were very unsound," and propose to state to the committee Elias Hick's very words, to show that they had good and sufficient cause for the course they had taken.

Nay, say the committee, we have nothing at all to do with the doctrines of E. Hicks, but our business and our concern is for the support of the order and Discipline of the Society. You had no right to open your lips against Elias Hicks. He stands as an approved minister, and carries as good a certificate as you do !

Such was the plea of E. Hicks and his friends on all occasions, to avoid an exposure and examination of his doctrines, and such is the plea of J. J. G. and his friends, to avoid the exposure and investigation of his doctrines.

But the Friends of J. J. G. say, that his doctrines are not so bad as those of E. H., and therefore the cases are not parallel. But how do we know which of the two systems are the most exceptionable, until the merits of them are examined ?

Do they choose to determine cases without an investigation and without evidence ?

If there are any who think that J. J. Gurney's case is good, why need they fear an examination to see whether it be better than that of E. Hicks, and how much ?*

---

* In the adoption of a principle of action in such cases, the question rests, not upon the excess of unsoundness, in the one case or in the other, but upon the existence of it, in relation to essential points.

The parallel of these cases is, their doctrines are both fundamentally unsound and erroneous, and the principle on which both of these persons have acted, is precisely the same, and that is, manifesting a determination to avoid a comparison of them with the doctrines of Friends, a course which all who have attempted an innovation upon our religious principles have pursued, that is to say, all who have proposed to themselves to carry the Society with them.

Here then is a sure test of motives,—all those writers whose intentions are honestly to set forth and to promote the true Christian doctrines as held by Friends, have ever been, in all readiness, to compare their own views with the standard writings of our Society. But on the contrary, those whose intentions are to modify or change the doctrines of Friends, have always without exception, studiously avoided a contrast of their own sentiments with those of the Society.

On whichever hand, therefore, the intentions of such have been "to remove the land marks," their aim and manner of doing it have run parallel to each other, have been obviously the same, to remove them unseen and unsuspected by the members at large, whilst he who doeth truth cometh to the light that his deeds may be made manifest, that they are wrought in God.

Elias Hicks and Joseph John Gurney have both professed and declared their own views to be in unison with the primitive doctrine of Friends in regard to the Saviour of men, if not in all points. But the former, however, appears to be wanting in his fidelity as to Christ's personal coming and attributes; and the latter in his fidelity as to his spiritual coming and dwelling in the heart of man. The latter has the fullest faith in his personal coming and atoning sacrifice for the remission of sins; the former as full in his spiritual coming for the renovation of the inner man, and a saving of him from a continuance in sin.

But both of these appear to be great debtors to the correct part of each other's doctrine ; each apparently holds to half, and each apparently rejects half of the Christian covenant, and therefore holding nothing in common with each other in relation to redemption by Christ. But still, each (professedly) holding to half the covenant in common with Friends.

OBJECTIONS ANSWERED.

There are those who have been, and continue to be, very liberal in their censures upon those who have conscientiously proclaimed a fast from imbibing certain defective doctrines abroad in the Society, finding fault with every course they have taken in the faithful discharge of what they believe to be their religious duty. At one time averring, that however great any evil might appear, their manner of exposing it is altogether improper. And at another time, charge the whole present difficulty in the Society, *not upon the evil and the authors of it,* but upon those who expose the evil, and upon the *manner* of doing it.

And the advocates of J. J. G. further state, that if those who reprobate his doctrines had forborne to do so, the present dissension would not have existed, and things among us would have remained quiet. Be it so. And so they might say, if the prophets in former times had held their peace, and quietly suffered Israel to depart from the doctrine of the Lord's covenant with them, then the dissensions between the faithful and the unfaithful might have been avoided, and a quiet agreement in the lapse of principle enjoyed, at least until the judgments of the Lord were poured out upon them.

And so, if those called Protestants had stifled their convictions, and kept still, then the persecutions and burning of martyrs would not have transpired.

Again, if George Fox and his friends had been disobedient to Divine manifestations and requirings, in preaching again the inward power, life and light of primitive Christianity, in contravention with priestcraft, then all the outward persecutions, imprisonments and martyrdoms which they suffered might have been avoided !

And lastly, if those who maintained sound doctrines against Elias Hicks and his followers, had chosen that kind of peace and unity so loudly called for by the latter, in preference to the true principles and doctrines of Truth, then the cruel dissensions and sore troubles which ensued might have been avoided.

Who then, in consideration of all these religious dissensions, shall we make chargeable with the appalling results which followed?

Shall we charge the calamities of early times upon the prophets who could not hold their peace when the testimonies of that covenant were profaned? Or, shall we charge all the blood of all the martyrs upon a Wickliffe and a Huss, a Luther and a Calvin, because they withstood the Romish superstitions and atrocities? Or shall we charge it where it belongs, upon the pope and his insidious hierarchy? Or shall we charge the great dissensions and cruel persecutions which fell out in the days of our first Friends upon George Fox and his cotemporaries, because the doctrines which they preached and their opposition to a hireling ministry led to those dissensions?

Again, shall we charge upon those who reprobated and withstood the doctrines of Elias Hicks with the great confusion which took place at Mount Pleasant and at New York, when that fearful schism was consummated at those places, seeing that if those doctrines of E. H. had not been controverted, those events would not have transpired.

No more than they, therefore, are those who reprobate false doctrines *in the same way and manner* in this day, chargeable with the consequences which follow; but those by whom the offence cometh— the author and the abettors of him and his doctrines, they are they on whom the vast responsibility rests! And more especially in those places where such have the ascendency, should they be disposed to close up every avenue through which the society at large may obtain correct information of the soundness or unsoundness of such doctrines as are offered to their acceptance.

But there are among us, those who suggest, if rightly understood, that it is not so much the want of occasion, more or less, for reprobating the doctrines of J. J. G., nor of the right of doing so, that they object; but that it is the *manner* in which some have spoken against J. J. G. or his doctrines, that they *disapprove.*

To which the writer replies, that seeing the doctrines alluded to are easily proved to be fundamentally unsound, and tangibly perversive of Quakerism, he feels fully warranted in claiming the authority and example of those who have *heretofore,* in the very *same manner,* spoken and testified against doctrines which were also unsound and perversive of Quakerism, as well as against the authors and holders of those doctrines. He is now referring to the authority of William Almy, Rowland Greene, Abel Collins, Thomas Howland, William Jenkins, and a great number of other Friends, at the time of the Hicksite controversy.

These friends appeared to be conscientiously concerned to guard the members of our Society against imbibing the defective doctrines, which were then spreading both in New England and to the westward. And two of the number mentioned, travelled westward in the ministry at that time, and were often known, in the *same manner,* to warn

11*

Friends against imbibing the unsound doctrines then spreading in the society, whilst they were out on religious service.

The *manner* of the Friends appealed to above, was to speak and testify against the *unsound doctrines* then advocated; and their *example* and *manner* has been followed by some concerned Friends of the present day, to guard the society against defective views that are offered to their acceptance.

Again, there are some who refer to the authority of numbers as a reason for their choice of ground in the present controversy; and others to the credibility of the character and standing of those to whom they had been accustomed to look as leading Friends.

Reasons like these, undoubtedly, have a powerful effect upon the mind of man—upon his affections and passions. But the wise and conscientious believer, so soon as he finds that either numbers or character, are placed in competition with *principles*, however great the number, or conspicuous the character, he is awakened to a greater necessity of a firm resolution and decision in favor of the truth and sound principles, regardless of the consequences which may follow.

Had it not been for such honest resolution and decision of character, firmly adhered to by the first few protestant reformers, what would have become of the reformation from popery? It would never have been. And but for such derision in George Fox, and a few other congenial spirits against protestant Babylon, Quakerism had probably never existed.

But these few solitary individuals in the midst of a great nation, and in the midst of nations, bound in the covenant of a glorious hope; were enabled to maintain the truth against the opposition and resistance of all the domination of earthly power, against the many—the solitary few against the *mighty,* the *noble,* the *honorable,* because He who must be obeyed, rather than all men, had commanded them, and was with them in the work whereunto he had called them.

Again, if numbers or names are to govern principle, must we not then, by the same rule, abandon Quakerism altogether, although it hath, under that name, existed for near two centuries, and led thousands to glory triumphant, because the whole society is but a little handful compared with the whole body of Christian professors? Inasmuch, too, as among others we know there are many mighty, many noble, and many great men, whose intimacy and friendship has become so exceedingly enticing to some among the Quakers.

Finally, because the great body of those under our name, (including many eminent men,) upon Long Island, and divers other places in New York, and elsewhere, adhered to an unsound man and his sentiments. Ought those few who remained, to have gone with them, because their number was small?*

---

* During the pendency of the editor's case before the society, much pains have been taken to defame his character, sending abroad over the Yearly Meeting, as well as elsewhere, a great variety of unfounded reports, in order no doubt, to enlist if possible, the whole society against him, so that his excommunication might be the more easily affected.

And since that has been accomplished, some of the same and other unfounded stories are most industriously circulated; as it appears for the purpose of obtaining a full assent or justification in the minds of Friends, of the cruel measures thus consummated upon an afflicted brother.

But through the kindness of his Friends, he has had the opportunity of refuting many of these reports,—all that have reached him; and so far as he knows, to the satisfaction of all those who have been so good as to give him the opportunity of doing so. He has always encouraged enquiries and investigations into those reports, and still does encourage them, although, like the Apostle, he would rather glory in his infirmities than to take praise to himself, or to attempt to hide them from the Searcher of Hearts, or from his beloved Friends, whose reproofs, when given as directed by the Saviour, he

The Yearly and Quarterly Meeting's Committees have said and reported, that their treatment towards J. W. has been in kindness and great tenderness ; and these reports have been widely spread by themselves and others, not only in New England, but otherwhere, as many of his readers will bear witness.

But if the reader has given attention to the foregoing narrative of the proceedings of these Committees, and marked the unreasonable privations, and unkind usages to which they have subjected J. W., he must have been prepared before coming to this article to reprobate, in no unhesitating manner, these most unhallowed pretentions to kindness and tenderness.

They refused to allow him the company and assistance of any of his near Friends, when under the painful endurance of their reprimands, and even that of his wife ; and such refusal as this was persisted in to the last, although the right was often requested, and by means of disability was often needful.

The reader will have seen, that they refused him altogether, his right of access to the *records*, so needful to the preparation of his case in vindication of his proceedings, and to prove the wrongs that were inflicted upon him.

The reader will also have seen, that they sought an advantage over him, by demanding answers to irrelevant questions—that they shifted their ground divers times, in order to prevent and interrupt the course of his defence,—that they proffered him anonymous papers in order to annoy him,—that

would desire to profit by. And his fervent prayer is, that when God sees iniquity in him, that He would do it away—that He would ever awaken and quicken his conscience to a ready perception of all that offends Him, and to cause that judgment should have its perfect work.

they accused him of *falsehood,* touching the premises of his letter to them, and virtually pronounced those premises to be a fabrication, and thus charging him with that which they could never prove, otherwise than by a reiteration of the same charges; and charges too, which were not maintainable,—that they accused him in large companies with stubbornness, and of being possessed of a dark and hard heart.

In short, their treatment of him on all occasions, so far from tenderness, has been but the confirmation of a determination to prostrate his standing,—some of which movements have been noticed in this work.

RECORDS.

The appellant had several times applied to the clerk of the Quarterly Meeting of ministers and elders for a copy of the minute, by which their committee was appointed and authorized for service, in the restoration of unity and harmony, but he refused to give it, without direction from the meeting. The Select Quarterly Meeting was therefore applied to for liberty to their clerk to furnish a copy as aforesaid ; but it refused to give such liberty.

When the investigation of his case before the committee of his own Monthly Meeting approached, one of that committee requested the Yearly Meeting's Committee, some of whom were expected to be in attendance, to bring with them a copy of the minute as above, and also from the clerk's files, South Kingston Select Meeting's account of its state, as presented to the Quarter in the 5th month, 1840. When the committee met, a paper was brought, purporting to be a copy of said minute ; but the account from South Kingston was not produced.

The appellant, having been present when the

minute was made, and being at that time apprehensive of the intentions of the movers of this measure, took especial notice of the wording of the minute, and had also heard it read once or twice afterwards, by the committee, in the early part of its proceedings ; and could not, therefore, now believe that the paper now produced, was a true copy of the *original minute ;* but still thought it most prudent, not to disclose his apprehensions at this time, not knowing but the discrepancy might possibly occur incidentally. But the account not being brought, the appellant proposed sending a messenger to the clerk's office for it, unless the Yearly Meeting's Committee would admit its clearness in relation to unity, and which they acceded to, rather than to have the account presented.

He now concluded to do the best he could with things as they were, intending if another occasion should offer for it, to call for the book itself, and to be sure to have the account present.

Accordingly, when his appeal was pending before the Quarterly Meeting's Committee, and the time of meeting not far distant, the appellant applied in writing to the respondents, (one of whom was the keeper of the papers, and was the clerk of the Select Quarterly Meeting,) to produce before the Quarterly Meeting's Committee on the appeal, the books of records which contained the minutes of Rhode Island Quarterly Meeting of Ministers and Elders, held in the 5th month, 1840, and also the accounts from South Kingston Select Meeting which was presented at that meeting : being in their possession, and essential in the trial of the case.

In due time, while the appeal was in progress, before the Quarterly Meeting's Committee, the respondents were asked to lay on the table the book and papers called for by the appellant,—after some hesitation they said, they were not present ; but offered such an extract as before. The appellant now complained of the injustice in withholding from him his right of an evidence so essential in his case. The respondents replied by saying, "*Does John Wilbur think that we will bring evidence here, to destroy our own case?*" And subsequently repeated the same again!

The appellant now enquired, whether a public officer could withhold books or papers pertaining to his office, in a case on trial, though their presence might subject himself to a decision not to his own advantage?

But most of the committee apparently, like Gallio, cared for none of these things; nor did they so much as say to the clerk of the Select Quarterly Meeting, that the appellant had a right to call for that book—and that he, the clerk, had laid himself liable for refusing to produce it.

Being of this temperament, the Quarterly Meeting's Committee of course decided the case against the appellant. But he was now more fully confirmed than before, that the discrepancy was not merely incidental; but the record had either undergone some mutilation or was garbled in copying!

Therefore, previous to the Yearly Meeting where his appeal was to be finally decided, the appellant called at the house of the clerk of the Select Quarterly Meeting, who was also one of the respondents from the Quarterly to the Yearly Meeting, and found him at leisure; and there plead with him for justice, and the right which is due to all men, and which the discipline gives and provides for all who appeal to its decision, but found his mind closed against all entreaty for justice. The appellant now desired him to turn to the minute in question, and to let him just see it; but he would not. He then asked him, if he would not carry the book and South Kingston account to the Yearly Meeting, but he would give no encouragement of doing so. The appellant then told him, that if he persisted in a refusal to do so, he should have a right to say that his copy was not a true copy of the *original* minute, and they might expect him to challenge it as spurious, before the committee of the Yearly Meeting; and that he might expect him further to prove it by the question which they put at Providence, to wit: "Does John Wilbur think that we will bring evidence to destroy our own case? 11" An interrogative and declarative of their own, clearly and fully proving that the book contains evidence *against them,* which the extract they brought did not.

When Yearly Meeting came they did persist in the same course, and carried not the book and document as requested; but with a hope, as it appeared, to work on the credulity of the committee on the case, they produced what they called a copy by the clerk, and a duplicate, said to be taken from the records by another of the respondents, and so far as the appellant knows, might be a copy of a mutilated record as it now stands, but not of it, in its original form, which, if brought forward must unavoidably, as they said at Providence, *destroy their own case.* Or did they not rather mean that the exposure of some marks of an officious hand upon the face of that minute with the document from South Kingston brought to view, *would destroy* (what they called) *their own case?* And better he thinks to call it their own case, rather than truth's cause.

But the appellant did refuse to acknowledge these pretended copies; they not being the evidence which the nature of this case, and state of things now called for, but a mere evasion of duty, and violation of good faith. Was it ever known before, that any people under our name had become so lost to a sense of justice, and the honor of the cause of truth, and had so conducted towards an individual member, as to refuse that their deeds should be brought to the light? Or, that refused to disclose to his proper judges, their usage toward him? The appellant believes not.

He now made objection to these papers, purporting to be copies of record, and protested against them, as spurious documents; and consequently, showing that the committee of the Select Quarterly Meeting, who had been the instigators and chief actors in this unjust course of persecution, had entirely neglected and departed from the recorded business of their appointment: and without cause, and without any discipline to warrant it, made an unprovoked attack upon him, whilst in the proper exercise of his duty in the support of our discipline, and therefore had no cause at all to complain of his vindication in his letter, or of his reprobating unsound doctrines of their author.*

SUBORDINATION TO THE BODY.

In all compacts or associations, individuals stand by mutual agreement in subordination to bodies, so long as those bodies sustain and protect the interest and rights of those individuals, agreeable to the rules or laws of that compact. If such general compact consist of branches composed of divers individuals, those branches, in like manner, stand in the condition of subordination to the general compact or association.

Such association being formed and mutually entered into, or voluntarily acknowledged by every individual member of it, for the benefit of each, be-

---

* Some months previous to the publication of this statement, the editor wrote to one of the Yearly Meeting's Standing Committee, (who was also one of the last respondents. and the keeper of their papers in this case,) requesting the loan of them for a short time in order for the completion of a fair record of the whole transaction; but could not obtain them. Hence, some of their objections could not be so directly met and answered; and this narrative is therefore somewhat less complete than it would otherwise have been.

ing wholly made up of individuals, and bound by its constitution and laws as premised, for the *benefit* and *interests* of its members, as well as to protect their *rights*—the responsibility, therefore, is mutual.

This responsibility rests upon the whole, in proportion to the authority or number, whether of the supreme body or its branches ; or whether of individuals. If the supreme body consist of a thousand individuals, its breach of trust, or breach of the conditions of its order, (if such transpire,) is in the same proportion greater than that of a single individual.

If a branch of that body consist of an hundred individuals, and acts by the power of that number, its breach of order is in the same ratio greater than that of an individual. Hence, the perverting or violating of the rules of such association, tending to the overthrow of such body, is dangerous in direct proportion to the powers and number of the body which abuses the rules of its original and mutual stipulations.

Thus the danger attending a serious disease of the head or the chest, is vastly greater than that which affects a single member of the human body. But if the association be wholly of a religious character, the considerations involved are of a higher order and of greater consequence,—if purely Christian, Christ presides, and his law is the governing rule of that compact ; as it is of every member of it, if he be a follower of Christ.

If such body be purely Christian, and so remain, no one can be required to resign or forego his obligations to Christ ; nor can a follower of Christ violate his law, and the obligation due to *him*, at the bidding of man ;—nor yet can a body, so being and so remaining, require one of its members to disregard or violate his allegiance to Christ.

But, touching the question of certainty in ascertaining the mind of Truth, and its pointings (wheth-

er we allude to the church or its members) in case
of a loss of the true anointing the early and spirit-
ually-endued members of the Society of Friends,
plainly recorded their views of the Christian doctrines, and also instituted a discipline and church
government for the establishment of doctrine as
well as practice in the future government of the
church. Such discipline and such doctrines, ordained of the Truth, have been acknowledged as a test
of faith and conduct by the Society for nearly two
centuries.

Whatever body of men, therefore, whether superior or subordinate, claiming ecclesiastical authority,
or to be a Yearly, or Quarterly Meeting, of such
Society; if they violate and disregard the rules,
regulations and doctrines of that Society, in any important points, and persist in it, are not to be considered nor accredited as the body of Christ, nor
can they belong to the Society of Friends; but are
a spurious body, and therefore not entitled to any
authority under the doctrines and discipline of the
ancient Society of Friends.

Bodies professing Christianity are as much bound
to act conscientiously and in the fear of the Lord as
individuals; and if all the individuals composing
such bodies so act, then there will be no misrule nor
oppression exercised by that body; nor occasion for
giving or receiving a plaudit for the quieting of one
anothers' consciences, nor of laying plans for turning away backward the judgment of truth.

But it has been made to appear by the foregoing
narration of facts which have transpired, that both
the superior and inferior bodies, under the name of
Friends, have disregarded and trodden down the
good order and discipline of the Society; and
through the ruling members (in whose acts these
bodies have united,) have also supported the author
or authors of unsound doctrines: and under these
flagrant abuses it is, that they reiterate the cry of

subordination to the body—subordination to the
body !! And no sin is more spoken of by them in
our hearing, as being of so deep a dye, as insubordination to the body—as insubordination to their
own wills and decisions !

But if *their* construction of the word, as to its
meaning, is correct, they themselves are chargeable
with insubordination, both to the Doctrines and Discipline of the Society of Friends, and they are now
called upon to clear themselves from this charge;
and if they can do it, all the upright will be made
glad. To do this, however, they must condemn
and revoke their proceedings *en masse*, against
South Kingston Monthly Meeting and its members,
as well as in other cases; and they must also condemn their support and defence of an unsound
writer. But this we know, that they who call themselves apostles and are not, and they who call
themselves Jews and are not, (however great their
number, and high their profession,) are not the *body*
of *Christ*, but are what He, who was dead and is
alive, declares them to be, as recorded in the Revelations. See chapter 2nd. No more are those who
say they are Quakers and are not—those who make
the profession, but have denied the faith by their
works,—we say, no more are these the body of
Christ; nor have they any more right to bind men's
consciences than had that body which called itself
the *Church or the Body of Christ* in the middle
ages: touching which we have shown that the
more corrupt the body, the louder the cry and the
more rigorous the measures to enforce subordination or obedience to the desires and will of the
body.

This cry of insubordination to the body, is by no
means new. It was raised against those undaunted
worthies who dissented from the false doctrines and
corrupt practices of the Romish Church, and who
faithfully testified against them; and for which they

endured every species of persecution, not excepting death itself.

Again, for the same crime the early Friends were arraigned, and persecuted, and put to death. And at the time of the Hicksite controversy, subordination to the body was loudly proclaimed and insisted on, and several valuable Friends were placed under dealing, and finally disowned from the Society for this alleged high crime. And now again the cry of insubordination is raised against those who dissent from and testify against the unsound doctrines spread abroad among us; and these are in turn subjected to the penalty of dealing and disownment.

Now, let us deliberate upon this claim of unconditional subordination, so strongly insisted on by the Yearly Meeting's Committee; and on their behalf by others amongst us; and reflect on the consequences to which it must inevitably lead, if admitted and acted on in the Society of Friends; never heard of in a sound and healthy state of the Church: but if her condition become otherwise, no marvel then that claims should be made by her rulers, for the prostration of the *rights* of subordinate meetings and individuals.

In coincidence with such claims, we have been told by prominent men, (employed in carrying out this doctrine of absolute subordination to the body,) that *it is our duty to yield our opinions to the body on all occasions; even if we know ourselves to be right, and the whole body to be wrong !!*

And then, to quiet our consciences, they tell us, that if we will only submit to all their dictation, no blame will attach to us; but that the responsibility will rest upon the body! And truly there appears to be no shrinking, on their part, from taking such responsibility.

This doctrine, if continued to be adhered to and finished, will undoubtedly bring us directly back

again to the ground maintained by the Papal
Hierarchy, in the middle ages; whose rulers undoubtedly supposed that their high standing and
authority in the body, and ecclesiastical distinction, would be a warrantee for whatever they
might list, and give credence to their unrighteous
proceedings.

But can it be believed, in this boasted age, that
justice and judgment, truth and righteousness, will
waive their claim to the abuse of ecclesiastical authority among men? Or even to a standing committee, or to any deputation whatever, from a Yearly Meeting of the Society under our name?

Nay, verily,—the higher the standing of any body
of men, the more reprehensible their misrule and the
more displeasing in the sight of God.

CONCLUSION :

Containing an affectionate invitation to all the
honest-hearted under our name, to hold fast the profession of the Christian faith, as recognized and
most surely believed by all our faithful predecessors
in the truth, as it is in Jesus Christ our Lord.

In this concluding address, I will not intrude upon
the reader's time with a specific recapitulation of
the foregoing proceedings, brought to view in vindication of the course taken in the support and defence of our Christian principles and discipline; the
importance of which I hope he will be enabled duly
to appreciate. But in this invitation, the object of
my desire and concern is, to persuade and exhort
all (and it is in the feelings of much brotherly love
and with a lively hope) to be entreated to come
forward more and more in a practical consummation of the obedience of that faith which leads to
the saving knowledge of God, through the revelation of Him who died for our sins and rose again
for our reconciliation unto God; and who also was

and is and yet to be, the Lord from Heaven, a quickening Spirit.

And first, permit me to say to you, my dear friends, that however very dear to me the rights and privileges of the militant church, in a condition owned of God ; yet, (if otherwise,) how much dearer ought to be, (and not to me only, but into every one of her children,) the love of God and the owning of his approving presence, which are the fruits of the one living faith in the Son of God, and in the fundamental and inalienable doctrines of the Gospel of Christ, with the testimonies and discipline of the true church ; a faithful conformity whereunto through obedience, being indispensable as a test of membership in that body, of which Christ is the Head; and therefore of the greatest consequence to every one who would desire to be a member of the true church.

And we, of the present generation, are entrusted with the keeping of this faith, and those testimonies, through *our* day, and are bound by the strongest obligations, (inasmuch as our way has been made more easy, by the delivery into our hands of these testimonies, pure and entire, by our predecessors,) to act our part faithfully, through the Lord's assistance, and tender mercies ; not only in the scrupulously upholding of them ourselves, through our day and time, as a righteous standard and testimony to all men ; but to deliver and hand them down to the succeeding generation, undiminished and without abatement ; so that those who follow after may rejoice and gather strength by means of our unflinching uprightness and willingness to endure all things for the sake of Him who gave them to the church; and to bear the cross and to despise the shame, in the faithful endurance of self-denial in this, a day of lightly esteeming and treading down of the holy testimony of the cross of Christ, which is the power of God and wisdom of God ; and remains to be a

mystery which has been hid for ages from the wise
and prudent,—from all the carnal professors of every
age,—but revealed to the humble, and the lowly,
and self-denying followers of the Lamb, of every
generation.

And the importance, that we as a people, who
have advanced in the faith of vital Christianity beyond others of the protestant reformation, should
hold fast to the testimonies that we were at the first
entrusted with, (and without the fear of man,) is
strikingly apparent ; lest we through a culpable relaxation should give countenance and strength to
the apostacy of such other denominations as are
retrograding into a sorrowful declension from their
own first principles, and thereby should bring condemnation upon ourselves on their account.

How sorrowful will it be, my dear Friends, if
we, either willingly or heedlessly fall irrecoverably
into the degenerating current of the day, and with
the multitude go back again to the house from
whence our forefathers came out, (through the cost
of great tribulations,) and which return must be to
the utter loss of our own souls, and to the great reproach of the holy profession handed down to us by
our worthy predecessors in the truth, and would be
crucifying to ourselves the Son of God afresh, and
putting him to an open shame.

As reasons for the goodly exercise of care, in
watching over ourselves and guarding the church
against the smaller as well as greater inlets of a
departure from sound doctrine and correct practices, we may once more recur to the view of things
which have transpired heretofore, as alluded to in
the preface of this narrative, both in ancient and
modern times, in which was noticed the sad declension of the church, under both dispensations, in relation to the Lord's statutes and doctrines delivered
to her, showing that the former, though established
of the Almighty himself, did not only become the

degenerate plant of a strange vine unto Him, but finally persecuted and wickedly put his messengers to death, and finally slew the Son and sent of God, before the measure of her iniquity was full. And that the latter, even under the gospel and name of Him who came not to destroy men's lives but to save them, persecuted the messengers whom he had sent to warn them of their iniquities, and put them to death without mercy.

And the question was asked, and may again well be asked, whether the church now is better, and more secure against the danger of an apostate condition, than the primitive Christian church was? Will it not be acknowledged that the same enticements are now in the hands of the enemy as heretofore; and the same proneness to evil in men now as then, to wit, the love of pleasure—the love of the world—the love of power and other degenerating propensities; and are not these as deadly now to true religion as they ever were in any age of the world?

But we know it is so. Then, O then! let every one gird up the loins of his mind, and watch— watch and pray lest we enter into temptation, and fall by the subtle delusions of the wicked one. Oh, Friends l let us dwell in the light of the Lord, that so we may see the snares of the enemy and avoid them—let us draw near and dwell in Him who is light, and in whom there is no darkness at all : and as we come to see in him, the councils of wisdom, and are made to understand his will, let us obey, whether it be in acting or in forbearing to act— whether it be in the small or in the great sacrifices, remembering that believing and obeying in the one, is the same in the sight of God, as the believing and obeying in the other. Then despise not the day of small things, but keep the convenant of obedience in the little as in the much, for the reward is as certain in the one as in the other, even peace and joy in

12

the Holy Ghost,—for it is as we are faithful in the little, that we shall be made rulers over more, and be prepared to do more and more ; and so shall our strength be increased from less to more, and as our eye is kept single to the light of the Lord in our own souls, waiting upon Him, and keeping the word of his patience in that covenant, which is as sure by night as by day—as sure in the night of trial and temptation, as in the day of deliverance and rejoicing. Hence faith and patience in the disciple's experience, are a treasure of great price, and con-tribute, even more largely to his growth in the saving knowledge of God, than in his more joyous seasons of feasting upon the good things of his Master's table.

Zion can only be redeemed through judgment, and her converts by righteousness ;—by being plunged into the river of judgment: this must be known in the experience of every member of the true church. He must witness the sanctifying baptism and power of the Holy Ghost ; and immutable justice towards all men, must be the obvious characteristic of his life and conversation, showing mercy to others as he would desire God would show mercy to him. And in so walking in the fear of the Lord, it is only that we evince by our fruits, that we love Him above all, and our neighbor as ourselves.

By the inward operation of the judgment and power of God, it is, that the members are instructed and prepared for service in the church—to be way-marks and ensamples to all men.

And among the many and important services assigned to the members respectively, there are none peradventure of greater usefulness, or of a higher order, than that of the gospel ministry—a service, than which, none has been more grossly abused— than which, no one has been more sacrilegiously counterfeited. If true and apostolic, not received of man nor by man, but by the revelation of Jesus Christ—as such, it is a great blessing to the church —if false, and learned only of man and by man, and should prevail in the body under our name, it will prove an unfailing means of a degeneracy and estrangement from God, and a lapse into dead formality; and will greatly tend to draw away *from* God unto men.

So far as we know, the Society of Friends is the only people, among all the Christian denominations, since the primitive ages, who profess to preach the gospel only as the Spirit giveth utterance—who wait for the promise of the Father on all occasions as Christ taught his disciples, to wit :—who believe it requisite to tarry until they be endued with power from on high, before they attempt to preach in God's great and holy name.

Hence the testimony of Friends, touching this high and holy calling, is at this day the most primitive, noble and dignified testimony in the world, being the only one which recognizes a sensible, direct intercourse and communication between the heavens and the earth ; or in other words, from God to the children of men.

Inasmuch, then, as the Society of Friends are the only people who hold fast to the faith, that Christianity itself has not diminished, nor fallen off, nor its gifts and graces been withdrawn from the true church, since the day when the Lord told his disciples, that the Spirit which should succeed his personal presence with them, should instruct them in all things, and bring all things to their remembrance ; or since the day when he promised that he would abide with them for ever, even unto the end of the world ;—how desirable and indispensable for us, in the fulfillment of ancient prophecy, " they shall all know me," &c., and for the unspeakable benefit of the church, as well as of the world at large, that we hold fast the profession of this faith without wavering—this faith of the continued dispensation of the gift of the Holy Ghost unto them who wait for him in sincerity and humility, and believe in his power.

But this gift of God's grace and Holy Spirit, is by no means exclusively given to gospel ministers, but flows from the Vine, which is the fountain of life, to every living branch;—from Christ to every member of his body. And all the true members, whatever their respective callings are, as their hearts are open to receive, are by the anointing of his Spirit taught and instructed to fulfil their duties and callings conformable to the will of God, and are blessed with immediate access to him, through the mediation of Christ, and without the intervention of any man.

And it is as impossible for the church of Christ to remain such, and to be a living body, without the savor and circulation of the Spirit and life of Christ, as for a tree to remain green and fruitful without the circulation of sap and nourishment from the root and from the body ; or as for a man to exist in the vigor of life, without the circulation from the heart, of that blood which is the life of man.

But to return to the exercise of the gospel ministry. I feel concerned to exhort all, who are called to that solemn service, faithfully and patiently to wait, and to rely on Him alone who is the Great Minister of the sanctuary and true tabernacle which God hath pitched and not man, both for the opening and the shutting.—for strength,—for mouth and wisdom—tongue and utterance. And, above all things, having no confidence in themselves, or in the endowment of man's wisdom ; but tarry, I entreat you, (as you would desire your own furtherance, and that of your brethren,) tarry at Jerusalem until ye be endued with power from on high ; for under the dominion of this power, (it only is) as it is waited for in the simplicity and integrity of the soul, that the work will prosper and bring peace and joy to those who are thus exercised in it : and will redound to the glory of God and the consolation of his people, whether the measure of the gift be less or more. Never, O never! let the desire for words, either in yourselves or in others, beguile you into an unsanctified offering—beguile you into a spurious ministry, or the offering of strange fire. Oh! how lamentable the condition of those where a lifeless ministry prevails! How deadening to an assembly of Quaker worshippers, for if it come not from God, though it may please the ear, or lead to head knowledge, it is no better than a sounding brass and a tinkling cymbal ! How much better in the sight of God, and for the church, is silent worship, than the annoyance of a spurious ministry !

The skill and artifice of man, in framing a beautiful discourse, if it be but in man's wisdom and learning, contributes no more to the honor of God, or the salvation of souls, than would man's sagacity in forming a beautiful image of things above or things below: he can, of himself, no more breathe the breath of life into the one than into the other. And without a portion of the Divine life, which is the gift of God and testimony of Jesus, preaching is no more saving, than any other mere image of good things.

Hence the necessity that Christ's ministers, seeing they are but men, should abide with the Lord Jesus in the inner court of the heart, and "with him in his tribulations, that so they may know of his doctrines," and how to preach them,—that they may be instructed in the counsel of his will, for it is here, in the heart, that "whatsoever is to be known of him is made manifest,"—pertaining to his own glorious kingdom and the salvation of souls ; which is at times made known to the messengers of his covenant, for their own qualification to minister, and for the watering and refreshing of "those who serve him," as well as for the reproof and instruction of "those who serve him not," to his own holy and blessed acceptance.

And it is only by patiently enduring the baptism of Christ and of his judgments, to the subjugation of the will of the flesh in themselves, that they can be good stewards of the manifold grace of God, and fully prepared to divide the word aright among his people, and clearly to discern between the precious and the vile, under whatever covering such states may exist, or under whatever appearance or professions men may make; these true messengers of Christ, will not be misled, by what men have been, or by what they now profess to be.

Wherefore, my dear fellow-pilgrims in this high calling of God, grudge not, I beseech you, the conflict, or the reproaches, of drinking deeply of the Saviour's bitter cup, nor the endurance of his fiery baptisms, (for his own received him not, but slew him, and denied him,) seeing that so great salvation is the result of suffering, and awaits the faithful and unflinching labors of those who are prepared by the ordeal of his power; and who have labored and have not fainted, and who have borne the burden through the heat of the day. And remember who it was, and from whence they came, whom John saw round about the throne of God, who had washed their robes and had made them white in the blood of the Lamb.

And oh! that all under our name of all classes, who name the name of Jesus, may never name Him unworthily or deceitfully, but, by departing from all iniquity, might honor him, having his fear always before their eyes, walking in all humility and lowliness before him, that so their example may do honor to the high and holy name of the Great Author of our salvation, and to the exalted profession we are making among men.

And how, above all things, is the Christian's experience in that power of God which overcomes the world, enlarged, by frequently and continually seeking and feeling after him with the whole heart, undivided and unreserved. Oh! fellow-probationer, forget not thy morning oblation, before thy head is raised from thy pillow, but approach the altar of his sacrifices in thine own heart, for thou mayest there witness in the silence of celestial excellence, the flame of his love and holy presence to kindle upon thy offering :- and then when thou goest by the way, He will also go along with thee, and when thou liest down he will keep thee, and as thy desires are unto him, he will bless thy evening sacrifices : and again, when thy slumbers are broken, in the silent watches of the night, then let not thy thoughts go astray upon things that perish, but keep and gather them inward, and stay them upon Him whose presence fills the universe ; and he will become to thee the chiefest among ten thousand. But when he delayeth to come unto thee, then fasting and mourning will be thy lot; and " great searching of heart," and fearful enquiry, why he has forsaken thee, and whether thou hast not sinned against him, and gone backward, and left thy first love! Oh! this is the way by which all the holy men of old, and our worthy predecessors gained the experience of the knowledge and way of the Lord ; and if thou would gain a heavenly treasure like theirs, and follow their footsteps, to a blessed establishment in the unchangeable truth, then be faithful and relax not from a daily exercise in seeking Him, and staying thy mind upon him ; girding up thy loins and watching for the morning, possessing thy soul in the patience of God ; confessing to him thy sins and short comings, and asking forgiveness through Him who is the Mediator of God's covenant for reconciliation with thee : and behold he will, when it please him, and in the right time, shorten and dispel the hour and power of darkness and distress, and cause the true light again to shine into thy soul and round about thee, and will again arise himself with power and great glory, as from the gloom of the sepulchre, and will cause thy soul to rise with him, with joy unspeakable and full of praise.

Thus described is some of the true Christian's experience, and the practical ground of his coming to the saving knowledge of God, through the revelation of Jesus Christ, and by the means of keeping a single eye to the light, and watching unto prayer without ceasing, whereby the mind is stayed and kept alive unto God, and preserved in the hour of temptation, and from being seduced and led away " by every wind of doctrine," as mere superficial professors are.

Hence, when this blessed experience is attained and abode in by a follower of Christ, his mind will not be beguiled with false doctrines or misled by designing men, though such doctrines be preached in the eloquence of the wisest, or even by an angel from heaven, because the witness is in himself, and this witness for God will evermore, as do the holy Scriptures, contradict and deny all false and delusive doctrine, because the disciple dwells with him who is light, and in whom there is no darkness at all. And therefore thus abiding in the light, no man can deceive him, nor yet the wicked one, hough he might assume the appearance of an angel of light.

But when men begin to hate the light, and to depart from it, because their deeds are become evil, then their vision is darkened, and they can scarcely distinguish between an ignus fatus, or the counterfeit radiance of the fallen angel, from the clear shining of the light of the Lord, and are therefore exposed to the imposition of false doctrines proffered to them in the wisdom of the serpent, by his deceitful working, and by his transformations are undistinguished by those "whose vision is not clear."

How lamentable the condition of those, viewing things as they do, with a clouded imagination, or through an inverted medium, and therefore are led to call light darkness, and darkness light; good, evil; and evil, good; just like the same sort of people in the prophet's time. Here we see the great powers of transformation in the hands of the wicked one. And never better pleased was he, as would appear, nor his kingdom better served in any age, than by his success in alluring and beguiling the servants of the Lord, to become and to be his servants; and the more eminent in their former station the more so in the latter, as fully demonstrated by events which have transpired.

And how deplorable the state of those who are transformed from the image of God to a condition of unrighteousness—from the love of God to the love of the world—from the fear of God to the fear of man, and the desire of pleasing God exchanged for a greater desire of pleasing men.

A condition in which man is ashamed acceptably to acknowledge the Redeemer before a man who shall die, and the son of man who shall perish.

Of those who regard men more than they regard Him, he will be ashamed before his Father and the holy angels, and will not therefore be a mediator between *them* and their God, whom they have despised, and have more lightly esteemed Him than they have esteemed men.

With such there must be a fearful looking for of judgment, and the righteous indignation of God's displeasure, because they have more lightly esteemed the favor of, and fear of God, than the persons and friendship of men, which is idolatry and great offence in His sight.

Our Lord and Saviour describes the contrast between the fear of man and the fear of God in a very striking manner, and gives forth His command to fear God rather than man, in despite of the utmost that man can do : " Fear not them that kill the body, and after that have no more that they can do ; but I will forewarn you, whom ye ought to fear—fear Him who after he hath killed, hath power to cast into hell," and emphatically adds, " Yea, I say unto you, fear Him." And this command stands unabated, and is as obligatory on us as on his followers in that day.

Although men now have not power, by the laws of the land, to kill the body, or to take men's lives on account of their fidelity to God, yet there are those who have power and disposition to persecute, and to take from us that which had been almost as dear as life itself to us—our places, our rights, and our privileges in the outward visible church. A process plainly distinguishable from the law of Christ, as will appear by a recurrence to the pattern of church government, as well as the doctrines received and acknowledged aforetime by the whole body, under the acknowledged guidance of the spirit of Christ.

Therefore, when those who teach us doctrines, and hold the rein of church government over us, shall have unhappily departed from that pattern, then fear them not, nor reverence them, for they will begin to deny the Master's coming, and to beat the men servants and the maid servants, and to lord it over the heritage of God.

Now, here is the difference, those who are ordained of the Holy Ghost to teach and to rule in his church, are both to be regarded and honored, so long as they rule in righteousness. But when their garments become defiled with enmity or the love of power, or the love of filthy lucre, or their eye become evil, then their hearts are become dark, and their hands full of oppression, and their arm but an arm of flesh. And he that continueth to transfer to them the honor which only belongeth unto God, or to trust in them, is accursed of the Lord, though *they* may shine as stars of great magnitude over the tabernacles of Esau; they are no longer to be called by the name of Jacob, nor surnamed by the name of Israel, so long as they disregard Israel's statutes and testimonies.

Hence we see the necessity of wisdom from above, and a clear discernment of the states and conditions of men, aside from prepossession, favor or friendship; aside from relationship and all *former* estimations, outward circumstances or outward appearances; and aside too from the estimation of others. When the condition of men is seen in the light, and their views, practices and motives are not answerable to the pattern as above, then let the loyal disciple of him in whom there is no shadow of turning, and who is to give account, and bear a faithful testimony against such in all meekness and lowliness, move in the fear of the Lord, and trust in his providence and power, and then he has nothing to fear from men, nor from a host of the mighty, for as he so continue and abide in the everlasting patience in the secret place of the Almighty, whose refuge will be round about him, and his banner over him; and for all the sufferings, revilings and evil reports which he shall have to endure, the reward from his blessed Master's hand will be an hundred fold in this present world, and that which is to come, everlasting life.

And the writer is induced to believe, through the opening of truth, that a remnant will be spared from the "flood of mighty waters overflowing," whilst "the beauty which is on the head of the fat valley shall be a fading flower, and as the hasty fruit before the summer, which when he that looketh upon it, seeth; while it is yet in his hand he eateth it up." "In that day shall the Lord of hosts be for a crown of glory, and for a diadem of beauty unto the residue of His people, and for a spirit of judgment to him that sitteth in judgment, and for strength to them that turn the battle to the gate, and many shall run to and fro, and the knowledge of the Lord shall be increased, and judgment shall run down as waters, and righteousness as a river—the wilderness shall become as Eden, and the desert as the garden of the Lord. Aliens shall be thy ploughmen, and strangers shall stand and feed the flock, and nations that knew not thee shall run unto thee because of the Lord thy God."

It has been seen by divers of the Lord's messengers in our Israel, both earlier and later, that a great declension and sifting time would take place among us, and that a remarkable reformation and better day would succeed.

The former we have already seen sorrowfully to have been progressing, in a departure from truth's testimonies and doctrines, by the insidious working of the enemy, drawing away from the true faith, both on the right hand and on the left. And is believed that the day is near, (if the Lord's purposes are not frustrated through fear or unfaithfulness in these who have been spared and called to begin the work,) when the foregoing declarations of the prophets will be verified and fulfilled in the succession of faithful messengers and standard bearers, and of a better day; and of the advancement and upholding of truth's dignified testimonies to the honor of God's great, and glorious, and holy name.

JOHN WILBUR.

Hopkinton, R. I., 1st month 16th, 1845.

APPENDIX,

CONTAINING A

COMPARISON OF SOME OF THE DOCTRINAL VIEWS

OF

J. J. GURNEY,

WITH THOSE OF SEVERAL STANDARD WRITERS AMONG
THE EARLY FRIENDS, AND SEVERAL TESTIMONIES
AND LETTERS RELATIVE

TO THE

DOCTRINES AND CONDITION

OF THE

SOCIETY OF FRIENDS.

"I am satisfied that there is a spirit at work, which would lay waste
the ancient profession and doctrines of our religious Society, and draw
Friends away from the spirituality of that which they have once
known. and many are catched with it."—(*Jonathan Evans' Memo-
rials of deceased Friends. Published* 1842. *page* 71.)

"I let him know that I did not consider it unfriendly, or contrary to
Discipline, to make a statement of the doctrines he published, as I considered it as a species of public property.—(*Joseph Whitall's Conversation with Elias Hicks. See Foster's Reports, p.* 215.)

APPENDIX, &c.

OF THE TRUE SOURCE OF ALL DIVINE KNOWLEDGE.

J. J. Gurney (Portable Evidences, p. 31) : "Now the information which the Bible gives, respecting the Supreme Being, whether considered as a harmonious whole, or viewed in its principal details, is to be found *originally* in the Bible *alone*."

(id. p. 35.) " It is the Bible, and the Bible *only*, which declares a standard of morals, universally applicable to our need, and liable to no change."

(p. 101.) " Now it is in the Scriptures only that the attributes of our Heavenly Father are *fully made known to us*."

(Address to the Mechanics of Manchester, p. 6.) " This delightful science [Geology] has done much to confirm the Scripture record, and to complete that *natural* proof of a Supreme intelligent Being, *on which all religion hinges*."

Contrast the above with

Robert Barclay (Apol. Prop. II. p. 17) : " Seeing no man knoweth the Father but the Son, and he to whom the Son revealeth Him ; and seeing the revelation of the Son is in and by the Spirit ; therefore the testimony of the Spirit is that alone by which the true knowledge of God hath been, is, and can be only revealed."

(p. 20.) " For the better understanding, then, of this proposition, we do distinguish betwixt the certain knowledge of God, and the uncertain; betwixt the *spiritual* knowledge and the *literal*; the saving heart knowledge, and the soaring head knowledge. The last, we confess, may be divers ways obtained; but the first, by no other way than the *inward immediate* manifestation and revelation of God's Spirit, shining in and upon the heart, enlightening and opening the understanding. None have any true ground to believe they have attained it, who have it not by this revelation of God's Spirit."

(p. 26.) " I would, however, not be understood, as if hereby I excluded those other means of knowledge from any use or service to man; it is far from me so to judge, as, concerning the Scriptures, in the next proposition will more plainly appear. The question is not, what may be profitable or helpful, but what is absolutely necessary. Many things may contribute to further a work, which yet are not the main thing that makes the work go on. The sum, then, of what is said, amounts to this : that where the true inward knowledge of God is, through the revelation of his Spirit, *there is all;* neither is there an absolute necessity of any other. But where the best, highest, and most profound knowledge is, *without this,* there is nothing, as to the obtaining the great end of salvation."

William Penn (Rise and Progress, p. 27): " I have already touched upon their fundamental principle, which is as the *corner stone* of their fabric; and indeed, to speak eminently and properly, their characteristic, or *main distinguishing* point or principle, viz : the light of Christ within, as God's gift for man's salvation. This, I say, is as the root of the goodly tree of doctrines that grew and branched out from it, which I shall now mention," &c. &c.

George Fox (Journal, Leeds edit. Vol. I. p. 92): "My desires after the Lord grew stronger, and zeal in the *pure* knowledge of God, and of Christ alone, without the help of any man, book or writing. For though I read the Scriptures that spoke of Christ and of God ;

yet *I knew him not, but by revelation*, as He who hath the key did open, and as the Father of Life drew me to his Son by his Spirit."

William Penn (Pref. to Prim. Christ. Revived): "By this short ensuing treatise, thou wilt perceive the subject of it, viz: the light of Christ in man, as the manifestation of God's love for man's happiness ; now, forasmuch as this is the peculiar testimony and characteristic of the people called Quakers ; their great fundamental in religion; that by which they have been *distinguished* from other professors of Christianity in their time, and to which they refer all people about faith, worship, and practice, both in their ministry and writings ; that as the fingers shoot out of the hand, and the branches from the body of the tree, so true religion, in all the parts and articles of it, *springs from this divine principle in man.*"

FAITH.

J. J. Gurney (Essays, p. 345. 6 Amer. edit.): " Were I the most solitary of hermits, or cast, like the shipwrecked mariner, on an uninhabited island, I could not live at all, did I not, in a multitude of instances, exercise the principle of faith. I must be led about by probabilities.

" But it is in social and civil life, more particularly, that the principle of *faith* is called into action, and every one who has reflected on the subject, must be well aware, that were it not for the willing admission of those things which are not philosophically certain, but only in various degrees probable, and more especially for a due reliance on *testimony*, the whole frame work of society would be disorganized and subverted. *Faith* is an indispensable link in that mighty chain of divine wisdom and providence, which binds together man to man, family to family, and nation to nation : and without it, there could be no order or union in the intellectual part of God's visible creation. Such being the state of the case, there can be nothing opposed to true reason and philosophy in the perfectly corresponding fact, that under the moral and spiritual government of God, and in order to that religious life which is alone productive of eternal happiness, men are required to bring *the same principle* into action, and to regulate their dispositions and conduct not merely by their knowledge of that which is certain, but more especially and more extensively by their belief of that which is probable."

(p. 353.) "Faith draws near unto that God whom *reason* has discovered," &c.—" but as long as *these* noble *faculties of the human mind* are kept," &c.

(p. 357.) " It is a *reliance* of the soul, on the *incarnate* Son, who conducts the great scheme appointed for our salvation."

(p. 359.) " Although this trust in God may, through grace, be exercised by persons who possess no other information on divine subjects, than that which they derive from *natural* religion, yet the declarations of Scripture respecting faith, have been, in all ages, addressed to that part of mankind, who have enjoyed the light of an *outward revelation.*"

(p. 360.) " This faith is the means through which we receive the Holy Spirit, by whom we are regenerated and sanctified. Lastly, a saving faith in Jesus is not merely intellectual, it *springs from* the *heart*, works by love, gradually accepts the Saviour in all his offices, and gently constrains the Christian to take up his daily cross and follow Christ."

(Address to Mechanics of Manchester, p. 7): " But you ask me on what moral and religious knowledge is founded? I answer, *on that which is the basis of every other branch of knowledge—belief.*"

Contrast the above with

Robert Barclay (Apol. Prop. II. pp. 33 & 34, American edit.) : " The fourth thing affirmed is, that these revelations [the immediate revelation of Christ by the Holy Spirit] were the objects of the saints' faith of old.

This will easily appear by the definition of *faith*, and considering what its object is ; for which we shall not dive into the curious and various notions of the school-men, but stay on the plain and positive words of the apostle Paul, who (Heb. xi.) describes it two ways : ' Faith (saith he) is the substance of things hoped for, the evidence of things not seen ;' which, as the apostle illustrateth it in the same chapter by many examples, is no other but a *firm* and certain belief of the mind, whereby it *resteth*, and in a sense possesseth the substance of some things hoped for, through its confidence in the promise of God; and thus the soul hath a *most firm evidence*, by its faith, of things not yet seen or come to pass. The object of this faith is the *promise, word,* or *testimony of God*, speaking *in the mind*. Hence it hath been generally affirmed, that the object of faith is *Deus loquens*, &c., that is, God speaking, &c., which is also manifest from all those examples deduced by the apostle throughout that whole chapter, whose faith was founded neither upon any outward testimony, nor upon the voice or writing of man, but upon the revelation of God's will manifest unto them and in them."

(p. 37.) " Moreover, if the *faith* of the ancients were not one and the same with ours, i. e. agreeing in *substance* therewith, and receiving the same definition, it had been impertinent for the apostle (Heb. xi.) to have illustrated the definition of our faith by the examples of that of the ancients, or to go about to move us by the example of Abraham, if Abraham's faith were different in nature from ours. Nor doth any difference arise hence, because they believed in Christ with respect to his appearance outwardly as future, and we as already appeared ; for neither did they then so believe in him to come, as not to feel him present with them, and witness him near; seeing the apostle saith, ' They all drank of that spiritual rock which followed them, which rock was Christ; nor do we so believe concerning his appearance past, as not also to feel and know him *present with us*, and to feed upon him, ' except Christ (saith the apostle) be in you, ye are reprobates ;' so that both our faith is one, terminating in one and the same thing"————

William Penn (Prim. Christ Rev. Chap. XI.) : " Yet we are very ready to declare to the whole world, that we cannot think men and women can be saved by their *belief* of the one [Christ's coming in the flesh] without the sense and experience of the other [His inward and spiritual appearance]."

George Fox (Journal, Leeds edit. Vol. II. p. 217) : " They whose faith doth not stand *in the power of God,* cannot exalt his kingdom that stands in power; therefore every one's faith must stand in the power of God. All that are in the *true faith,* that *stands in the power of God,* will judge them as carnal, and judge down that carnal part in them that cries up Paul or Apollos; that their faith may stand in the power of God, and that they may exalt Christ, the author of it. For every one's eye ought to be to Jesus ; and every just man and woman may live by their faith, which Jesus Christ is the author and finisher of. By this faith every man and woman may see God, who is invisible ; this faith gives the victory, and by it he hath access to God. So every one's faith and hope standing in the power of God, all therein have unity, victory, and access to God's throne of grace ; in which faith they please God. By this faith they are saved, by this faith they obtain the good report, and subdue all the mountains that have been betwixt them and God."

Isaac Penington (Works, Vol. I. p. 272) : " What then is that faith which is the gift of God ? It is that power of believing which springs out of the seed of eternal life ; and leaves the heart, not with notions of knowledge, but with the power of life. The other faith is drawn out of man's nature, by considerations which affect the natural part, and is kept alive by natural exercises of reading, hearing, praying, studying, meditating in that part ; but *this* springs out of a seed of life given, and grows up in the life of that seed, and feeds on nothing but the flesh and blood of Christ ; in which is the living virtue, and immortal nourishment of that which is immortal. This faith, at its first entrance, strikes that part dead in which the other faith did grow, and by its growth perfects that death, and raiseth up a life which is of another nature than ever entered into the heart of man to conceive."

(p. 274.) " The *true faith* (the faith of the gospel, the faith of the elect, the faith which saves the sinner from sin, and makes him more than a conqueror over sin and the powers of darkness) is a belief in the nature of God; which belief giveth entrance into, fixeth in, and causeth an abiding in that nature. Unbelief entereth into death, and fixeth in the death; faith giveth entrance into, and fixeth in the life. Faith is an ingrafting into the vine, a partaking of the nature of the vine, a sucking of the juice of life from the vine ; which nothing is able to do but the faith, but the belief in the nature. So then faith is not a believing the history of the Scriptures, or a believing that Christ died for sinners in general, or for me in particular; for all this may be done by the unbelieving nature (like the Jew); but a uniting to the nature of God in Christ, which the unbeliever starts from in the midst of his believing of these. Yet I do not deny that all these things are to be believed, *and* are believed *with* the true faith ; but this I affirm, that they also may be believed without the true faith ; and that such a belief of these doth not determine a man to be a believer in the sight of God, but only the union with the nature of that life from whence all these sprang, and in which alone they have their true value."

Jos. Phipps (Original and Present State of Man, p. 152) : " Gospel faith in man believes the truth of all that is revealed by the Spirit, both in the heart, and in the sacred writings; because it feels it, savors it, and is one with it. It not only assents to the scriptural accounts of the incarnation, and whole process of Christ in Judea ; but it also receives his internal appearance, consents to his operation, and concurs with it. That faith which stands wholly upon hearsay, tradition, reading, or imagination, is but a distant kind of ineffectual credence, which permits the soul to remain in the bondage of corruption. The wicked may go

this length towards gospel faith ; but the *true faith* lays
hold of, and cleaves to the Spirit of Truth, in its inward
manifestations ; wherein it stands, and whereby it
grows, till the heart is purified, the world overcome,
and salvation obtained. This faith is as a flame of pure
love in the heart to God. It presseth towards him,
panteth after him, resigns to him, confides and lives in
him. The mystery of it is held in a pure conscience,
and in the effective power of the everlasting gospel, &c.
&c. It is the faith by which the members of Christ
truly live, and abide as such. It is their invincible
shield ; and the knowledge of *Christ in them* is the proof
of their possessing it. Abundance is said of the nature,
power, and effects of this all-conquering faith ; but I
hope this will be sufficient to show, though, in its *complete* sense, it *includes* a belief of all that is said of Christ,
and by Christ, in Holy Writ, it goes deeper, and ariseth
not in man merely from the man, but takes its birth
and receives its increase from the operation of the Holy
Spirit in him; which works by it to the sanctification of
the heart, and the production of every Christian virtue."

UNIVERSAL AND SAVING LIGHT.

J. J. Gurney (Essays, American edit. p. 366) : " The
multitude of the Gentiles, who gave themselves up to
idolatrous and other vicious practices, were condemned
for this very reason, that they sinned against the *light
of nature*—and both practised and promoted iniquity,
although they knew the judgment of God, that they
which commit such things are worthy of death."—[In
a note at the bottom of the page] " I beg it may be
understood, that by *the light of nature*, I mean, simply,
the light which God *has communicated to the souls of men*,
independently of an outwardly revealed religion."

(p. 392.) " God has written his moral law on the
hearts of all men, or in other words, has *interwoven a
sense of it with their very nature.*"

(Portable Evidences, p. 23.) "Yet it must be allowed
that it is chiefly through revelation that we are thus led
to reason from creation and providence, and that *merely*

natural religion, even with the additional light of tradition, has left the heathen world in all ages, in a state of *great darkness* respecting the Supreme Being."

(p. 164:) " Their case is not to be confounded with that of the uninstructed *heathen*, who have never heard the truth. To these [viz. instructed persons] the gospel has been preached," [plainly implying that it has not to the others.]

Contrast the above with

George Fox (Journal, Vol. I. p. 112) : " I saw that Christ died for all men, and was a propitiation for all; and enlightened all men and women with his divine and saving light, and that none could be a true believer, but who believed in it. I saw that the grace of God, *which brings salvation*, had appeared to all men, and that the manifestation of the Spirit of God was given to every man to profit withal."

(p. 224:) " I declared to them, that *every one that cometh into the world,* was enlightened by Christ the life ; by which light they *might see their sins, and Christ*, who was come to save them from their sins, and died for them."

(p. 420.) " Now I was speaking of the heavenly, divine light of Christ, with which he enlightens every one that cometh into the world, to give them the knowledge of the glory of God in the face of Christ Jesus their Saviour."

Robert Barclay (Apol. Prop. V. & VI.) : " And this *light* enlighteneth the hearts of all for a time, in order to salvation ; and this is it which reproves the sin of all individuals, and *would work out the salvation of all*, if not resisted. Nor is it less universal than the seed of sin, being the purchase of his death, who tasted death for every man, &c. For as hence it well follows that some of the old philosophers might have been saved, so also may some, who by Providence are cast into those remote parts of the world where the knowledge of the history is wanting, be made partakers of the divine mystery, if they receive and resist not that grace, a manifestation whereof is given to every man to profit withal. This most certain doctrine being then received, that there is an *evangelical and saving light and grace in all*, the universality of the love and mercy of God towards mankind, both in the death of his beloved Son, the Lord Jesus Christ, and in the manifestation of the Light in the heart, is established and confirmed, against all the objections of such as deny it. Therefore, Christ hath tasted death for *every man*; not only for all kinds of men, as some vainly talk, but for every man of all kinds; the benefit of whose offering is not only extended to such who have the distinct outward knowledge of His death and sufferings as the same is declared in the Scriptures, but even unto those who are necessarily excluded from the benefit of this knowledge by some inevitable accident; which knowledge we willingly confess to be very profitable and comfortable, but not absolutely needful unto such from whom God himself hath withheld it; yet they may be made partakers of the mystery of His death, though ignorant of the history, if they suffer his seed and light, enlightening their hearts, to take place, *in which light, communion with the Father and the Son is enjoyed,*" &c.

THE " GOSPEL."

J. J. Gurney (Essay on Love to God. p. 5): " In effecting this blessed change, &c. the Holy Spirit makes use of the Gospel of our Lord Jesus Christ, as his grand, appointed instrument. *That Gospel written in the Holy Scriptures*, and preached by the Lord's messengers, is a spiritual weapon of heavenly mould; and when *wielded* by a divine hand, it penetrates the heart, and *becomes* 'the power of God unto salvation.'"

Contrast with

Robert Barclay (Apol. Prop. V. & VI. p. 168.): " Thirdly, this saving spiritual light is the Gospel, which the apostle saith expressly is preached *in every creature under heaven*; even that very Gospel whereof Paul was made a minister, Col. i. 23. For the Gospel is *not* a mere *declaration* of good things, being the *power of God unto salvation to all those that believe*, Rom. i. 16. Though the outward declaration of the Gospel be taken sometimes for the Gospel, yet it is but figuratively, and by a metonymy. For, to speak properly, the Gospel is this inward power and life which preacheth *glad tidings in the hearts of all men*, offering salvation unto them, and seeking to redeem them from their iniquities, and therefore it is said to be preached in every creature under heaven : whereas there are many thousands of men and women to whom the outward Gospel was never preached."

George Fox (Journal, Vol. I. p. 251) : "Waiting in the light, you will receive the power of God, which is the Gospel of peace ; that you may be shod with it, and know that in one another, which raiseth up the seed of God," &c.

(p. 401.) "For though ye have the four books, yet the *Gospel* is hid to you ; who are strangling at the work of God, and do not believe that Christ hath enlightened every one that cometh into the world."

(Vol. II. p. 25.) "In their reasoning, they said, 'the gospel was the four books of Matthew, Mark, Luke, and John,' and they called it *natural*. I told them, 'the Gospel was the power of God, which was preached before Matthew, Mark, Luke, and John, or any of them were printed or written ; and it was preached to every creature, (of which a great part might never see, nor hear of those four books) so that every creature was to obey the power of God ; for Christ, the spiritual man, would judge the world according to the Gospel, that is, according to his invisible power.'"

OF THE SCRIPTURES AND THE HOLY SPIRIT.

J. J. Gurney (Essay on Love to God, p. 5) : "In effecting this blessed change in the affections of fallen man, the Holy Spirit makes use of the *Gospel* of our

13

Lord Jesus Christ *as his grand appointed instrument. That Gospel, written in the Holy Scriptures,* and preached by the Lord's messengers,' &c.

(p. 39.) " The love of Christ is indeed an animating subject, full of joy and sublimity; and to dwell on its principal features, *under the guidance of Scripture,* must be regarded as one of our happiest privileges."

(Strictures on Truth Vindicated, p. 24): " The comparison which *some* of the early Friends were accustomed to institute between the Spirit as the primary rule, and the Scriptures as the secondary one, was *not intended,* as I conceive, to apply to the question of *authority,* but only to that of *order,* and *dignity.*"

(Essay on Love to God, p. 25.) " What a blessing, that his holiness is established beyond the possibility of a doubt, by that *intuitive* rule of right, which in characters more or less legible, he has condescended to write, by his Spirit, on the hearts of all men! It is in the Holy Scriptures, however, that the theology of nature is cleared and confirmed." " Let us, then, under the *guidance of prophets and apostles,* learn to contemplate God as our Father," &c.

(Essays, Amer. edit. p. 383) " In the fulfilment of the *written prophecy,* in the wisdom of the *written doctrine,* in the purity of the *written law,*—in the harmony of the contents of the Bible amidst almost endless variety,—and in its efficacy, as the *principal means* employed by Divine Providence for the *illumination, conversion,* and *spiritual* edification of man, the enquirer cannot fail to perceive unquestionable indications of the divine origin of Holy Writ." " Therefore, the person who searches for that which is *revealed* may safely direct his unhesitating attention to that which is written."

(Portable Evidences, p. 3. edit. 1832.) " But the moral and spiritual *force* of the Sacred Volume is that which chiefly serves to fasten its contents on the mind of every honest inquirer, whether more or less educated, and to produce a settled conviction of its divine origin.'

(p. 5.) " It [the Bible] is a text book for moral and religious teaching, *which knows no rival,* and to the use and application of which there appears no limit."—

" Whatsoever, in the preaching or writings of modern Christians, has *any tendency* to convert, purify, and save the souls of men, never fails to be found in its *original* form, in the Bible."

(p. 31.) " Now the information which the Bible gives, respecting the Supreme Being, whether considered as a harmonious whole, or viewed in its principal details, is to be found *originally* in the Bible *alone.*"

(p. 33.) " The moral law, as *revealed in Scripture*, partakes of the character of its author, &c. It applies to *all* circumstances, comprehends *all* conditions, regulates *all* motives, *directs and controls all overt-acts.*"

(p. 69.) " In the Bible all is simple, powerful, and practicable. While enough is hidden to humble us under a sense of our own ignorance, *enough* is revealed to direct our faith, and *regulate our conduct.*"

(p. 91.) " They [the Scriptures] unfold the law of God in *all its strength* and *spirituality* in *all* the glorious *variety* of its *details.*"

(p. 101.) " Now it is in the Scriptures only that the attributes of our Heavenly Father are fully made known to us. And therefore it is only through the religion of the Bible, that we can obtain an *adequate notion* of sin."

(p. 105.) " The Bible, which *alone fully reveals* the nature and character of sin, expressly declares," &c.

(p. 170.) " When we open the volume of Scripture, and propose that interpretation of its contents—*especially* of its more mysterious parts—which is demanded by the plain laws of criticism—laws which good sense has established, and which are familiar to every scholar—we again appeal to enlightened reason," &c. &c.

(Portable Evidences, p. 100.) " But it is only through the medium of revealed religion [meaning, obviously from the context, the Bible] that we obtain a proper conception of the nature of sin, or are enabled to form a right estimate of the moral condition of mankind."

(Address to Manchester Mechanics, p. 6.) " Moral and religious knowledge ! And where is this to be obtained ? Certainly we may furnish our minds with some considerable portions of it by reading the book of nature and providence ; but there is another book which must be regarded as its *depository*—a book in which *all things, moral* and *spiritual*, belonging to the welfare of man, are *fully* unfolded."—" I believe it is also true that the law of God is written, in characters *more or less legible*, on the hearts of all men. *But* for a *full* account of his glorious attributes—for the *knowledge of religion* in *all* its beauty, and strength, and completeness,—we must have recourse to the Bible—we *must meditate* on the written word. *There* the *whole* moral law is delineated with a pencil of heavenly light," &c. &c.

(Sketch of Wilberforce, p. 25.) " Dr. Doddridge's Rise and Progress, and Wilberforce's own Book on Christianity—whatsoever there is of a converting nature in these and such other works, is *originally* expressed *only* in the Bible "

Contrast the above with

Robert Barclay (Apol. Prop. III.): " Nevertheless, because they [the Holy Scriptures] are only a declaration of the Fountain, and *not* the *fountain* itself, therefore they are not to be esteemed the principal ground of all truth and knowledge, nor yet the adequate primary rule of faith and manners. Yet because they give a true and faithful testimony of the first foundation, they are and may be esteemed a secondary rule, subordinate to the spirit, from which they have all their excellency and certainty—for as by the inward testimony of the Spirit we do alone truly know them, so they testify, that the Spirit is that Guide by which the saints are led into all truth; therefore, according to the Scriptures, the *Spirit* is the first and principal leader."

(p. 74.) " The principal rule of Christians under the Gospel is not an outward letter, nor law outwardly written and delivered, but an inward spiritual law, *engraven in the heart, the law of the Spirit of Life, the word that is nigh in the heart and in the mouth.*" " That which is given to Christians for a rule and guide, must needs be so full, that it may clearly and distinctly guide and order them *in all things* and occurrences that may fall out. But in that there are numberless things, with regard to their circumstances, which particular Christians may be concerned in, for which there can be no particular rule had in the Scriptures ; therefore the Scriptures cannot be a rule to them"—" What Scripture-rule shall inform me, whether it be my duty to preach in this or that place, in France or England, Holland or Germany?" &c. " The general rules of the Scriptures, viz. to be diligent in my duty, &c. can give me no light in this thing."

" Through and by the clearness which that Spirit gives us it is, that we are only best rid of those difficulties that occur to us concerning the Scriptures." " The real and undoubted experience whereof, I myself have been a witness of," &c.

" If it be then asked me, whether I think hereby to render the Scriptures altogether uncertain, or useless— I answer, not at all. The proposition itself declares how much I esteem them ; and provided that to the Spirit from which they came, be but granted that place which the Scriptures themselves give it, I do freely concede to the Scriptures the second place, even whatsoever they say of themselves. It is to be observed, that it is only the spiritual man that can make a right use of them— as for the others, the apostle Peter plainly declares, that the unstable and unlearned wrest them to their own destruction : these were they that were unlearned in the divine and heavenly learning of the Spirit, *not in human and school literature.*"

(Quakerism Confirmed, Barclay's Works, Vol. III. p. 106.) " Now as to the second branch of their argument, that the Scriptures are a sufficient objective revelation of all things necessary to salvation ; *this we altogether deny,* as is said. For although the Scriptures are a full-enough declaration of all doctrines and principles, both essential and integral of Christian religion ; yet our souls need a more near and immediate discovery of God than the Scripture, which is but a report of him, that he may feed and nourish us by his divine manifestations."

(Apol. Prop. II. p. 66.) " As the description of the light of the sun, or of curious colors, to a blind man, who, though of the largest capacity, cannot so well understand it by the most acute and lively description, as a child can by seeing them ; so neither can the natural man, of the largest capacity, by the best words, *even*

Scripture words, so well understand the mysteries of God's kingdom, as the least and weakest child who tasteth them, by having them revealed *inwardly* and *objectively* by the Spirit."

George Fox (Journal, vol. I., p. 187.): "I directed them to the Divine light of Christ and his spirit in their hearts, which would let them see *all the evil thoughts, words, and actions*, that they had thought, spoken, and acted; by which *light* they might see their sin, and also their Saviour Christ Jesus, to save them from their sins. This I told them was the first step to peace, even to stand still in the *light* that *showed them their sins* and transgressions; by which they might come to see how they were in the fall of old Adam, in darkness and death, strangers to the convenant of promise, and without God in the world; and by the same *light* they might see Christ, that died for them, to be their Redeemer and Saviour, and their way to God."

Page 429, [nearly in the same terms.]

I. Penington (Works, vol. I., p. 20.): "In my heart and soul I honor the Scriptures, and long to read them throughout with the pure eye, and in the pure light of the living spirit of God: but the Lord preserve me from reading one line of them in my own will, or *interpreting any part of them according to my own understanding*, but only as I am guided, led, and enlightened by him, in the will and understanding which comes from him. And here all Scripture, every writing of God's spirit, which is from the breath of his life, is profitable to build up and perfect the man of God."

(Works, vol. I., p. 277.): "That eye that can read the Scriptures with the light of its own understanding; that can consider and debate, and take up senses and meanings of it, without the immediate life and power; that is the eye that may gather what it can from the letter, but shall never see into the life, nor taste of the true knowledge; for Christ, who alone opens and gives the knowledge, hides the pearl from that eye."

JUSTIFICATION.

J. J. Gurney (Essays, American edition, p. 357.): " From these premises it follows, that in the order of the grace of God, *justification precedes sanctification*, and that the faith in Jesus Christ, by which the ungodly are justified, has respect, in a very pre-eminent manner, to the atonement which he has made for the sins of the world."

(p. 358.) " While however the *justification* of the sinner, through faith in a crucified Redeemer, *precedes* the work of *sanctification*, its close and inseparable connexion with that work is evinced by the fact, that in the economy of God's spiritual government *this very faith* is the constituted *means, through which* we *obtain* the gift of the Holy Spirit."

Contrast the above with—

Richard Claridge (Works, as quoted, Friends, vol. XI., p. 231.) : " If we attend to the order of the apostle's testimony (1 Cor. vi : 2,) we *must* be washed and *sanctified, before* we can be *justified.* And if we come to witness the efficacious work of the spirit of Christ, in our cleansing and sanctification, we shall know ourselves to be in a state of justification and not till then. For though Christ be a propitiation for the sins of the whole world, yet no man can comfortably apply him as such to his own soul, but as he *first* experiences the *sanctifying* work of the spirit."

" The Antinomian insisted much upon the priority of justification to sanctification, alleging that men are first justified, and then sanctified. R. Claridge replied, that complete justification denoted a being made inwardly just, by putting an end to sin, finishing transgression, and bringing in Christ's everlasting righteousness ; and this being the work of the spirit in sanctification, *sanctification must* of *necessity* precede our justification."

R. Barclay (Apol. Prop. VII., p. 196.): " As many as resist not this *light*, but receive the same, it becomes

in them an holy, pure and spiritual birth, bringing forth
holiness, righteousness, purity, and all those other blessed fruits which are acceptable to God : by which holy
birth, to wit: *Jesus Chr·st formed* within us, and working his work in us, as we are sanctified, so are we
justified in the sight of God," &c.

(p. 217.) " Therefore, as none are said to be sanctified that are really unholy, while they are such ; so
neither can any be truly said to be *justified*, while they
actually remain unjust," &c.

(p. 223.) "Having thus sufficiently proved, that by
justification is to be understood a *really* being *made
righteous*, I do boldly affirm, and that not only from a
notional knowledge, but from a real, inward, experi-
mental feeling of the thing, that the immediate, near-
est, or *formal cause* (if we must in condescension to
some use this word) of a man's justification in the sight
of God, is, the *revelation of Jesus Christ in the soul*,
(*changing, altering* and *renewing the mind*, by whom
even the author of this inward work) thus formed and
revealed, we are truly justified and accepted in the
sight of God," &c.

(p. 225.) " That it is by this revelation of Jesus
Christ, and the new creation in us, that we are justified, doth evidently appear from that excellent saying
of the apostle," &c.   " According to his mercy he hath
saved us, by the washing of regeneration and renewing of the Holy Ghost," &c.   " Now, that whereby
we are saved, that we are also no doubt justified by;
which words are in this respect synonymous.   Here
the apostle clearly ascribes the *immediate* cause of justification to this inward work of *regeneration*, which is
Jesus Christ revealed in the soul, as being that which
formally states us in a capacity of being reconciled with
God," &c.

William Penn (Primitive Christianity Revived.—
Works, Vol. V., p. 310.) : " We *cannot believe* that
Christ's death and sufferings *so* satisfy God, or justify
men, as that they are *thereby* accepted of God : they
are, indeed, thereby put into a *state capable* of being
accepted of God, and, through the obedience of faith,
and sanctification of the spirit, are in a state of accept-

ance; for we can never think a man justified before God, while self-condemned," &c.

(p. 311.) "In short, justification consists of two parts, or hath a two-fold consideration, viz : justification from the guilt of sin and justification from the *power* and *pollution* of sin, and in *this* sense justification gives a man a full and clear acceptance before God; for want of *this latter* part it is, that so many souls, religiously inclined, are often under doubts, scruples, and despondencies, notwithstanding all that their teachers tell them of the extent and efficacy of the *first* part of justification. And it is too general an unhappiness among the professors of Christianity, that they are too apt to cloak their own active and passive disobedience with the active and passive *obedience* of Christ :—The first part of justification we do reverently and humbly acknowledge, is only for the sake of the death and sufferings of Christ : nothing *we* can do, though by the operation of the Holy Spirit, being able to cancel old debts, or wipe out old scores; it is the power and efficacy of that propitiatory offering, *upon faith and repentance*, that justifies us from the sins that are *past ;* and it is the power of Christ's spirit in our hearts, that purifies and makes us acceptable before God. For till the heart of man is purged from sin, God will never accept of it. He reproves, rebukes, and condemns those that entertain sin there, and therefore such cannot be said to be in a *justified* state; condemnation and justification being contraries ; so that they that hold themselves in a justified state by the active and passive obedience of Christ, while they are not actively and passively obedient to the *spirit* of Christ Jesus, are under a *strong* and dangerous delusion."

1. Penington (Works, Vol. I., p. 96.) : " Mark then, the justification or redemption is not by believing of a thing done without man (though that also is to be believed) but by *receiving* Him *into the heart.*"

13*

IMPUTATIVE RIGHTEOUSNESS.

J. J. Gurney (Portable Evidences, p. 58): "Yet surely it is because of his [Christ's] infinite worth and dignity in the glorious Godhead, that Christ becomes ' *our* righteousness,' and that his righteousness, *imputed* to believers, procures for them the reward of a happy immortality."

(p. 138.) "In himself indeed as a transgressor from his birth, he [man] is *vile* and *polluted*, but by the blood of Jesus sprinkled on his heart, his conscience *is* purged from every dead work; and having obtained an interest in the Saviour of men, he *wears a robe* of righteousness in which there is no spot."

(Essays, p. 390.) "Our *only claim* on the heavenly inheritance therefore consists in this; that God is pleased to *impute* to those who believe, the perfect righteousness of our Lord Jesus Christ."

Contrast the above with—

Robert Barclay (Truth Cleared, &c., Works, Vol. I, p. 177.): "Thy last argument from 2 Cor. v: 21, is most absurd and impious, for accordingly it would follow, that as Christ was made sin for us, or suffered for our sins, who himself had no sin, no not in the least, so we may be made righteous before God, though we have no righteousness, no holiness, no faith, no repentance, no mortification, no good thing wrought in us. And doth not this strengthen the wicked, ungodly and profane in their presumption, to have title to Christ's righteousness?" We find the apostle makes a far better inference from Christ, his dying for us, 2 Cor. vi: 15. 'He died for all, that they who live, might not any longer live to themselves, but to God;' yea, and every where he holdeth forth inward holiness and righteousness, as that without which no man can lay claim to Christ.' 'If any man be in Christ, he is a new creature;' but he doth not say, God reputes him a new creature, though he be not really renewed."

I. Penington (Works, Vol. I , p. 97.): "He whom God maketh righteous, was ungodly *before* He made him righteous. There was nothing but unrighteousness could be imputed to him in transgression, before He gave him His Son, and *made him righteous* in his Son; for nothing is righteous with God but Christ, and man only as he is taken into his righteousness; which is done not by a believing from the bare letter, but by a receiving of faith *in the life.*"

(p. 97.) "Faith is the gift of God, and this gift justifies; this is that which God imputeth for righteousness The faith is in the blood, and the blood in the Son; and in the *true receiving* of the Son, both the faith and the blood are known and felt. These are true words, though *hard to the fleshly ear.*"

THE SABBATH.

J. J. Gurney (on the Sabbath, p. X.): "In applying to the Christian's day of rest and worship, the name of *Sabbath,* I consider that I am fully justified both by the simple meaning of the word, &c."

(p. 1.) The *moral* and therefore permanent nature of that divine institution," &c. &c.

(p. 85.) "And the day on which Jesus rose from the dead, had been *hallowed* by the Lord himself," &c. &c.

(p. 85.) "The Lord of the Sabbath was again *honoring* the *day* which He had *chosen for himself.*"

(p. 102.) "On this hallowed day we are bound by a sacred obligation," &c. &c.

(p. 104.) "The whole man ought *then* to be presented, a living sacrifice unto God."

(p. 107.) "Although these assemblies [in the middle of the week] are the means of much edification, they are seldom found to serve the purpose of social worship and communion, in their full extent."

(Contribution to a Lady's Album, Norwich, 1827, p. 5): "No person of serious reflection would, I presume, object to those outward institutions—such as the *Sabbath day,* appointed hours and places of meeting,

&c. &c., which are *essential*, in the order of Providence, to the *congregational* worship of the Deity," &c &c.

Contrast the above with—

Robert Barclay (Apol. Prop. XI., p. 340): "We may not therefore think with the papists, that these days are *holy*, and lead people into a superstitious observation of them; being persuaded that *all* days are *alike holy* in the sight of God." "We not seeing any ground in Scripture for it, *cannot* be so *superstitious* as *to believe*, that either the Jewish Sabbath now continues, or that the *first day* of the week is the antitype thereof, or *the true Christian Sabbath*; which with Calvin we believe to have a more spiritual sense, and therefore we know *no moral obligation* by the fourth commandment, or elsewhere, to keep the first day of the week more than any other, or any holiness inherent in it. But first, forasmuch as it is necessary that there be some time set apart for the saints to meet together to wait upon God; and that secondly, it is fit that at some times they be freed from their other outward affairs; and that thirdly, reason and equity doth allow that servants and beasts have some time allowed them to be eased from their continued labor; and that fourthly, it appears that the apostles and primitive Christians did use the *first day* of *the week* for these purposes; we find ourselves sufficiently moved for these causes to do so also, without superstitiously straining the Scriptures for another reason, which, that it is not to be there found, many Protestants, yea, Calvin himself, upon the fourth command, hath abundantly evinced. And though we therefor meet, and abstain from working upon this day, yet doth that not hinder us from having meetings also for worship at other times."

(Truth Cleared, &c., Works, p. 204, Vol. I.): "And the Lord's people have frequent times, more than once a week, wherein, laying aside their outward affairs for a season, they may and do meet together to wait upon the Lord, and be quickened. refreshed, and instructed by Him, and worship Him in his spirit, and may be useful unto one another in exhortation, or admonition, or any other way, as the Lord shall furnish." "And it were said, if the Lord had only allowed but one day of seven unto this effect." "And our souls do oft bless the Lord, in allowing us many times of refreshment and strengthening, to the establishing and confirming us in his love and life, and disburdening our minds of earthly things much more frequently than in one day of seven," &c. &c.

George Fox (Journal, Vol. II., p. 188): "For we were redeemed out of days by Christ Jesus, and brought into the day which hath sprung from on high, and are come into him who is Lord of the Jewish Sabbath, and the substance of the Jews' signs."—See also Discipline of Philadelphia Yearly Meeting on this subject.

PRAYER.

J. J. Gurney, (Observations, p. 291, 7th edit.): "No one can, with any show of reason, deny that our Lord's precept respecting our entering into the closet—shutting the door—and praying to our Father, who seeth in secret, is to be understood *literally;* and therefore such a practice, as far as circumstances allow, is universally incumbent upon Christians. If we would grow in grace, and in the knowledge of our Lord Jesus Christ, it must be our frequent practice—especially at the commencement and end of each day—to retire into solitude, and there seek for ability to pour out our prayers to the Lord, with a diligent and fervent spirit. Nor ought we to forget, that we may be *assisted* in the performance of this Christian duty, by kneeling down in a deliberate and solemn manner, &c. (p. 292.) "To the occasional use of the prayer which our Lord condescended to recite, I cannot conceive that any reflecting Christian can for a moment object: *and I believe that our children ought to be accustomed to it from early life.*"

(On Love to God, p 77.) "With respect to our children, more particularly, it is surely our duty, by watchful instruction, and sometimes by uniting with them in their private religious exercises, *to train them*

in the habit of daily prayer—just as we see the parent
bird, by frequent example and experiment, teaching
and inducing her young ones to use the wings which
God has given them."

Contrast the above with

Robert Barclay, (Apol. Prop. XI. p. 364.) "We find
that Jesus Christ, the author of the Christian religion,
prescribes no set form of worship to his children.
Note. If any object here, *that the Lord's prayer is a
prescribed form of prayer, and therefore of worship given
by Christ to his children*, I answer, first, this cannot be
objected by any sort of Christians that I know, because
there are none who use not other prayers, or that limit
their worship to this. Secondly, this was commanded
to the disciples, while yet weak, before they had received the dispensation of the Gospel; not that they
should only use it in praying, but that He might show
them by one example, how that their prayers ought to
be short, and not like the long prayers of the Pharisees.
And that this was the use of it, appears by all their
prayers, which divers saints afterwards made use of,
whereof the Scripture makes mention; *for none made
use of this, neither repeated it, but used other words*, according as the thing required, and *as the spirit gave
utterance.* Thirdly, that this ought to be so understood,
appears from Rom. viii. 26, where the Apostle saith,
'We know not what we should pray for as we ought,
but the spirit itself maketh intercession for us,' &c.
But if this prayer had been such a prescribed form of
prayer to the church, that had not been true, neither
had they been ignorant what to pray, nor should they
have needed the help of the spirit to teach them." (p.
392.) "Our adversaries, whose *religion* is all for the
most part *outside*, and such whose acts are the mere
product of man's natural will and abilities, as they can
preach, so can they pray when they please, and therefore have their set particular prayers. I meddle not
with the controversies among themselves concerning
this, some of them being for *set prayers* as a *liturgy*,
others for such as are conceived *extempore:* it suffices

me that all of them agree in this,—that the motions
and influence of the spirit of God are not necessary to
be previous thereunto; and therefore, they have *set
times* in their public worship, as before and after preaching, and in their *private* devotion, as *morning and evening*, and before and after meat, and other such occasions, at which they precisely set about the performing
of their prayers, by speaking words to God, whether
they feel any motion or influence of the spirit or not;
so that some of the chiefest have confessed that they
have thus prayed without the motions or assistance of
the spirit, acknowledging that they sinned in so doing;
yet they said they looked upon it as their duty so to do,
though to pray without the spirit be sin.   We freely
confess that prayer is both very profitable, and a necessary duty commanded, and fit to be practised frequently by all Christians; but as we can do nothing without
Christ, so neither can we pray without the concurrence
and assistance of his Spirit.   But that the state of the
controversy may be the better understood, let it be
considered, first, that prayer is two-fold, *inward* and
outward.   Inward prayer is that secret turning of the
mind towards God, whereby, being secretly touched
and awakened by the light of Christ in the conscience,
and so bowed down under the sense of its iniquities,
unworthiness, and misery, it looks up to God, and joining with the secret shinings of the *seed of God*, it
breathes toward Him, and is constantly breathing forth
some secret desires and aspirations towards Him.   It
is in this sense that we are so frequently in Scripture
commanded to *pray continually*, which cannot be understood of outward prayer, because it were impossible
that men should be always upon their knees, expressing words of prayer; and this would hinder them from
the exercise of those duties no less positively commanded.   *Outward* prayer is, when as the spirit, being thus
in the exercise of inward retirement, and *feeling* the
breathing of the spirit of God to arise powerfully in
the soul, *receives strength and liberty* by a *superadded*
motion and influence to bring forth either audible sighs,
groans, or *words*, and that either in public assemblies, or in private, or at meat, &c.   As then *inward*

prayer is necessary *at all times*, so, so long as the day of every man's visitation lasteth, he never wants some influence, less or more, for the practice of it ; because he no sooner retires in his mind, and considers himself in God's presence, but he finds himself in the practice of it. The outward exercise of prayer, as needing a *greater* and *superadded* influence and motion of the Spirit, as it cannot be continually practised, so neither can it be so readily, so as to be effectually performed, until his mind be some time acquainted with the inward," &c. (p. 397.) " If any man know not how to pray, neither can do it without the help of the Spirit, then it is *to no purpose* for him, but altogether *unprofitable*, to pray without it."

I. Penington (Works, Vol I. p. 21) : " Mark, *all prayer and supplication* must be in the Spirit ; Yea, it must be *always* in the Spirit, which speaks in the heart to God, and makes the intercession, or it is no prayer. If a man speak ever so much from his own spirit, with ever so much earnestness and affection, yet it is no prayer, no true prayer, but only so far as the Spirit moves to it, and so far as the Spirit leads and guides in it."

ON WORSHIP.

J. J. Gurney (On the Sabbath. p. 105) : " In frequenting the solemn assemblies of the Lord's people, we ought to cultivate a joyful and thankful Spirit ; to *train* our minds to a *vivid perception* of the beauty of holiness ; and to *delight ourselves* in the worship of God. Let us ever remember that on these occasions we meet *for the purpose* of commemorating the glories of creation, the wisdom and goodness of providence, and the wonders of redeeming love."

(Sketch of Wilberforce, Norwich, p. 7. 1838.) " In the autumn of 1816, I well remember going over from the place of my own residence in the neighborhood of Norwich, partly for the purpose of seeing so great a man, and partly for that of persuading him to *join our party*, at the time of the approaching anniversaries of the Norfolk Bible and Church Missionary Societies."

Contrast the above with—

Robert Barclay (Apol. Prop. XI. p. 351, &c.): "We judge it the duty of all to be diligent in the assembling of themselves together—and when assembled, the great work of one and all ought to be to *wait upon God;* and returning *out of their own thoughts and imaginations,* to feel the Lord's presence, and know a *gathering into his name* indeed, where he is *in the midst,* according to his promise. And as every one is *thus* gathered, and so met together inwardly in their spirits, as well as outwardly in their persons, there the secret power and virtue of life is known to refresh the soul, and the pure motions and breathings of God's Spirit are felt to arise ; from which, as words of declaration, prayers or praises arise, the acceptable worship is known, which edifies the church, and is well pleasing to God. And no man here limits the Spirit of God ; but every one puts that forth which the Lord puts into their hearts : and it is uttered forth, *not in man's will and wisdom,* but in the evidence and demonstration of the Spirit, and of power. Yea, though there be not a word spoken. yet is the true spiritual worship performed, and the body of Christ edified ; yea, it may, and hath often fallen out among us, that divers meetings have passed without one word ; and yet our souls have been greatly edified and refreshed, and our hearts wonderfully overcome with the secret sense of God's power and spirit."

William Penn (Primitive Christianity Revived, chap. X.): " As the Lord wrought effectually, by his divine grace, in the hearts of this people, so he thereby brought them to a divine *worship* and ministry : Christ's words they came to experience, viz., that God was a Spirit, and that he would therefore be worshipped in the spirit, and in the truth, and that such worshippers the Father would seek to worship him ? For, bowing to the convictions of the Spirit in themselves, in their daily course of living, by which they were brought to eschew that which was made manifest to them to be evil, and to do that which was good, they, in their assembling together, sat down and waited for the preparation of

his Holy Spirit, both to let them see their own states
and conditions before the Lord, and to worship Him
acceptably; and as they were sensible of wants, or
shortness, or infirmities, so in the secret of their own
hearts, prayer would spring to God, through Jesus
Christ, to help, assist and supply: but they did not
dare to ' awaken their beloved before his time,' or approach the throne of the King of Glory, till he held
out his sceptre ; or. take thought what they should
say, or *after their own*, or *other men's* studied words and
forms ; for this were to offer strange fire, &c." So that
it is this people's principle, that fire must come from
heaven, life' and power from God, to enable the soul to
pour out itself acceptably before him. And when a
coal from His holy altar touches our lips, then can we
pray and praise Him as we ought to do."

I. Penington (Works Vol. II. p. 249.): " What is the
worship, or what are the sacrifices, which the true
worshippers offer up to God in this holy place ?—
Answer.—the gifts of His Spirit. . These they offer
up, and nothing else. The breathings which the
Father gives into the heart of the child, they are
breathed back unto Him in the same spirit of life ; in
the living sense, in the quickening power. Nothing
of man's wisdom, nothing of man's invention, nothing
according to man's will, nothing that would please the
flesh, or seem glorious in its eye, is offered up there ;
but the exhortations, or directions, or reproofs, that
spring up in God's light, in God's wisdom, they are
given forth in the leadings, and by the guidance of His
Spirit, and they reach to the hearts of those to whom
He pleased to direct them. And this is the ground of
such meetings, and breakings, and convictions of soul,
(and such like inward operations) as are frequently
found in such assemblies. For the living God is there,
and the dread of His power overspreads the hearts of
such as are gathered into and assembled in His name ;
and the life springs in the earthen vessels, and the
Saviour is precious to all that have their spiritual
senses."

RESURRECTION.

J. J. Gurney (Essays, p. 134) : " With respect to the impenitent wicked, their *lot during the separate state,* is described as one of pain or punishment, &c."

(p. 141.) " He [man] has within him a never dying spirit ; and *even that part of him* which is destined to moulder in the grave, shall in the end be found the *seed* of a *spiritual body,* and shall be *clothed* with incorruption and immortality."

(Portable Evidences, p. 151.) " As it relates to the faithful followers of Christ, *the resurrection of the body* clearly forms a part of the scheme of redemption. It is represented in Scripture as *the last step* to the fullness of their happiness, &c.

Contrast this with

George Fox (Doctrinal Works, p. 466) : " Is not this your condition, that make such a work about the body of Christ, and with what bodies people shall be raised up; and the Apostle saith to such: " Thou fool, that which thou sowest is not quickened except it die; and that which thou sowest, thou sowest *not that body that shall be.*" So he tells here plainly it is not the same, and calls thee a fool that questionest. If thou sowest wheat or other corn, let the husbandmen answer thee in this."

(p. 467.) " And the apostle further saith, ' Behold I show you a mystery ; we shall not all sleep, but we shall *be changed.*' Mark—*be changed. So not the same :* which the husbandman will teach thee."

(p. 946.) " And Christ saith, ' Verily I say unto you, except a corn of wheat fall into the ground and die, it abideth alone ; but if it die, it bringeth forth much fruit.' So, what the husbandman soweth, whether wheat or other seed, he soweth—mark—he soweth *not* that body that shall be ; but God giveth it a body as it pleaseth Him and to every seed its own body," &c.

Wm Penn (Testimony to the Truth of God, Works, Vol. 3, p. 523) : " Because from the authority of Holy Scripture, as well as right reason, we deny the resurrection of the same gross and corruptible body, and are neither over inquisitive nor critical about what bodies we shall have at the resurrection, leaving it to the Lord, to give us such bodies as he pleases, (and with that we are well pleased and satisfied, and wish all others were so too;) from hence we are made not only deniers of the resurrection of any body at all, however spiritual or glorified, but eternal rewards too."

(Defence of Gospel Truths, Works, Vol. 3, p. 549): "Here it is we are cautious, and tread softly, remembering what the apostle says to the curious and inquisitive upon this head. ' But some man will say, how are the dead raised up, and with what bodies do they come?

Thou fool, thou sowest not that body which shall be, but bare grain. But God giveth it a body as it hath pleased him, and to every seed its own body.' Here is the ground of our caution, which the bishop is pleased to call suppression, and others, denying of the resurrection. (We have indeed been negative to the gross conceit of people concerning the rising of this carnal body we carry about with us, which better agrees with the Koran of Mahomet, than the gospel of Christ: but that there is a resurrection of the just and unjust to rewards and punishment, we have ever believed." Bodies we shall have, *but not the same,* says the apostle, and so believes the Quaker."

THE ATONEMENT.

J. J. Gurney (Essay on Love to God, p. 40): "Behold the glorious partner of the Father's throne, freely opening his bosom to the *vials of His wrath,* groaning and bleeding on the cross," &c.

(p. 45.) "Let us call to mind, that in that hour of unutterable desertion, the *righteous vengeance* of God, against a guilty world, was poured forth upon the innocent substitute."

[How does this agree with the text, "God so *loved* the world, that he gave His only begotten Son," &c.?—Ed.]

ON THE FATHER, SON, AND HOLY SPIRIT.

J. J. Gurney (Essays, pp. 108, 109.): " The very pointed allusions made by our Saviour to the *personality* of the Holy Spirit are in exact accordance with the mode of expression which was often adopted, in relation to the same subject, by his inspired disciples. From various passages in the Book of Acts, and the Epistles, we can scarcely do otherwise than deduce the inference, that these servants of the Lord regarded the Holy Spirit as one possessing *personal* powers, and requiring a *personal* allegiance."

(Ibid. p. 110.) " Such is the scriptural evidence of which we are in possession, that the Father is God, that the Son is God, that the Holy Spirit is God. Having considered this evidence, we may now proceed to take a view of some additional passages in the New Testament, in which the Father, the Son, and the Holy Ghost, whose deity is thus *distinctively* and *separately* *indicated*, are presented to our attention as the united sources of the Christian's help and consolation, the united objects of the Christian's belief and obedience. This description is indeed applicable to the passages already cited from the Gospel of John, in relation to the *personality* of the Holy Ghost," &c.

(Essays, pp. 112, 113.) " In order to obtain a just and comprehensive view of the whole subject, (as far as it is revealed to us) it is necessary also to advert to the order of that relation in which they are ever represented as standing one towards another. The Father is the first; the Son is the second; the Holy Spirit is the third. The Son is subordinate to the Father, because he is of the Father—the only begotten Son of God. The Holy Spirit is subordinate to the Father and the Son, because he is the Father's and the Son's; see Matt. iii. 16, and Rom. viii. 9. The Father sends the Son. The Father and the Son send the Holy Spirit, John xv. 26."

(Ibid. p. 113.) " *The Holy Spirit* is the operative power, through whom the Father and the Son carry on the work of mercy, and exercise their dominion of the souls of men.   It is *He* who enlightens, converts, renews, consoles, and purifies the heirs of salvation. The Father is, in the deepest and most comprehensive sense of the expressions, the Creator—the Son, the Redeemer—the Holy Spirit, the Sanctifier.   The Father originates, the Son mediates, the Holy Sprit consummates."

(Essays, p. 393.): "On a careful perusal of the whole of that Sacred Volume, he [an honest inquirer after truth] is led to take a view, first, of the *natural* and moral attributes of the Supreme Being; secondly, of the *personality* and unity, *in Him*, of the Father, the Son, and the Spirit," &c.

(Portable Evidences, p. 74. Boston edit. 1833.) " When our Saviour was about to quit this lower world, he commanded his disciples to go and teach all nations, baptizing them into the name of the 'Father, and of the Son, and of the Holy Ghost;' from which expressions we learn that these servants of God were to baptize their converts into that faith, of which the Father, the Son, and the Spirit, are the inseparable objects. Now since it cannot for a moment be imagined that a mere attribute or influence could be presented to us, as a joint object of our faith with the Father and the Son, this passage *must be regarded as containing a clear evidence of the personality of the Spirit.*"

Compare the foregoing with

George Fox : " And it is the Spirit that beareth witness, because the Spirit is truth; for there are three that bear record in heaven, the Father, the Word, and the Holy Ghost, and these three are One; and there are three which bear record in earth, &c. 1 John v. 6, 7.   And now let none be offended, because we do not call them by those unscriptural names of Trinity, and *Three Persons,* which are not Scripture words."— See Evans' Exposition, pp. 2, 3.

Barclay (ibid. p. 5.): " Again, according to his [Brown's] custom, though I condemn the Socinians, he will be insinuating that I agree with him: to whose notions of the Spirit, albeit I assent not, yet I desire to know of him, in what Scripture he finds these words that the Spirit is a distinct person of the Trinity."

William Penn (ibid. p. 7.) : "But they are very tender of quitting scripture terms and phrases for schoolmen's, such as distinct and separate persons and subsistences, &c. are ; from whence people are apt to entertain gross ideas of the Father, Son, and Holy Ghost."

I. Penington (ibid. p. 10.).: "That there are 'three that bear record in heaven, the Father, the Word, and the Holy Spirit;' that these three are *distinct*, as *three several beings or Persons*; this they read not; but in the same place, they read 'they are one.'"

Francis Howgill (ibid. p. 12) : "First, concerning the Trinity, thou sayest, they confess the Father, Son, and Holy Ghost, and yet they deny the Trinity, and those to be three distinct persons ; for confutation of this, thou bringest Heb. i. 3—He is the express image of his Father's person."

" Thy Trinity is an old Popish term, and we love to keep to *sound words ;* but by Trinity, I suppose thou meanest three, and thy own words shall confute thee. Thou confessest we say, there is Father, Son, and Holy Ghost, and yet but *one God,* or one eternal being or substance, in which they all subsist ; but thy word *distinct* is thy own, and not the Spirit's ; yet to distinguish betwixt Father, Son, and Spirit, we deny not : and as for Heb. i. 3, it is in another translation rendered, the express image of his substance ; for *Person* is too gross a word to express an Eternal and Divine Being in ; and if thou dost hold three distinct substances, thou errest in thy judgment, for that were to make three Gods."

William Chandler, Alexander Pyott, Jos. Hodges, and others (ibid. p. 17.) : "We believe that great mystery, that they are three that bear record in heaven, the Father, Son, and Holy Ghost, and that these three are one being and substance "

R. Claridge (ibid. 2. 21.): "Therefore in this, and all other articles of faith and doctrines of religion, in common to be believed, in order to eternal salvation, let not the *opinions*, explications, or conceptions of men which are often dubious, various, or erroneous, be esteemed a rule or standard, but let every one rely on the divine testimony of the Holy Scriptures, which declare that God is one, and that there is none other besides Him; and that the One God is Father, Son, and Holy Spirit; or, as it is expressed, 1 John v. 7— 'The Father, the Word, and the Holy Ghost.'

"And as we distinguish between a Scripture Trinity, Father, Son, and Holy Ghost, which we unfeignedly believe; and that humanly devised Trinity of three *distinct*, and *separate persons*, which *we receive not*, because the Holy Scriptures make no mention of it."

Thus spoke our ancient Friends; and that the Society still continues to hold this doctrine may be inferred from the following extract, taken from Foster's Reports, Volume I. p. 292:

Cross-Examination of Thomas Evans.

Question. "If you hold that there is no contrariety of will in them, do you hold that they are, in any manner, distinct?"

Answer. "We have always *denied* that the Deity consisted of *distinct* and separate persons: and while we have believed that there were three, have as uniformly maintained that those three are One."

Counsel. "The question is not fully answered."

Witness. "If the Counsel will explain his meaning of the term *distinct*, as used in the question, I will endeavor to answer it further."

Counsel. "The question is, Do you hold that they *are in any manner distinct?*"

Witness. "I have already stated that the Society of Friends do not believe that there are *distinct and sepa-*

rate persons in the Godhead; and have answered him in Scripture terms as regards what the Society do believe," &c.

MORAL SENSE, ETC.

J. J. Gurney (Essays, p. 365.) " It will, I presume, be without difficulty allowed, that these observations are in a general, yet very important sense, applicable to all men, whether they are partakers in the benefit of an outward revelation, or are left to that which is usually *described as the light of nature.* If we admit that mankind, without an outward revelation, are nevertheless sinners, we must also admit that mankind, without such a revelation, are nevertheless in possession of the law of God; for we are expressly told by one apostle, that 'where no law is, there is no transgression;' (Rom. iv. 15.) and by another, that sin is the transgression of the law; (1 John iii. 4.) declarations which obviously correspond with the dictates of sound reason.

" The law to which I now allude, and which is universally bestowed upon men, is that *moral sense of right and wrong*, by which the natural conscience is directed and illuminated, and which, unless perverted by prejudice, or seared by the fatal operation of vice, it never fails to bear witness."*

J. J. Gurney (Strictures on " Truth Vindicated," p. 25.) : " To denominate our Lord Jesus Christ a Rule, as does this author in the last mentioned extract, involves the danger of a very fatal heresy; it obviously tends to divest him of his personality, and to convert him into a principle.

" In the mean time, the author of the Truth Vindicated, does not hesitate to insinuate that without any instruction whatsoever in Christianity, every creature

---

* " For my own part, I beg it may be understood, that ' by the light of nature,' I mean, simply, the light which God has communicated to the souls of men independently of on outwardly revealed religion."—NOTE, at p. 365 and 366.

under heaven may have the saving knowledge of the
' gospel of life and salvation through Jesus Christ.' "

(Essays, p. 361.) " Prone to iniquity, and *transgres-
sors from the womb*, we are alienated from God, who is
the source of all happiness ; and, in the world to come,
eternal separation from him, and, therefore, eternal
misery is the consequence of our evil doings."

(Portable Evidences, p. 165.) "In himself indeed, as
a *transgressor from his birth*, he is vile and polluted, but
by the blood of Jesus sprinked on his heart, his conscience is purged from every dead work ; and having
obtained an interest in the Saviour of men, he wears a
robe of righteousness in which there is no spot."

Robert Barclay (Apol. Prop. V. & VI. p. 177.) : "And
certainly hence it is, even because this light seed and
grace that appears in the heart of man is so little regarded, and so much overlooked, that so few know
Christ brought forth in them."

(p. 178.) " Some will have it to be *reason ;* some, a
natural conscience ; some, *certain reliques of God's image
that remained in* Adam. So that Christ, as He met
with opposition from all kinds of professors in his outward appearance, doth now also in the inward."

(ibid. p. 182.) " It [the saving grace] testifies that it
is no natural principle or light, but saith plainly, it
brings salvation."

(ibid. Prop. XI. p. 382.) " For we must cease to do
evil, ere we learn to do well ; and *this meddling in
things* spiritual *by man's own* natural understanding, is
one of the greatest and *most dangerous evils that man* is
incident to ; being that which occasioned our first parents' fall, to wit, a forwardness to desire to know
things, and a meddling with them, both without and
contrary to the Lord's command."

(ibid. Prop. IV. p. 95.) " Nevertheless, this *seed is
not imputed to infants*, until by transgression they
actually join themselves therewith ; for they are by nature the *children of wrath*, who walk according to the
power of the prince of the air, the spirit that now
worketh in the children of disobedience, having their

conversation in the lusts of the flesh, fulfilling the desires of the flesh and the mind.'

(ibid. p. 104.) " Than which testimonies there is nothing more positive ; since to infants there is no law, seeing as such they are utterly incapable of it ; the law cannot reach any but such as have in some measure less or more the exercise of their understanding, which infants have not."

Phipps (Original and Present State of Man, p. 32.) : " All the personal instructions and writings of the prophets, apostles, and their cotemporaries, taken in their full extent, have never been any thing near so universal amongst mankind as this grace and power of God; for it always hath been, and is present to every individual in all nations and throughout all generations."

THE ANOINTING—CHRIST IN MAN.

J. J. Gurney (Brief Remarks, p. 8.) : " For the same reason we cannot but object to the doctrine that Christ is the Anointing. Truly he is the Anointed of the Father, and the Anointer of his own people; but who on that account would think of identifying him with the Anointing? that is, with the enlightening, qualifying influence of the Holy Spirit?

" This peculiar notion is also occasionally applied amongst us, to a highly important passage in the Epistle of Paul to the Colossians, where he speaks of the ' mystery which hath been hid from ages and generations, but now is made manifest unto the saints,' to whom he adds, God would make known what is the riches of the glory of this mystery among the Gentiles, which is ' Christ in you the hope of glory,' Col. i. 26. The words ' Christ in you,' are often recited by mistake, as ' Christ within ;' and these expressions are sometimes used amongst us as a synonyme for the light of the Spirit of Christ in the heart—a view which some have imagined to be supported by the apostle's treating the whole subject as a ' mystery.' Hence it necessarily follows, that the light of the Spirit of Christ in the heart, is the same as Christ himself, and is represented as the hope of glory. The plain fact, however, appears to be, that the mystery of which the apostle is speaking, is that of the incarnation of the Son of God, a subject which had indeed been typically shadowed forth to the Jews, but had been totally concealed from the Gentiles ; kept secret since the world began, but was now made known to the saints, (1 Tim. iii. 16.) and without controversy great is the mystery of godliness. God was manifested in the flesh, justified in the Spirit, seen of angels, preached unto the Gentiles, believed on in the world, received up into glory. No sooner did the Gentiles, by a living faith, accept the Saviour, who was thus preached unto them ; no sooner did they receive him into their hearts, that he might rule there by his Spirit, than Christ was *in* them the hope of glory, Eph. iii. 17, ' that Christ may dwell in your hearts by faith ;' and 2 Cor. xiii, 5, ' Know ye not your ownselves, how that Jesus Christ is in you, except ye be reprobates ?' So also John vi. 56, ' He that eateth my flesh and drinketh my blood, dwelleth in me and I in him ;' John xvii. 26, ' That the love wherewith thou hast loved me, may be in them and I in them.'

" The true view of this subject, and in particular of the passage now cited from Colossians, is briefly but happily stated in the General Epistle from our last Yearly Meeting : 'As the Holy Spirit influences our hearts, and enlightens our understandings, we are brought to a lively apprehension of the character and offices of the Messiah, and Christ received by faith into the soul, and, ruling there by his Spirit, becomes our sure and only hope of glory.' Here then is a full testimony to vital, practical, inward religion, but no mysticism. These mistakes, especially John i, 9, and Col. i. 26—28, have often been made by persons who cordially accept the Lord Jesus Christ in all his gracious offices, both as God and man.

" Thus the errors themselves have naturally enough been suffered to pass with but little notice. But with some who have seceded from us in America, they have evidently *been the means of aiding* that tremendous process in heresy, by which the Eternal Word, or Son of God, is gradually converted into a mere influence, and finally becomes nothing at all but a seed sown in the hearts of all men."

Contrast the above with

Barclay ($_{A}$polog$_{Y}$, p. 52.): " The apostle proposeth this anointing in them, as a more certain touch-stone for them to discern and try seducers by, even than his own writings."

(pp. 138, 139.) *" But we understand a spiritual, hea-venly, and invisible principle, in which God, as Father, Son, and Spirit dwells*; a measure of which divine and glorious life is *in all men* as a *seed*, which of its own na-ture draws, invites, and inclines to God; and this, some call *vehiculum Dei*, or the *spiritual body of Christ, the flesh and blood of Christ, which came down from heaven,* of which all the saints do feed, and are thereby nour-ished unto eternal life.

" And as this seed is received in the heart, and suf-fered to bring forth its natural and proper effect, Christ comes to be formed and raised, of which the Scripture makes so much mention, calling it the *new man, Christ within, the hope of glory.* This is that Christ within, which we are heard so much to speak and declare of, every where preaching him up, and exhorting people to believe in the *light*, and obey it, that they may come to know *Christ in them*, to deliver them from all sin.

"But by this, as we do not at all intend to *equal our-selves* to that holy man, the *Lord Jesus* Christ, who was born of the Virgin *Mary*, in whom all the fullness of the Godhead dwelt bodily, so neither do we *destroy the reality of his present existence*, as some have falsely ca-lumniated us. For though we affirm that Christ dwells in us, yet not immediately, but mediately, as he is in that *seed*, which is *in us*; whereas he, to wit, the *Eter-nal Word*, which was with God, and was God, dwelt immediately in that holy man.

" *We understand not this seed, light, or grace, to be an accident, as most men ignorantly do, but a real spiritual substance*, which the soul of man is capable to feel and apprehend, from which that real, spiritual, inward birth in believers arises, called *the new creature, the new man in the heart.* This seems strange to carnal-minded men, because they are not acquainted with it: but we know it, and are sensible of it, by a true and certain experience.

(pp. 142, 143, 144.) "We have said before, how that a *divine, spiritual, and supernatural light is in all men;* how that *that divine, supernatural light or seed, is* vehiculum Dei; how that *God and Christ dwelleth in it, and is never separated from it;* also how that as it is received and closed within the heart, Christ comes to be formed and brought forth; but we are far from ever having said, that Christ is thus formed in all men, or in the wicked; for that is a great attainment, which the apostle travailed that it might be brought forth in the Galatians.

"But in regard *Christ is in all men* as in a *seed,* yea, and that he never is nor can be separate from that *holy, pure seed* and *light* which is *in all men;* therefore may it be said, in a larger sense, that he is *in all,* &c.

"And forasmuch as Christ is called that *light that enlightens every man, the light of the world,* therefore the *light* is taken for *Christ,* who truly is the fountain of *light,* and hath his habitation in it forever.

"Thus the *light of Christ* is sometimes called *Christ,* i. e. that in which Christ is, and from which he is never separated."

THE SEED.

J. J. Gurney (Brief Remarks, p. 10.): "That this parable (of the mustard seed) was intended to set forth the small beginnings of Christianity in the world, and its subsequent extension and victory, can scarcely be doubted by any sober commentator; and we may freely allow that it also bears an allusion to the growth in grace of the *individual* believer in Jesus;—but that the mustard seed is here equivalent to Christ himself in his inward appearance to the soul, is surely a notion, without the smallest foundation either in reason or Scripture. The seed which the sower went forth to sow, in another parable, as explained by our Lord as signifying the word of divine truth as it is *preached* and *heard.* It cannot therefore signify Christ, who in his character of a prophet, or preacher, is represented as the sower ; and equally obvious is it, that it cannot be identical (as some persons appear to imagine) with the light of the Spirit of Christ in the hearts of all men.

"The influence of the Holy Spirit, through which. the *believer* is born again, may probably be represented by the term ' seed.' In 1 Peter i. 2, 3, ' Being born again, not of corruptible *seed*, but of incorruptible, by the word of God which liveth and abideth forever ;' and this *grace* abiding in the *heart* of the *believer*, appears to be spoken of under the same term in 1 John iii. 9 : ' Whomsoever is born of God doth not commit sin, for his seed remaineth in him, and he cannot sin, because he is born of God.' "

Contrast with

George Fox (Sewell's History, Vol. II. p. 490. Philadelphia edit.) : " All is well, the seed of God reigns over all, and over death itself." " And though," continued he, " I am weak in body, yet the power of God is over all, and the Lord reigns over all disorderly spirits." " He used often, even in his preaching, when he spoke of Christ, to call Him the Seed; therefore, those that were with him very well knew what he meant when he spoke of the ' Seed.'

"Again, about four or five hours before his death, being asked how he did, he answered, ' Do not heed, the power of the Lord is above all sickness and death ; the Seed reigns, blessed be the Lord !' "

OF THE BODY AND BLOOD OF CHRIST.

J. J. Gurney (Brief Remarks, p. 13.) : After commenting at large on John vi. he says—"Hence it follows, that the bread which Christ gives us to eat is his flesh, which he offered upon the cross for the sins of the whole world. As eating the bread of life is identical with believing in Christ, the incarnate Son of God, so

eating his flesh is identical with such a belief in him as
is especially directed to his atoning sacrifice.

"Our Lord's meaning becomes yet more indisputa-
ble, when he pursues his use of this expressive figure,
and adds to the eating of his flesh, the drinking of his
blood : ' Verily, I say unto you, Except ye eat the flesh
of the Son of Man, and drink his blood, ye have no life
in you. He that eateth my flesh, and drinketh my
blood, dwelleth in me, and I in him,' ver. 53—56.
That the flesh and blood of Christ are here spoken of
in relation to his incarnation and atoning sacrifice, is
made abundantly clear by the comparison of all the
other passages in the New Testament, and especially
in the writings of this apostle, in which mention is made
of that flesh or of that blood.

These passages are numerous; and on a careful examination of them, it will be found that the *flesh*
always means his human body—that body which was
born, died, and rose again—and that his blood *always*
means his very blood, which was his natural life, and
which was naturally shed on the cross for the remission of sin."

Contrast with

Barclay (Apology, p. 446:) : " The *body* then of
Christ, which believers partake of, is *spiritual*, and not
carnal; and his *blood*, which they drink of, is *pure* and
heavenly, and not *human* or *elementary*, as *Augustine* also
affirms of the *body of Christ*, which is eaten, in his
Tractat. Psalm 98. *Except a man eat my flesh, he hath
not in him life eternal:* and he saith, *The words which I
speak unto you are Spirit and life;* understand spiritually
what I have spoken.

Ye shall not eat of this body which ye see, and drink
this blood which they shall spill, which crucify me—I
am the living bread, who have descended from heaven.
He calls himself the bread, who descended from heaven, exhorting that we might believe in him, &c.

If it be asked then, *What that body, what that* flesh
and blood is ?

I answer; It is that *heavenly seed*, that *divine, spirit-*

ual, celestial substance, of which we spake before in the *fifth* and *sixth propositions*. This is that *spiritual body of Christ*, whereby and through which he communicateth *life to men*, and *salvation to as many as believe in him*, and *receive him ;* and whereby also man comes to have fellowship and communion with God."

GURNEY-ISMS, ETC.

J. J. Gurney (Portable Evidences, pp. 109, 110.): " Furnished as we are by the Author of our being with a *moral principle*, it is impossible for us to conceive that God will reward and punish mankind in a future world, by any other than the *moral rule.* We should be utterly at a loss to account for the contrary, which would be directly opposed to that sense of *right and wrong, which He has so graciously interwoven with our very nature.*"

(Ibid. p. 123.) " All men have sinned against the law of God, as it is written on their hearts ; and those on whom the Scriptures are bestowed, have sinned against the same law as it is more largely unfolded in the sacred volume."

(Ibid. pp. 121, 122.) : " Now where but in the Sacred writings, shall we look for a full account of the holiness and comprehensiveness of the law of God ? Where, but in them, shall we learn the lesson of its variety and completeness ; of its spiritual and searching nature ; of its divine control, not only over our words and actions, but over our thoughts, motives, and dispositions ?"

(Note at bottom of page 20, of Strictures on " Truth Vindicated.") " Had R. Barclay lived to witness the result of the labors of many eminent biblical critics, during the last 150 years, he would have entertained a higher view than he appears to have done, of the substantial correctness of the text of the Old and New Testaments."

(Portable Evidence, p. 109.) " Now I conceive that in the agreement between the law written on the heart, and the law written in the book, and in the *extension* of the *latter* beyond the *natural* limits of the former, we

14*

have two cogent and distinct evidences, that the Scriptures are the book of God."

(Misinterpretations of Scripture as published in the Inquirer, Vol. I. No. 7, p. 195.) " The idea was at one time rather prevalent among the members of our Society, that when the Apostle used the term, ' a more sure word of prophecy,' he was alluding not to any word written, but to that Divine illuminating influence by which the prophets were inspired, and which guides the Christian believer 'into all truth.' Such a view of the passage is, indeed, *but seldom* insisted upon at the present day ; but as it is sometimes advanced, I think it *right to acknowledge my own sentiment*, that it is at variance with the simplicity which we ought always to maintain in the perusal and interpretation of the Sacred writings. That the ' very sure word of prophecy' was that which had been uttered and written, is evident from the immediate context, in which the Apostle distinguishes the word from the day star in the heart, and at the same time identifies it (as I conceive) with prophecy of the Scripture."

(Ibid. p. 198.) " The misinterpretation which I wish to notice is, that of several writers who appear to suppose that because Christ is called the light, (i e. the enlightener,) he is therefore to be identified with the influence which he bestows ; in short, that the light of the Spirit of God in the heart of man is itself actually Christ. The obvious tendency of this mistake is, to deprive the Saviour of his *personal* attributes, and to reduce Him to the rank of a principle."

(Ibid. p. 194.) " It is unquestionably our duty to exercise diligence and care, in order to obtain a right understanding of the sacred volume ; for this, like every other book, must *be interpreted in accordance with the known principles of language, and not without reference to innumerable facts and circumstances which throw light on its meaning*."

Contrast these sentiments with

Penington (Works, Part I. p. 8.) : " But poor man having lost the life, what should he do ? he can do no other, but cry up the letter, and make as good shift with it as he can, though his soul the meanwhile is starved, and lies in famine and death for want of the bread of life, and a wrong thing is fed."

Geo. Fox (Journal, Vol. 1. p. 32.) : " He [the Priest] took for his text these words of Peter, ' We have also a more sure word of prophecy, whereunto ye do well that ye take heed, as unto a light that shineth in a dark place, until the day dawn, and the day star arise in your hearts.' He told the people this was the Scriptures, by which they were to try all doctrines, religions, and opinions. Now the Lord's power was so mighty upon me, and so strong in me, that I could not hold ; but was made to cry out, ' Oh ! no ; it is not the Scriptures;' and told them it was the Holy Spirit, by which the holy men of God gave forth the Scriptures, whereby opinions, religions, and judgments were to be tried ; for it led into all truth, and so gave the knowledge of all truth. The Jews had the Scriptures, yet resisted the Holy Ghost, and rejected Christ, the bright morning star. They persecuted him and his Apostles, and took upon them to try their doctrines by the Scriptures, but erred in judgment, and did not try them right ; because they tried without the Holy Ghost."

Barclay (Apology, p. 147.) : " So we confess also, that conscience is an excellent thing, where it is rightly informed and enlightened : wherefore some of us have fitly compared it to the lantern, and the light of Christ to a candle ; a lantern is useful, when a clear candle burns and shines in it ; but otherwise is of no use. To the light of Christ then in the conscience, and not to man's *natural* conscience, it is that we continually commend men ; that, not this is it that we preach up, and direct people to, as a most certain guide into life eternal. Lastly, this light, seed, &c., appears to be no power or natural faculty of man's mind ; because a man that is in his health can, when he pleases, stir up, move, and exercise the faculties of his soul ; he is absolute master of them ; and except there be some natural cause or impediment in the way, he can use them at his pleasure ; but this *light and seed of God in man,* he cannot move and stir up when he pleaseth ; but it moves, blows, and strives with man, as the Lord seeth meet."

Geo. Fox (Journal, Vol. I. p. 111.): " I was sent to turn people from darkness to the light, that they might receive Christ Jesus ; for to as many as should receive him in his light, I saw he would give power to become the sons of God ; which I had obtained by receiving Christ. I was to direct people to the Spirit, that gave forth the Scriptures, by which they might be led up to all truth, and up to Christ and God, as those had been who gave them forth. I was to turn them to the grace of God, and to the truth in the heart, which came by Jesus ; that by this grace they might be taught, which would bring them salvation, that their hearts might be established by it, their words might be seasoned, and all might come to know their salvation nigh. I saw that Christ died for all men, was a propitiation for all, and enlightened all men and women with his divine and saving light ; and that none could be true believers, but those that believed therein. I saw that the grace of God, which brings salvation, had appeared to all men, and that the manifestation of the Spirit of God was given to every man, to profit withal. These things I did not see by the help of man, nor by the letter ; though they are written in the letter ; but I saw them in the light of the Lord Jesus Christ, and by his *immediate spirit* and *power,* as did the holy men of God by whom the Holy *Scriptures were written.*"

(Ibid. p. 212.) " Another time, this priest came to a meeting, and fell to jangling. First, he said, ' The Scriptures were the word of God.' I told him, they were the *words of God,* but not Christ, the word ; and bid him prove by Scripture what he said."

J. J. Gurney (Brief Remarks, p. 15.): " And as it is appointed unto men once to die ; but after this the judgment : so Christ was once offered to bear the sins of many ; and unto them who look for him shall he appear the second time without sin unto salvation.

Heb. ix : 27, 28. It is generally allowed and I think it is very obvious that the second appearing of Christ, here mentioned is nothing more nor less than his future coming in glory, to judge the quick and dead."

Discipline of New England, (Yearly Meeting, p. 74.): " And to his spiritual appearance in the heart, for ' unto them that look for Him shall He appear the second time, without sin, unto salvation.'"

J. J. Gurney. " Were I required to define Quakerism, I would not describe it as the system so elaborately wrought out by a Barclay, or as the doctrine and maxims of a Penn, or as the deep and refined views of a Penington ; for all these authors have their defects as well as their excellencies ; I should call it the religion of the New Testament of our Lord and Saviour Jesus Christ, without dimunition, without addition, and without compromise."

See concluding paragraph of his misinterpretation of Scripture.

J. Penington says, " Now mark, see if this be not a clear thing, He that giveth any other meaning of any Scripture, than what is the true, proper meaning thereof, he both addeth and diminisheth ; he takes away the true sense, he addeth a sense that is not true. The Spirit of the Lord is the true expositor of Scripture, he never addeth nor diminisheth : but man (being without the Spirit) doth but guess, doth but imagine, doth but study or invent a meaning, and so he is ever adding or diminishing."

―――――

NOTE.—The Publisher of this Narrative, is indebted to a much esteemed Friend for most of the foregoing extracts.

LETTERS, &c.

In the following letters a very few verbal alterations and transpositions have been made, not only
for a grammatical improvement, but to make a few
sentences more explicit to the understanding of the
reader. Yet these are substantially literal copies of
the original letters, and on a comparison will be
found, entirely, to coincide with the *sense* of the
original:

LETTER I.

To —— ——.

My Dear Friends :—Notwithstanding the lively
continuation of that interest which I have truly for
a long time felt for you and your prosperity in
things of an eternal moment ; and although I have
been aware of some discrepancy of views for most
of the year past between you and myself, and a
great grief has it been to me, because considerations
of great importance are involved therein : yet I have
never until very recently, felt even a liberty to address you on the subject. But now the way for
such service seems to open pretty clearly ; so much
so that you have of late been almost continually
present to the view of my mind, with interesting
and living desires for your as for my own preserva-

tion in the truth. And however little is the qualification of which I am possessed for such an attempt, yet as I am now convinced that a conformity to this attraction to duty, if attended to in simplicity and meekness, will bring peace, I no longer withhold.

I need not tell you how clearly the Apostle Paul made a unity of faith and doctrine the test of fellowship, nor of how beautifully he describes the agreement and fitness of the members of the body one with another so that it might be one perfect harmonious whole. Nor how the Gospel, or standard of Truth's doctrines are to be the believer's only rallying point, to the exclusion of all other doctrines, although such other may be promulgated by the greatest of men, or even by an angel from heaven; as in Galatians 1—8, "But though *we*, or an angel from heaven, preach any other Gospel unto you than that which we have [already] preached unto you, let him be accursed."

And so decided and earnest in this avowal, was the Apostle, that he confirms it by a reiteration of the same in the very next verse; and then adds, "for do I now persuade men, or God? or do I seek to please men? for if I yet pleased men, I should not be the servant of Christ."

Can any work or device of men, however imitative or skillful in the display of goodness and wisdom, ever make amends for a defection in faith and doctrine, orreconcile unto Christ? See Mat. 7—22. "Many will say to me in that day, Lord! Lord! have we not prophecied in thy name? and in thy name have cast out devils; and in thy name done many wonderful works?" Nor does he go about to deny their having done those works: no, but he says, "then will I profess unto them, I never knew you!"

The one thing needful was wanting, the knowledge of Christ; a knowledge which gathers and unites his whole household into one, in heart and mind, doing and believing as one man doeth and believeth.

But to come more directly to the subject of this letter, I will confess unto you, that I still feel much uneasiness in relation to many of the doctrinal views of J. J. Gurney, the Friend who is here from England in the capacity of a minister ; and of which uneasiness I informed him at the time of our last Yearly Meeting. And so far from attempting an explanation, for mine and others' satisfaction, he entered promptly into a summary defence and justification of the same ; and attempted sheltering himself under his certificate from London, and plead that we have no right to call in question any thing which he had written previous to that time, a point in which we found ourselves [at issue ; unless, indeed, he had condemned his defective writings which are among *us*, here as well as there, before the certificate was granted; for his wrongs to the Society were here as well as there, and cannot be amended without a condemnation made as public as the writings themselves.

I could not dispute his idea, that Friends in London had sanctioned his doctrines by granting him a certificate of unity. But that other Yearly Meetings which are not subordinate but independent bodies, should be bound by such an inadvertent cover of defective doctrines by them, is an assumption altogether in my apprehension absurd.

The great question with us is, whether he has ever condemned and made satisfaction to Friends for those doctrines, agreeable to the usages of our Christian Discipline, or whether they yet remain to be his own. This question was fully decided by himself during the interview which I had with him. He said that his " writings contained no doctrines but such as were sound and conformable to Quakerism !" Hence we are bound by his own veracity to believe that every thing to be found in his books is yet a true transcript of his own sentiments. But have we a right thus plainly to handle the character and doctrines of a travelling minister well recommended—a man so pleasing and interesting as well as religious? No! unless he has put *himself* in competition with the Society ;—with our principles and testimonies.

If he have volunteered, and made public his name and sentiments, they are ours, [public property,] and there is no delicacy or impropriety in thus informing one another, and of developing to one another, the character of them, and the danger which thereby awaits the Society and its distinguishing doctrines.

If such right were taken from us, then the safety, if not the existence of this Society must soon be at an end !

No individual has a right to claim the sparing of his character, at the expense of the whole Society and its doctrines, or to the dishonor or displeasure of Him who dispensed these doctrines to this people. For indeed, my dear friends, I account it no small thing for an individual to arraign the whole company of our early and deeply experienced Friends in matters of faith and doctrine, and thus to reprobate their principles. But you will probably be surprised at such allusions as these, unless you have read his works ;—if you have, attentively, I know your knowledge of our principles, and that your intelligence is such, that you will perceive there is no breach of charity in these remarks, being equally concerned with myself, as I trust you are, that the pure Christian doctrines of our early Friends may be kept and remain inviolate and without abatement.

We know that every one of those noted individuals who have in our time attempted an innovation upon our principles, claimed for themselves, and their friends claimed for them, the application and protection of our excellent discipline, relative to love and unity, and detraction ; and no great honor to them either, to lay their unhallowed hands upon those Christian provisions, and to apply them to an unhallowed purpose, to lay a suspicion of their designs and to obviate detection. Some of them also when abroad with certificates, and friends expressed dissatisfaction with their doctrines, claimed the protection of their credentials, and appealed to the authority of their friends at home !

[But whether you have been conversant with the writings alluded to or not, I will extract a few out of the many exceptionable passages, and present for your view and consideration; and if there should be any doubts in your minds relative to any one of them, you will please compare them with Fox, Barclay and Penn : for however *he* may deny the testimonies of these, I am assured that you will not. [Here followed the extracts. The reader is referred to those contained in the following letter, which are substantially the same.

The copy of the preceding letter in my hands is without date, but is believed to have been written in the 4th month of 1839, and signed by

JOHN WILBUR.

LETTER II.

HOPKINTON, 10th of 11th mo., 1838.
My Dear Friend, —— ——— :
Within these few days a little inclination has sprung up in my mind, to suggest a few considerations to thee, relative to the important question which transpired during our Yearly Meeting ; and

as much time has elapsed for deliberation thereon, I feel that I can address thee with the more freedom. And if I understand the question it was this :— " *Whether a Certificate granted to a travelling minister, from a body of Friends to which we are not subordinate, is an entire foreclosure of a recognizance of doctrines fundamentally incorrect, and known to exist in the sentiments of the bearer of such credentials ?* Or, in other words, *whether it be requisite, that whatever one Yearly Meeting adopts, all others are bound to receive and approve ?* A rule or principle, my dear friend, if this question is determined in the affirmative, which will amount to the assumption, that if one of those independent bodies should unhappily become apostate in principle, (a calamity which has been known to befal the best of bodies,) then are all of those bodies unavoidably rendered obnoxious to the same apostacy.* Hence, if an alliance, or correspondence, one with another unavoidably subjects Yearly Meetings to such consequences, were it not better that such alliance should not exist? But inasmuch as I esteem the proposition incorrect, I would not suspend an intercourse between Yearly Meetings ; but that each should know its own standing and abide on the sure foundation, by a constant recurrence to the pattern of first principles, independent of each other's fidelity or misgivings ;—and then a mutual intercourse under the Divine superintendency, will tend to the strengthening and edifying of one another not to the perversion, but to the confirmation of sound principles as they are in Christ Jesus our Ho-

---

* If such certificate protects the bearer, forecloses all enquiry, and adopts his doctrine at home, (as by himself claimed,) then his returning certificates, if such be granted from all the Yearly Meetings, by the same rule must protect him from all impeachment, and establish his doctrines throughout the whole Society!

ly Head. And there is another case besides that
of apostacy from original Quakerism, possible to occur, which might serve as an obstruction to the
service of a minister from abroad with a good certificate, namely—should he be found chargeable
with mal-conduct which transpired previous to his
liberation, but unknown to the body which liberated
him, and afterwards coming to the knowledge of
Friends where he goes. These supposed cases are
adduced upon general principles, simply to show
that incidents may occur, in which full credence
might be necessarily withholden from a minister
producing a full certificate. Furthermore, a third
case may occur and be plainly tangible, independent of the authority which liberated a minister,
namely, when he is found to be fundamentally defective in principle at any time during his visit
abroad ; and in which case neither the credibility
of the meeting recommending, or its certificate, can
be rightfully brought forward in defence of the
person or his principles ; whether known or unknown to the liberating body, belongs not to the
enquiry, but whether he actually hold such principles.

Nevertheless, such person ought to be aware that
his claiming the sanction of his own Yearly Meeting, reflects no honor upon that body. The truth
itself is to be the test and standard of such decision ;
and his doctrine must be compared with the doctrines of Christianity as found recorded in the Holy
Scriptures, and with which those of our Society,
from the first are believed to be in full accordance :
and whosoever departs from that belief departs
from Quakerism, however good he may suppose his
claim to Christianity. And if the fact of his defection
is clearly known and understood, whether through
the medium of his own written and recorded declarations, or by his oral testimonies delivered in public or private, his liability, and the course to be

taken by his friends, and the conclusions to be drawn *are the same—undeniably the same.*

But the Society of Friends in this country has always placed a stronger guard upon the Press, than upon the Gallery ; because recorded and published defections are generally productive of the greater evil, for the reason that such are the more tangible, and reduced to a more permanent form than those put forth orally. A conclusion evinced by the order of Society in prohibiting an author from printing his doctrinal views without an official approval first obtained ;—a restraint not laid upon oral testimony.

And now, my beloved Friend, I will come more directly to the very important case in question; but before proceeding to identify and enumerate some of the impediments which are deemed to lie in the way of the conspicuous stranger now in our land, I will speak a word or two of the rights of every member of the compact, if not his duty to guard against all unrighteousness—to ask for an explanation of any avowals or doctrines which he does not comprehend, or understand to be in accordance with Christianity, (by whomsoever, or in what manner soever advanced) and to expect reasonable satisfaction to be made ; and on a *refusal* thereof, to bear his testimony honestly against it, for the clearing of his own mind. and that he may not be a partaker with such, of their deeds.

And if I mistake not, it will be made plainly to appear that the person alluded to, has volunteered in the profession of doctrines, obviously at variance with the acknowledged and established tenets of the Society ; and thereby placed himself at issue with every sound member of the body in matters of faith and practice ; and until he retract the same, has never a right to complain of a prompt defence of our principles, though it could only be done at the expense of his religious character ; and better so than omitted at the expense of the whole body, and of the testimonies of truth, agreeably to the Scripture, that it is better for one member to suffer, than that the whole body should suffer.

If it were so that a member of our Society, under any circumstances whatever in which he might be placed, being unsound, cannot be approached, or impeached, or asked to explain, and to make satisfaction for things which give uneasiness, then the Society must be in great jeopardy ! If any man among us has an exclusive privilege of writing and preaching such doctrines as he listeth, and the least of the flock not allowed to be satisfied, then it would seem, that the safety of the Society, if not of its existence, as a Quaker fraternity, is in a perilous condition.   Are we not informed by the published account, that one of the notable witnesses on the trial with the Hicksites in New Jersey, was asked the question, whether any Friend was considered to have a right to call on a minister travelling with a certificate, for an explanation of his avowals, or to call them in question ? To which I think the answer was, *that any member, or even a child, was always considered to have such a right.*   But Judge Ewing suggested the idea that the writings of Elias Hicks were better evidence against him than oral declaration.

I will now adduce a few articles from his (Joseph John Gurney's) own doctrines and confessions of faith ; and if called for, the works, and pages, and discourses will be produced and pointed out. They are as followeth :

1st. That there is no correct divinity but that which is borrowed from the Bible.

2d. That the spirit is a person.

3d. That he believes in the resurrection of *the* body.

4th. That it is only by the Scriptures that we obtain a proper conception of the nature of sin.

5th. Justification by faith, and that faith independent of the Spirit, which regenerates the heart: and of obedience.

6th. He believes in delivering public discourses [or lectures] on Christianity, distinct from preaching.

7th. He believes in a form for prayer.

And in his last book called " Brief Remarks on an impartial interpretation of Scripture ;" he interprets the following highly important passages of Scripture in a manner contradictory and perversive of Robert Barclay's interpretation of the same passages, briefly noticed as follows:

1st. The Bible, the ' more sure word of prophecy.'

2d. He believes ' the Gospel of Christ [not] to be the Power of God unto salvation to every one which believeth,' but only an outward declaration, or record of that which is the Power of God.

3d. ' That was the true light which lighteth every man that cometh into the world.' From the tenor of his comments on this passage, his opinion appears to be, that Christ himself is not the Light which lighteth the heart, or inner man, but outwardly the ' enlightener.' He controverts the belief that He is himself the true Light which shines in man, and affirms that ' the obvious tendency of such an opinion, would be to deprive the Saviour of his personal attributes, and to reduce him to the rank of a principle,' a consequence often attempted, substantially, to be pressed upon our first Friends by their enemies, and as often refuted. Such objections to this our distinguished and evangelical doctrine, seems an attempted limitation, and attack upon Christ's character without knowledge ; and upon this blessed and essential manifestation and office of our Lord Jesus Christ. And whilst he professes to be guarding his personal attributes, his reasoning goes to deprive him of an attribute divine, and us of its indispensable benefit, even that of the immediate revelation of light and knowledge, whereby all his attributes, together with his Holy Will, are the better understood. The material sun, (made by the skill of attributes,) by pouring forth his animating beam upon the bosom of this world ever since its creation, has never yet deprived itself of its own image, or essential properties, or that portion of light and heat so essential to vegetation, sent forth from him the fountain of it; nor reduced itself 'to the rank of a principle.' And shall we say *less* of Him who made it such?

4th. He thinks that the seed, the parable of the mustard-seed, and the seed of the sower, relate only to the outward increase of the church, or of Christ's outward descent, and thus disagrees with Barclay, namely—that the seed alludes to a measure of light, grace, spirit or seed of the kingdom, word of God, &c.

5th. He argues that the *Name* of Father, Son and Spirit, do not allude to the *Power*.

6th. He believes that the partaking of the Lord's Supper is not a 'Communion of the Holy Ghost,' nor yet 'a participation of the Divine nature through faith,' as set forth by Friends in England,* but a participation of his material Body and Blood by faith.

7th. Is an attempt to divide Christ from his own Light, revelation, spirit and power, namely, that it is only Christ personally on which the Church is built.

8th. Is a continued hostility to the spiritual appearing and kingdom of Christ, with and in the hearts of his people, and says that ' His second appearance without sin unto salvation, *to them who look for Him*,' as declared by the Apostle, ' is no-

---

* About half a century ago.

thing more nor less than his future coming in glory to judge the quick and dead.'

These eight interpretations and their introductory and accompanying remarks constitute the whole tract, the object and purport whereof, cannot be easily misunderstood; admired and applauded by the Beaconites, and to all who receive and adopt these sentiments, they will have a direct tendency to lead them from the inner to the outer court of the Lord's house—from the spirit, life and power of that religion which is immediately revealed by Jesus Christ, in the soul and mind of man, to a more outward and literal religion, consisting of head, knowledge and notions, conceived in the wisdom of man, and understood by a carnal construction of the sacred volume—which is here exhibited through a brilliant display of learning, to the outdoing of all the former translators of the Holy Scriptures; and attaining to the great skill of exalting the Hebrew, Greek and Latin, over the head of Him who is not only Christ crucified, the wisdom of God and power of God, but is the light of the world, and whose life is the light of men; but to be looked for inwardly in the heart, and not (as he would seem [inclined] to have us think) outwardly and above it, by the understanding only.

The review of the above-named tract brings to mind some remarks of a late American writer, when in England, in relation to a class of men who as he says, " are endeavoring to revive many of the errors of Popery into the English Church, or to carry it back again to the state of things before the Reformation." He says, " I hardly need tell you that these views sprung up at Oxford, [the great seat of learning.]

" I was told," he continues, " that the originators of these views had been very *covertly* and cautiously bringing them out for a long time, and no one suspected the point to which they were aiming, till the whole thing stood revealed; and thus many had been entrapped unawares. The charms of poetry had been thrown around the doctrine, the attractions of learning, the plausibility of arguments, and the powers of gifted genius had been employed to give them currency. The abettors of them were men of distinguished scholarship—of great urbanity and blameless lives. Their influence at Oxford had been astonishingly great," &c.

Now, my dear friend, if such be a true picture of the means put in operation for the purpose of carrying back again the Episcopal Society to the faith of Popery, how much application or touching of the pencil will that picture require, to make it a fair delineation of the means now apparently in operation for the purpose of translating Quakerism back again to the Episcopal religion?

Our author, in his introduction to the tract aforesaid, strongly implicates the Society of Friends and its writers, with *mistakes and errors*, and says, " I am convinced that the sooner such errors are rectified, the better for the growth and prosperity of our little section of the Christian Church, small as they [these errors] may be regarded in their origin, consisting perhaps in an inaccurate view of a single word or sentence" [of Scripture.]

" These mistakes," he continues " are often found to spread their influence to a great extent, &c." By these remarks it is but rational to suppose that he was referring to those passages of Scripture which he subsequently comments upon in the same tract, and thereby plainly reprobates the faith and understanding of our standard writers upon the same passages.

Again, he seems not afraid boldly to charge Friends' views of Scripture passages, with *heresy*, with " being the means of aiding that tremendous lapse of *heresy* in America." Than which perhaps a keener and more unjust reproach and sarcasm has seldom been cast upon the faith of Friends by their bitterest enemies.

Now in solid consideration of the foregoing quotations, it would appear that until their Author come candidly forward and condemn his anti-quaker views and charges of *error* and *heresy* upon the Society, that his offering himself to us as a preacher of our principles, would seem as absurd and contradictory of order, as any two positions of practices can well be.

A want of conformity to the faith adopted by a religious body, has always been found the very root of disorder, and has been palpably productive of it in a great variety of instances. Witness the commotions in Ohio and New York Yearly Meetings, and let me ask *which party was chargeable with the disorder* ?—those who first propagated unsound principles; or those who withstood them? And I will ask again, had all a *right* to withstand them? If the ministers and elders failed to withstand those errors [as in many instances they did] had the common members and young people a right to withstand them?

The answer to these last questions, must undoubtedly turn upon the point of another, namely :—Whether the principles propagated by Elias Hicks were substantially at variance with the doctrines of the Society? And so it must be determined after all that can be said in the present case ;—If J. J. Gurney's doctrines are substantially at variance with the doctrine of Friends, then every member of the body has a right,—nay, it is the duty of all, whether young or old, to make a stand against them for the body's sake. But if his written sentiments are coincident with those always held by Friends, why is it that he does not openly and candidly explain them, and thereby put all our doubtings to rest? His evasions and refusals to do so give increased uneasiness, and render his views and intentions the more distrustful in the minds of many, and must continue to do so until he comply with so just a course and the good order which truth requires,— " first be reconciled to thy brother and *then* come and offer thy gift."

It is well known that Elias Hicks and his abettors, called loudly for order, and denied every body the right of questioning the protective authority of his credentials when abroad; pleading for unity, charity and harmony with great zeal, in order to suppress inquiry. The same order, love and unity was again called for with much earnestness by Elisha Bates and the Beaconites, whilst the great breach of candor and contradiction was in themselves, professing as they did to be sound friends, whilst their grand object was to undermine Quakerism—feigning to support that which they were pulling down;—calling for order to protect disorder !

In an interview with the subject of these strictures, I informed him that the minds of many friends, were possessed of fears in relation to the soundness of his writings, and that myself was one of that number ; and that he had no *occasion* to marvel if expression were sometimes given to those fears : but if the *occasion* of these fears could be removed out of the way, that all such fears and expressions would cease. He now clearly understood me to be calling upon him for a recantation, and immediately entered into a prompt defence and justification of the said writings—supposed there might be some expressions which Friends did not understand, but that there was nothing in his doctrines at variance with Quakerism !—but complained of the unfairness of Friends, as he deemed it, for sending his last book over here to hurt his service, yet seemed not at all disposed to concede a single sentiment which it contained. He plead that it was not *published*, but only printed for private distribution to the ministers and elders. But I asked him if he did not present

it to the Morning Meeting in order for publication ?
To which he replied that he read it to the Morning
Meeting, and they separated it from another work
presented at the same time ; but laid no prohibition
upon his printing it upon his own responsibility ?

Now, can we suppose that he would prepare it
for the press, and finally carry it over the heads of
that body, and print it for the ministers and elders,
unless it was a correct transcript of his own sentiments. Nor does he make any pretension that I
have ever heard, that the views are not his own.
In the last paragraph of this book he says,

" Were I required to define Quakerism, I would
not describe it as the system so elaborately wrought
out by a Barclay, or as the doctrine and maxims of
a Penn, or as the deep and refined views of a Pennington ; for all these authors have their defects as
well as their excellencies ;—I should call it the religion of the New Testament, &c."

From which proposition these several conclusions do naturally result, 1st. If Jos. J. Gurney's
Quakerism is at variance from Barclay, Penn and
Pennington, it must be of a spurious kind, and not
entitled to the name ; for there is no other legitimate Quakerism, but that adopted and defined by
them and their coinciding cotemporaries ; and the
name belongs only to a people of their peculiar principles.* 2d. The charge of defection here laid
upon Barclay, Penn and Pennington, leaves his
readers entirely at liberty to place them on a level,
or even below a Wickliffe, a Baxter, or a Bunyan, in
point of Christian faith ; for it may be truly said,
that these last had their *excellencies* as well as their
defects. 3. This proposition is so shaped that it

---

* And for any, as we have heretofore thought, to claim credence
under this name without a conformity to its whole creed, is making
rather free with that which belongeth not to them.

plainly denies to the doctrine of Barclay, Penn and Pennington an accordance with the doctrines of the New Testament.

Finally, if his printed works, (as above shown, defended and justified by himself) are to be admitted as a test of his faith, there can hardly be a doubt in the mind of any candid reader, of his readiness of mind for the Society of Friends to make an obvious change (in some, at least) of their fundamental doctrines, from those originally acknowledged. And probably, as he suggests, *so he thinks*, that the sooner such change is made, (or as he calls it a correction of error) the better for the growth of our little section of the Christian Church! But my dear friend, I trust there are a few yet among us, who are so entirely satisfied that Quakerism is in unison with primitive Christianity, (and I can but hope that thyself and wife are of this number) that they will, regardless of consequences, cleave to it without abatement and without a compromise— will faithfully watch, guard and testify against all innovations, and every doctrine which stands at variance with the faith of the true Gospel of life and peace as held by our worthy predecessors, let those opposing doctrines be advanced and advocated by whom they may, and under whatever circumstances they may be advanced:—and unto how much suffering of reproach soever the adherence of these, to first principles may expose them, it is to be hoped that a remnant at least will be found loyal to those principles.

The apprehension that thou might not be in possession of some of the information above adduced, led me the more to consider the propriety of fulfilling an attraction to duty in thus freely unfolding a view, (however imperfectly) of the present aspect of things, believing that such as thyself and wife ought not to be kept uninformed of those things

which have so direct a bearing upon the safety of
our Society.

And as we can hardly act in a manner purely
defensive against him who acts in a manner *offensive*
without a personal allusion to such an one who has
taken the field before us, thou wilt expect no further
apology on that score, it being no more than the
upholding of Truth's testimonies requires;—and in
that conclusion I rest, and am thy sincere friend,
hoping that if thou find any thing exceptionable
herein contained, that thou wilt freely remark upon
it, through the same medium of pen and paper.

JOHN WILBUR.

THOMAS SHILLITOE'S

*Testimony against the writings of Joseph John Gur-
ney, delivered by him three days before his de-
cease, taken down from his lips by ——— ———.*

" Thomas Shillitoe said, this testimony rested on
his mind, and he must have it committed to paper,
as he found his peace consisted in so doing, (addressing ———- ———-.) Thou wilt want a great
deal of time and patience to hear what I have got
to say, and it must be faithfully delivered, for I am
afraid at a future day it will devolve heavy upon
thy shoulders. It is extraordinary that thou
shouldst have come in at this juncture, for I have
been wanting my son-in-law to come in and put
down what I am now better satisfied should be received by thee from my mouth: And I therefore
declare, unequivocally against the generality of the
writings of Joseph John Gurney, as being non-
Quaker principles, not sound Quaker principles, but
Episcopalian ones ; and they have done great mis-
chief in our Society, and the Society will go gradu-

ally down if it yields to the further circulation of
that part of his works which they have in their
power to suppress; this is my firm belief. I have
labored under the weight of it for the last twelve
months, beyond what human nature is able to support, and the committee of the Morning Meeting
which passed that last work, (Gurney's Peculiarities, with a new title) must be willing to come forward to be sufficiently humble to acknowledge their
error. And the meeting for Sufferings must also
be willing to remove its authority in allowing it to
be given away to those not of our Society. I declare the author is an Episcopalian, not a Quaker.
I apprehend Joseph John Gurney is no Quaker in
principle. Episcopalian views were imbibed from
his education and still remain with him. I love the
man for the work's sake, so far as it goes, but he
has never been emptied from vessel to vessel, and
from sieve to sieve, nor known the baptism of the
Holy Ghost, and of fire to cleanse the floor of his
heart from his Episcopalian notions. He has spread
a linsey woolsey garment over our members; but
in a future day it will be stripped off, it will be too
short for them, as they will be without Jesus Christ
the Lord. This is my dying testimony, and I must
sign it. If I had been faithful I should have expressed it in the last Yearly Meeting of ministers and
elders, (1836,) but I hope I shall be forgiven. Oh
Lord, accept me with the best I have.

I have letters from America which confirm me
in the truths of every part of what I now state. I
believe there is not an individual member of our
Society in England, Scotland and Ireland, more willing to do good than Joseph John Gurney, but willingness is no qualification. This is my dying testimony to Quaker views, especially as to the ministry; what was anti-christ in George Fox's days is
anti-christ now. The clergy of this country, to
a man, every one of them, are anti-Christ so long

15*

as they wear the gowns and receive the pay, and
continue building up the people in the relicts of
popery, which the church of England left behind:
it will not do to speak of a man doing a great deal
for a little pay, and call him a minister of Christ. It
is a grievous thing that any minister in our Society
should so speak. They are anti-Christ still, since
they lead the people from Christ, and yet I love
some of them for the work's sake, so far as they go.

The writer was a neighbor of Thomas Shillitoe,
and came in unexpected : he does not entertain the
views Thomas Shillitoe did. Thomas Shillitoe's
daughter and grand-daughter were present at the
time the above was delivered."

A few copies have been circulated here (England,) the Friend was so remarkable in his day for
honest simplicity, and his dying testimony so striking and correct ; I have transcribed it for thy perusal, though to thee unknown, the narrative also is
very scarce. Truth needs to fear no exposure.
Error can't too soon be detected, the day calls for
unflinching integrity.

------

*To the members of the Yearly Meeting of Ministers
and Elders, [England.]*

Dear Friends :—In the feelings, as I apprehend,
of the pure love of the truth, it seems with me to express my fervent desire that those things which
tend to promote our peace, and things whereby we
may edify one another may prevail in our minds.
Some of you know that I manifested my concern
on account of the Morning Meeting. This concern
still remaining on my mind, I believe it right to
communicate something further on the subject. It
feels trying to me to have thus to plead with my
friends respecting the Morning Meeting ; but I believe I must say it has been a great trouble, both to

me and to many other Friends who love the truth, that the members of that meeting should have pass-ed such things as they have done in J. J. Gurney's writings, both in his works entitled Religious Pecu-liarities, &c., but more particularly in the revised edition with additions. In these publications there is that which I consider very contrary to the prin-ciples and doctrines which we, as a people, make profession of, and which we fully believe to be con-sistent with the Scriptures of truth. Also in his Essays on Christianity, which I suppose did not pass the Morning Meeting, there is much that is objectionable. In this publication, there is held forth that which Friends and many others have declared against as unsafe, dangerous and unauthorized by the Scriptures. I mean the speaking of the Father as a person, of the Son as a person, and of the Holy Spirit as a person. There are several extracts from Friend's writings in the first chapter of Thos. Evans' Exposition of the Faith of Friends, showing the inconsistency and unscriptural mode of so speak-ing. Richard Clarridge has also written a tract. giving, not only his own views upon it, but the views of many Friends and learned authors of different re-ligious denominations, such for instance as bishop Burnet, Calvin, Luther, Jeremy Taylor, Archbishop Tillotson and Usher, with many others whose sen-timents are well worthy of our attention.

The injury J. J. Gurney's writings have done, are likely still to do, to our Society, and to the cause of truth, seems to me to be very great, and I cannot but conclude that the affectionate part and the wisdom of man must have prevailed in the mind of the members, or they would not have suffers ed what they did to pass, and as respects the Essays, did not that work require the attention of the meeting for Sufferings, to whom is entrust-ed a general care of whatever may arise dur-ing the interval of the Yearly Meeting affecting our religious Society, and requiring its immediate attention. And should a work like this, so opposed to what the Society has always maintained, be permitted to be printed and published, and spread extensively as this has been, by any members, more especially by one in the station of a minister, without that meeting's declaring against it : seeing moreover that works coming from such an one, may, by those not acquainted with our principles, be thought consistent with them, whilst they are quite the reverse. It is my fervent desire, that Friends who have in any way been improperly influenced, may be favored to submit to the renewed baptism of the Holy Spirit, that so the Divine anointing which alone gives clearness of vision may be afforded them, and truth without mixture, supported and propagated.

For much mixture, and consequently much weakness, has got in, and has for some years prevailed among us. Otherwise, ——., ——., and ——. would not have been allowed to travel together—to hold such meetings, and to propagate such sentiments among the young people, as they have done, to the occasioning of a great burden and deep concern in the minds of the living members, where such meetings have been held. Neither would the Yearly Meeting of Ministers and Elders have given certificates of approval to E. Bates' preaching, which act was also a grievous burden to many well concerned Friends.

These things have rested much on my mind, particularly during my present illness, and it must be very evident that J. J. Gurney's interpretations of the Scripture are so contrary to those of the Society from its first commencement, that if his interpretations are to prevail, then the Society must change its ground, and become an inconsistent mixture of Quakerism and Episcopalianism. This I believe the great Head of the Church will never permit ;

but those who are unfaithful and turn aside, and prove themselves altogether unworthy to support the standard and testimonies of truth, will be rejected and scattered, whilst others will be brought in, and prepared, and qualified to unite in maintaining pure primitive Christianity, and in showing forth the Lord's praise among the nation.

These things deeply impressed and afflicted the minds of our dear Friends, Thomas Shillitoe and John Barclay, who are in mercy gathered to their everlasting rest. And now, in thus relieving my mind, I have a hope I shall, through the unmerited mercy of God in Christ Jesus, be favored to die in peace, to enter one of those mansions which our blessed Lord declared he went before to prepare for his followers, for those who not only believe in his outward appearance, but in fulfilling of his promise, that he would come again, and that he who was with them, should be in them, without which second appearance and faithful following of Him in spirit, and submitting to his purifying power, how can we be prepared for acceptance with him.

In looking over the foregoing address, you, my friends, are afresh brought very near to me, with feelings of fervent desire, that we may not be of the number of the wise and prudent, from whom our Lord said the things whereof he spake were hid, but rather that we may be of the babes, unto whom they are revealed, having our dependence on our Almighty Father for guidance, preservation and support, in the way to the kingdom of eternal rest and peace.

I remain your sincere friend,
GEORGE JONES.

Stockport, 9th of 5th month, 1839.

RALPH WARDLAW'S

Opinion of Joseph John Gurney.

Ralph Wardlaw, a Presbyterian priest of Scotland, called D. D. in letters which he has published, addressed to the Society of Friends, on some of their distinguishing principles, says: " I have given in copious extracts the views of J. J. Gurney, on the doctrine of justification. They are clear, simple, Scriptural—but are they Quakerism ? Let none be startled by the question; it is not a hasty, inconsiderate one. I shall show you there is room for it. There are large portions of the writings of this highly intelligent and devoted Friend, in which we entirely lose sight of the peculiarities of Quaker sentiments, and Quaker phraseology. He seems to lay aside his garb, or rather to divest the system of the costume in which before, it had invariably appeared. But for the occurrence of here and there a word, or phrase, which to those familiar with the language of the body, conveys more than others might at all think of, we go through entire sections with unmingled pleasure; losing the Friend in the Christian—almost forgetting even the *inward light.* I presume I speak according to truth, when I represent them as the first Quaker writings, at least of any eminence professing this character. He stands *per se* and (if I am not greatly mistaken) with no inconsiderable proportion of the more rigid Friends, who belong to the old school, and hold by the ancient Fathers of Quakerism, he has on this very account been *losing caste."* Page 195.

" The terms in which Mr. Gurney invariably speaks of the Holy Scriptures, and which it is my delight to see him using, are such as to convert those employed by him respecting the independent influence and guidance of the Holy Spirit, into little more than words without meaning." Page 351.

" My judgment and my feelings being in thorough accordance with those of Mr. Gurney, in all that he says of the paramount authority of the word of God as contained in the volume of Revelation, I cannot see how he can be in harmony with himself, till he has thrown aside the remnant of Quaker doctrine to which he still tenaciously clings. I mean this *immediate revelation*, under the modified designation by which he has chosen to qualify and recommend it. I cannot but fancy to myself the surprise and indignation with which some of the old Fathers of Quakerism would be stirred, by the attempts to explain away to so great an extent their most favorite dogmas, and to fritter down the meaning of their phraseology ; till there is hardly left a shred of distinction between them and the Christian world at large." Page 358.

" It would be unseemly presumption in me to dispute the accuracy of Mr. Gurney's statement respecting the views entertained by his own body : but really it is impossible to read the writings of the older Quakers—the Fathers of the family, without being sensible that there is a prodigious softening down on the part of this writer of their opinions and language." Page 365.

" Mr. Gurney conceives that every true Quaker is prepared cordially to acknowledge that the Holy Scriptures, and they alone, are a'divinely authorized record of all the doctrines which we are required to believe, and of all the moral principles that are to regulate our actions, not to mention the luminous declaration which they contain of our relative and particular duties.

" And indeed on this, and various other points, it cannot fail to strike the most superficial reader, what a perfect discordance there is between the writings of Mr. Gurney and those of the early Friends. I

am very far from wishing Mr. Gurney to take a
single step out of Quakerism, in points where Quakerism is true. In other points, however, he has
already taken several, and those, too, even larger
strides than any that now remain for him to take.
May the Divine Spirit be graciously pleased, by
means of that complete revelation, which he has
given to lead not him only but you, my friends, and
myself, and every fellow-Christian and fellow-man
around us into *all truth*." Page 367.